# NO TRADESMEN
## AND NO WOMEN

# NO TRADESMEN
## AND NO WOMEN

*The Origins of the British Civil Service*

MICHAEL COOLICAN

Biteback Publishing

First published in Great Britain in 2018 by
Biteback Publishing Ltd
Westminster Tower
3 Albert Embankment
London SE1 7SP
Copyright © Michael Coolican 2018

Michael Coolican has asserted his right under the Copyright, Designs and Patents Act 1988
to be identified as the author of this work.

Every reasonable effort has been made to trace copyright holders of material reproduced in this
book, but if any have been inadvertently overlooked the publisher would be glad to hear from them.

ISBN 978-1-78590-452-3

10 9 8 7 6 5 4 3 2 1

A CIP catalogue record for this book is available from the British Library.

Set in Adobe Caslon Pro

Printed and bound in Great Britain by
CPI Group (UK) Ltd, Croydon CR0 4YY

MIX
Paper from
responsible sources
FSC® C020471

# CONTENTS

# FOREWORD

I have long argued that if ministers knew more about past policy-making they would avoid repeating past failures, learn from earlier debates and discover options that are currently overlooked. That is an issue this book cogently addresses. I have also come to realise how valuable it would have been to know more about the way the civil service – the machine on which ministers depend – has developed. Mike Coolican traces the origins of the civil service in a way that, I believe, has not been attempted before – revealing how both its strengths and its weaknesses have evolved.

The story of its origins in the Middle Ages is a fascinating one. But Coolican's demonstration of how the Victorian reforms of the civil service generated a mindset and established the dominance of the gifted generalist over the qualified expert is of immense contemporary relevance. His account of the machinations by which those reforms were introduced reads like a whodunnit.

In my experience, the civil service contains many people of the highest calibre and dedication. Contrary to the picture portrayed in that wonderful TV series *Yes Minister*, civil servants loyally strive to translate a minister's agenda into practical policies. Nonetheless, there are systemic weaknesses in delivery and management of programmes, failures of project management and lack of specialist input to policy formation which have their roots in history. I commend this book to all those who are interested in policy-making and how it can be improved. However, it will also be of great interest to a much wider audience – all of us are affected by how government works and most of us want to know how it operates.

Above all, *No Tradesmen and No Women* is as entertaining as it is informative.

*The Rt Hon. Lord Lilley of Offa*
*October 2018*

# CHAPTER 1

# IN THE BEGINNING

On 25 May 2006, Home Secretary John Reid appeared before the House of Commons Home Affairs Committee. Reid had been Home Secretary for three weeks and was due to explain why some 1,000 foreign prisoners had not been considered for deportation at the end of their prison terms, despite court orders to that effect having been issued. Instead he astounded committee members by launching a vitriolic attack on staff at his Immigration and Nationality department, which he described as 'not fit for purpose'. Reid claimed the department was inadequate in regards to its systems, its leadership and its management, before adding that he had ordered a wholesale review of the department's structure, and warned that heads might roll.

In mentioning leadership and management, Reid had unerringly put his finger on a problem that affects not just the Home Office, but the entire British civil service. The bizarre goings-on at the Immigration and Nationality department were only an extreme example of the consequences of poor management and leadership which can be found in any government department. Performance reviews of government departments, carried out at the request of the Cabinet Secretary Gus O'Donnell, were published in December 2006 and suggested that the problem was getting worse in at least four departments, including the Cabinet Office itself.

The normal response of ministers and top civil servants to any manifestation of the results of poor management and leadership is to address the symptoms vigorously. But unless the underlying cause of the problem is also tackled, the symptoms will simply resurface elsewhere, to embarrass yet another minister or top civil servant. Since the problem is a service-wide one, it needs to be tackled on a service-wide basis if there is to be any hope of a solution. In the case of the Home Office, Reid opted for the conventional cosmetic approach and split the department in two. This involved a sharp tussle with other ministers, which no doubt made Reid feel good, and was a demonstrable piece of action to make him look good. However, it had no bearing on the problem itself, as Amber Rudd was to discover twelve years later, when she found herself mired in the controversy surrounding the Windrush generation and the way they had been treated by her Home Office officials.

The problem that John Reid and Amber Rudd faced was essentially that of a culture which, despite lip service to the contrary, places no value on management and leadership, or even on the need to understand what those terms mean. The problem is endemic to the civil service in Britain and has its origins in Victorian-era reforms, and in the varied agendas of those who carried forward those reforms. The details of the reforms and the agendas behind them are no longer widely appreciated, and that goes some way to explain the persistent failure of ministers and top officials to change the culture.

Inadequate leadership and management is not only a matter of concern to ministers who wish to avoid public embarrassment; it matters to all of us, since most of us in our contacts with government – paying taxes, claiming benefits, safeguarding our employment rights and complying with regulations – deal with the relatively junior civil servants who carry out the day-to-day work of departments. If these are poorly led and managed, and have to cope with grotesque systems, it will hugely affect their ability to deliver a decent service to the public.

It is important, however, to maintain a sense of proportion. Each day a vast government machine delivers a reasonably good service at airports, tribunals, courts, laboratories, schools and local offices all over the country, as well as in Whitehall itself. It is largely incorrupt, mostly effective and more often than not reasonably efficient. It is staffed by people who do not recognise themselves in the stereotypes of stand-up comic mockery, and it is overseen by politicians who are not all self-serving or morally deficient. But if delivering good government is a daily uphill battle against defective systems, poor management and virtually invisible leadership, then government departments will not be able to deliver the sort of service to which we are entitled, and which politicians continually promise to deliver.

No large organisation, whether in the private or public sector, can always run smoothly. But well-managed organisations identify and deal with their incompetents, over-promoted underperformers and freeloaders; they tackle misallocation of resources and ensure that they aren't doing unnecessary work. Badly managed organisations do none of these things. In the private sector, badly managed organisations go bankrupt. But the public sector does not go bankrupt, so when departments get into a hopeless mess (Child Support Agency, Criminal Records Bureau, National Asylum Support Service) they simply have to flounder on until someone sorts things out – by tackling the symptoms yet again.

In the UK, we have two distinct images of the civil service. One is of a collection of bowler-hatted buffoons and the other that of an urbane and brilliant set of intellectuals shimmering along Whitehall's corridors like the characters in a C. P. Snow novel. Having been a civil servant for forty years, I can confirm that these stereotypes are just that, and that most civil servants at all levels are well-educated, hard-working and conscientious, and that the majority of them make entertaining and interesting colleagues. Quite a lot of them, particularly in the more junior grades, excel at getting things done. The last person I worked with who wore a bowler hat to work retired back in the 1970s, and the mandarins stopped talking like characters from C. P. Snow novels at about the same time (well, most of them).

Despite their many similarities, however, there also exists a great divide between the very small number of top mandarins and the very great number of more junior staff, who do most of the work and who have the lion's share of day-to-day contact with the public. It is this division – the main outcome of the way recruitment to the British civil service was changed in Victorian England – which lies at the root of the culture of inadequate management and leadership identified by John Reid. The conventional wisdom is that this divide was the work of Sir Stafford Northcote and Sir Charles Trevelyan, but once you start poking around in the archives the story turns out to be rather more complicated. In this book I seek to explain the nature and consequences of the development of the civil service, to place the civil service in its modern context and to show what happens when the inherited structures are inadequate to cope with the tasks required of them.

The Victorians had a major impact on the civil service, and the consequences of the changes they made were all the more profound because the civil service was growing rapidly in size and scope, as successive administrations grappled with the complex issues thrown up by Britain's transition from a rural to an industrial economy. The departments of state upon which this growth was based were well-established organisations and, in some cases, a department's history would date back to at least the Normans. There were even indirect links back to the Roman civil service. The antiquity of some of these institutions affected not only how they evolved as public offices, but also how they responded to pressures for change in the ways they recruited and managed their staff. In order to understand how the Victorian reforms came about, it is important to have a basic understanding of some of the earlier history of English administration.

There is no evidence currently available to suggest that any institutions of government survived the collapse of Roman administration in Britain after the withdrawal of the legions in the fifth century AD. The waves of invaders that swept across the country after the Romans withdrew were initially organised on a tribal basis and had no need to develop any significant administrative machinery. Gradually, though, the tribes coalesced into minor kingdoms that gave rise to a need for more sophisticated administration.

By chance, the emergence of these kingdoms began at about the same time that St Augustine was sent to this country to convert the people to Christianity, and to become their religious leader. The rulers of the various Anglo-Saxon kingdoms, as they vied for hegemony, were thus able to draw on the administrative skills of the Church's leaders to give their hold on power greater robustness and stability. That the churchmen were able to provide such advice was partly due to the fact that they were intelligent and well-educated, but they also had a practical example of effective administration to draw from in the Church itself. The Church's effective organisational structure had its roots in the Roman Empire, with churchmen even borrowing words such as *diocese* and *curia* from the Romans. The strong Roman influence may have been due to many civil servants switching to administering the Church, following the collapse of the empire.

One important feature of the systems they helped to establish was that of the *curia regis*, the royal council, where the King could consult his chief advisors on matters of state. The concept of the *curia regis* proved to be a lasting one. It was adopted when the unification of England under one monarchy was achieved, and subsequently embraced by the Normans. The concept has undergone many changes over the centuries but it remains a part of the British administrative machinery in the form of the Privy Council.

There was another enduring legacy of the involvement of the Church in British administration. So prevalent was the use of the clergy in the business of the state that these officials became known as clerks, and the name stuck. Because of the preponderance of clergymen in their ranks, clerks were required to be celibate, and the requirement took time to disappear even after the balance had tipped heavily towards lay clerks. In England, the six clerks of the Chancery Court only obtained the freedom to marry early in the reign of Henry VIII.

Sparse though the records of Anglo-Saxon England are, enough of them remain to demonstrate that well before the Norman conquest some elements of central administration were already established in England. How and when these developments occurred is not known, but historical research has revealed the existence of some quite sophisticated administrative systems, particularly during the latter part of the Anglo-Saxon period. By the late tenth century, for example, most of the country had been divided into administrative units – shires and hundreds (shires and wapentakes in those areas of England that had been administered by the Danes). Key institutions of royal government – shire courts and hundred courts – had been established and were fully functional.

It can also be demonstrated that the shire and hundred courts were visited from time to time by the King's representatives, thus establishing the concept of inspection as a means of quality control. Two other key manifestations of effective administration – taxation and coinage – were also well developed in Anglo-Saxon England. At some point, the country – from the Midlands to the south coast – was comprehensively surveyed for taxation purposes and the later Anglo-Saxon rulers were able to collect taxes on a national basis. They also arranged for the issue of sound coinage. Although the evidence is subject to academic dispute, there seems to be little doubt that some later Anglo-Saxon monarchs managed to raise substantial sums of money (£20,000–£30,000 a year, about £200 million in current money) to finance military expenditure, including the provision of a standing fleet of some sixty warships. Their provisions for circulating sound coinage seem equally robust. The coins were minted locally but circulated widely. At several stages during the Anglo-Saxon period, existing coins were taken out of circulation and replaced by new issues; a quite sophisticated exercise.

Yet although there seems to be little doubt about the existence of central administrative policies, there is no evidence of a central administrative machine. The day-to-day administration of justice, taxation and coinage was entirely local. The sheriff of each shire was appointed by the King and below the sheriff were various office holders, such as the hundred-reeve and the geld (tax) collector, while at the bottom of the pile came the manor or village reeve.

But these were all local men (occasionally women) and their duties were not full-time ones. In many cases, the value of the post was the opportunity to keep a certain proportion of tax as compensation for the work (and odium) involved. Manor and village reeves seem to have been notorious for their oppressive ways. The continuity and extensive uniformity of the Anglo-Saxon administrative systems suggests that they were conceived centrally, but since no supporting evidence has been found this can only be conjecture.

It was the Normans who firmly established written records of central government in the country. They did so in a spectacular fashion when William the Conqueror, in winter 1085, launched a national audit from which the Domesday Book was compiled. This was a detailed record of the feudal tenure of the country, as it was before and after the conquest, and would be referred to time and again over the years in the resolution of disputes concerning land and charters – it was cited in a legal case as recently as 2006.

The compilation of the audit, which took only two years, involved a survey of virtually the whole of England apart from Winchester, the City of London and what is now Durham and Northumberland. According to contemporary sources, surveyors toured each county to establish the possessions of all the magnates, both lay and ecclesiastical, including their tenants, bondsmen and their animals, and any services due to them. Nothing escaped the surveyors' inquisitions. They counted not just the men and animals, but also the woodland, pastures, fisheries and fishponds, mills and ferries. In the same way that William the Conqueror's castles stamped his military authority on the land, so this operation established his central administrative capability. The King could now tell, down to the last farthing, how much his subjects were worth – and just how far he could squeeze them for taxes. But this was a one-off exercise carried out by teams of ecclesiastics and important laymen – there was still little in the way of permanent bureaucracy.

Such bureaucracy as there was existed within the royal household with offices such as the Wardrobe and the Chamber. These offices had originally been created to look after the monarch's personal needs, but they often became involved in the business of running the country. The first development of a recognisable bureaucracy was the establishment of the Exchequer during the reign of Henry I. It was followed by the development of the Chancery into a major administrative machine. The distinction is not a clear one, since the Exchequer and the Chancery were both part of the royal household, but they were clearly developed to deal with the administration of the country rather than the royal household, and thus they probably merit recognition as the first public offices. It would be easier to establish the point if written records existed, but despite the indisputable value to these early administrators of the Domesday Book, it was some time before it occurred to them that a systematic record of their own work would be equally valuable.

The first recording system was established in the early twelfth century with the production of the Exchequer Pipe Rolls, which sought to provide the monarch with an annual statement of financial accounts. In the second half of the century, the Exchequer began to keep copies of financial writs to check against the originals when subjecting the sheriffs to an annual inquisition on revenue-raising.

The Normans had continued the Anglo-Saxon system under which sheriffs were required to levy taxes for the King. The process by which money raised from taxes made its way into the coffers of Anglo-Saxon monarchs is not clear. The Normans required the sheriffs to account for the revenue at an oral inquisition at the Exchequer once a year. It was easier to prise money out of reluctant or duplicitous sheriffs if copies of writs could be compared with originals, and any fraudulent tampering with the original writs exposed.

A major step forward took place in the last decade of the twelfth century, when Archbishop of Canterbury Hubert Walter was appointed Chief Justiciar of England (the King's chief minister) and began the first systematic collection of legal records. Later, when Walter became Chancellor under King John, the keeping of Chancery rolls began. In these rolls, a record of royal charters, letters patent and royal correspondence was maintained. For the first time since the collapse of the Roman administration, the affairs of government in England were being recorded and kept safe; they are still available for inspection at the National Archives in Kew.

Although the Exchequer and the Chancery began their existence as part of the royal household, they gradually became independent during the thirteenth century. In part, this was due to the huge inconvenience of having administrators (and all their chests containing the rolls and all the paraphernalia of the seals) following the court as it travelled up and down the country. In part, also, there was a great benefit for those who did business with the Exchequer or Chancery in knowing where the officials could be found.

But if the establishment of these offices in permanent locations made life easier for some, it posed a major problem for the King – particularly in terms of providing him with access to ready money.

The state machinery had been built up over the years to mini-mise fraud rather than to facilitate spending by profligate warrior monarchs. The Exchequer and Chancery each had their own staff and would only act on documents that bore the appropriate seals. Their role was to follow proper form, and their procedures, re-flecting this, were cumbersome and slow. When money was paid into the Exchequer, the payee received a tally stick as his receipt (a tally was a piece of wood notched to represent a certain sum of money that was then split in half – one half would be retained as a record), but only after a raft of officials, including the writer, the cutter and the striker of the tally, and the Clerk of the Pells, who was responsible for keeping a written record of the transaction, had checked and cross-checked the records.

Getting money out was even worse. Whoever needed payment would first have to obtain a tally from the Exchequer, before taking it to a local receiver of revenue whom they would have to try to persuade to pay up. If the official in question had no ready money, the tally had to be returned and cancelled and a new tally issued.

The cumbersome processes of the Exchequer made life particu-larly difficult when the King was conducting a military campaign and needed his war chest to be kept replenished as he moved across the country. It was perhaps because of these problems that when Edward III created the Duchy of Lancaster for his son John of Gaunt, in 1361, the latter established an office (the Chancery Court of the Duchy of Lancaster) with far less bureaucratic proce-dures to handle the revenues from the Duchy's lands. There were local receivers and auditors and a single central receiver-general who answered to John of Gaunt. The records suggest that John of Gaunt was an effective manager, taking a close interest in the run-ning of his estates, and in his tenants – making sure, for example, that property was kept in good condition. John of Gaunt's Chan-cery Court was to influence later administrative developments.

When they could, English monarchs preferred to finance their activities through the royal household. The household was far more useful to the King, particularly when it came to raising money, as its processes were far swifter than those of the Exchequer. It was staffed by the King's personal servants, who would act on oral as well as written instructions from the monarch. They were far more concerned with keeping the King happy than with following any particular formal procedure. The household had one other great advantage as far as the monarch was concerned: the King's Council had no hand in its running, whereas they could and did have a say in the work of the Exchequer and Chancery. How much of a say the council had depended upon the relative strengths of the King and his great lay and ecclesiastical magnates. At times during the run-up to the Wars of the Roses, the council was effectively in control of all policy and day-to-day management of both the Exchequer and the Chancery. This meant that the administrative role of these departments grew in importance, and particularly that of the Exchequer, which attained a comprehensive grip on the country's finances.

The position was reversed after Edward IV's victory at the Battle of Barnet in 1471; the council lost its pre-eminent position and the royal household began a steady revival that culminated in the reign of the most powerful of England's medieval monarchs – Henry VII. Henry's genius was in securing the royal finances by channelling all the revenues from the Crown's lands into the royal household. Eventually, virtually all royal revenue and expenditure was handled by the household, and the Exchequer sank into obscurity.

The royal finances were controlled by the Treasurer of the Chamber, who was responsible for a huge budget of over £200,000 a year (some £400 million in today's money). A royal servant, he operated on instructions from the King, who checked the books thoroughly and signed every page to prove it. The system worked because Henry VII was a hard-working and diligent (as well as rapacious) ruler – but his son did not inherit those characteristics. Henry VIII's reluctance to buckle down to administration allowed the son of a butcher to become the grandest and most ostentatious church magnate ever to hold the office of Lord Chancellor.

Cardinal Thomas Wolsey took over the system of financial administration that had been so carefully crafted by Henry VII and his treasurers of the chamber, and rendered it even more informal, sometimes using his own servants rather than those of the royal household. He also made little pretence that his instructions to household staff originated from the King. Wolsey made few formal changes to the administrative machine – his main interest was foreign affairs – but he did develop the judicial role of the Court of Chancery and its administrative functions declined. His immediate successors as Chancellor, Sir Thomas More and Sir Thomas Audley, continued this trend and eventually the judicial system became quite separate from the administrative system. This split, which was an important milestone in the development of the country's administrative machinery, was not any conscious or formal development; it was no more than the outcome of the preferences of Wolsey, More and Audley for legal work.

The other major administrative developments of Henry VIII's reign were another result of a personal preference – in this case the King's desire for a new wife. Henry's decision to divorce his first wife, Catherine of Aragon, and marry Anne Boleyn led to a breach with the Catholic Church, one that would have numerous implications for the course of English history. It also resulted in two major changes to how the country was administered.

The first and most obvious change was that the breach with Rome brought an end to the role of the great ecclesiastical statesmen. From the moment when St Augustine had persuaded the King of Kent to become a Christian, the rulers of England had usually had several important clerics hovering at their elbows, offering advice and helping to deal with difficult Popes. Twelve Archbishops of Canterbury had held the post of Lord Chancellor, and six of them had been Lord Treasurer. Cardinal Wolsey was probably the most famous and most powerful of these prelates.

The issue of the annulment of the King's marriage should have posed no major problems for Wolsey, particularly since, only a few years earlier, Henry had robustly defended the seven sacraments against Protestant criticism and earned himself much papal goodwill, as well as the title 'Defender of the Faith'. But Wolsey had designs on the papacy, and sought to wrap the annulment within a wider strategy against the Holy Roman Emperor Charles V, who was the King of Spain and Catherine of Aragon's nephew and, following the sack of Rome by his troops, the effective jailer of the Pope. Wolsey's proposed strategy collapsed, and the annulment proceedings were recalled to Rome where they ground to a halt; Wolsey fell from power.

Wolsey's place as Chancellor was taken by a layman, Thomas Cromwell, who helped Henry sort out his love life. Cromwell seems to have been a committed Protestant (in a way that Henry certainly was not when the breach with Rome took place), and his impact on the religious reformation in England was profound. It was Cromwell's genius as an administrator, however, that brought about the second major change in how the country was administered. By the end of Henry VIII's reign, a distinctly medieval system of government had been transformed into a recognisably modern system; one that would be further developed during the reigns of Henry's three children and those of their Stuart successors.

Cromwell had an aptitude for bureaucratic work, and this sat happily with Henry's decided lack of interest in work of any sort. Cromwell, like Wolsey, came from humble stock. A bit of an adventurer, Cromwell married money and became a respectable merchant and banker. He entered the service of Wolsey, becoming one of his most trusted advisors, and for a time it seemed that he might share the cardinal's fate, but, in circumstances that are far from clear, Cromwell managed to obtain Henry VIII's favour. During the winter of 1529–30 he entered the King's service, having first become a Member of Parliament. By 1532, he was clearly Henry's main advisor. Cromwell was hard-working and had an eye and an inclination for detail that must often have irritated subordinates. But he was also an ideas man, and he instituted some major reforms of the administrative machine that he inherited from Wolsey.

Cromwell's model was the Court of the Duchy of Lancaster, which John of Gaunt had created to avoid the bureaucratic plodding of the Exchequer and Chancery. Cromwell's spur for action was the dissolution of the monasteries. This required a new administrative machine to manage the monastic properties and make provisions for displaced monks and nuns – particularly those too ill or too old to fend for themselves – as well as for settling the outstanding debts of the monasteries; it took the form of the Court of Augmentations, which was established by an Act of Parliament in 1536. The Court of Augmentations became responsible for managing the Crown's revenues arising from the dissolution of the monasteries, for exercising judicial authority, for determining all disputes over monastic property and for retaining permanent custody of all records relating to religious houses.

The Court of Augmentations was followed in 1540 by the establishment, again by Act of Parliament, of the Court of Wards (after a second Act was passed in 1541, it became known as the Court of Wards and Liveries). Wardship was a lucrative feudal relic that entitled the King to take custody of the lands of minors who were heirs to lands held in knight's service (on condition of performing military service) and to sell the minors (and their lands) in marriage to the highest bidder. It was a cross between an estate agency and a slave market and, with good reason, many families sought to evade its clutches. Cromwell realised that, if properly organised, wardship could add considerably to Henry's revenues. As both the Court of Wards and Court of Augmentations were established by Acts of Parliament, they were firmly within the area of national administration and outside that of the royal household. It became apparent that Cromwell wanted the offices of the royal household to dwindle in importance, and hoped to build up a bureaucratic organisation that did not depend (quite so much) upon the personal whim of the monarch. Even after Cromwell's fall from grace, his policy was still being followed with the establishment of yet another court, this time to deal with ecclesiastical revenues. The principle of an administrative machine independent of the royal household was firmly established.

But setting up new offices of state was not the limit of Cromwell's achievement. In 1534, he assumed the role of the King's Principal Secretary. Up to that point, the holders of this office, which dated from the reign of Richard II, had been responsible for managing the ruler's correspondence. To some extent, in the period after the Wars of the Roses, the holders had been employed in embassies to foreign courts. Cromwell, by his industry and effectiveness, turned the office into the hub of government, responsible for everything: finance, defence, foreign affairs and intelligence; overseas trade and the affairs of Ireland, Calais and the Channel Islands; and religion. No single official had ever exercised such control, and it is arguable that none since has done so either.

Although Cromwell worked hard, he could not manage this workload unaided. He had a staff of clerks who did much of the writing and who looked after the filing and record-keeping, for Cromwell was keen on keeping records and notes of meetings. It was yet another of his contributions to the development of effective administration. The value of the process was that it enabled a written record to be kept of what had been decided, by whom and why; it was a simple but effective way of ensuring continuity and fairness of treatment by reference to precedent, and, ultimately, of ensuring the accountability of bureaucrats for their actions. The process took time to get firmly established. In Queen Elizabeth I's reign, a question arose about the order of precedence in respect of the Chancellor of the Exchequer. No one knew the answer, 'only this is remembered by some auncient of the Court yet living … But by what authority or reason the Chancellor hath sitten in these several places it appeareth not in writing found'.

During the Middle Ages, human memory had been relied upon greatly; Cromwell's clerks and their successors increasingly used written records, all neatly indexed and filed. It was the foundation of good government. Because paper was scarce, incoming letters that demanded action were folded over; any blank space was used by the clerks to summarise the contents of the letter, and to suggest action or draft replies. They would pass these up the line, and whoever was competent to deal with the matter would indicate their approval or suggest other action; it was a system still in use at the Home Office in the nineteenth century.

Cromwell's exploitation of the role of Principal Secretary, and his creation of a supporting private office, laid the foundations for the growth of the role of the Secretary of State. The position crystallised in the closing months of Cromwell's power, when he was made a peer and two of his protégés, Thomas Wriothesley and Ralph Sadler, became joint secretaries. From then on, with a few exceptions in the early years, there would be two secretaries. Their offices eventually became those of the two Secretaries of State who were to become key ministers of the Crown during the seventeenth century.

Cromwell, like Wolsey, fell from power because of the King's romantic entanglements. Cromwell had plenty of enemies among the nobility, and when he incurred Henry's wrath following his involvement in Henry's disastrous marriage to Anne of Cleves, his enemies seized their opportunity. They persuaded Henry to execute Cromwell on a trumped-up charge of high treason. It was a rash decision that Henry quickly and deeply regretted, for he could find no one with the same abilities to take Cromwell's place.

There was one further development in the Tudor period that reinforced the demise of government via the royal household and paved the way for the organisation of government as we now recognise it. Cromwell's financial reforms had significantly sidelined the Exchequer by creating a number of new bodies to deal with revenues. In March 1552, during the reign of Edward VI, a commission was established 'for the survey and examination of the state of all his Majesties Courts of Revenue'. The commission produced a number of sound proposals for modernising procedures, and for cutting costs, but its members were nobbled by officials of the Exchequer, who sensed an opportunity to reclaim control of the revenues lost due to Cromwell's reforms.

Much of the effectiveness of the commission's report was set at naught by the obliging recommendation that most of the revenue should, once again, be managed by the Exchequer. Henry VIII died before the proposals could be enacted so it was not until late in 1553, when his daughter Mary became Queen, that legislation was passed. The clerks of the Duchy of Lancaster had been as tenacious in maintaining their independence as those of the Exchequer had been in seeking to claw back control, so the Duchy's revenues did not go to the Exchequer. But the last vestiges of revenue control by the royal household were firmly extinguished. This reform greatly enhanced the role of the Chancellor of the Exchequer, who had hitherto been only the keeper of the Exchequer's seal. The Act's schedules made it clear that the Chancellor was now the second most important officer after the Lord Treasurer. Effective work by one of Queen Elizabeth I's Chancellors of the Exchequer, Sir Walter Mildmay, who held the office for over twenty years, firmly established the commanding position of the post.

In the space of a little over fifty years, England had moved from an essentially medieval form of personal management that involved the King ruling through his personal household servants, to a modern system of the monarch ruling through a formal system of officials; a systematic and organised operation in which a bevy of clerks prepared papers for the Secretaries of State, who then advised the monarch (or took orders from him or her) and passed decisions down the line for execution. It was a robust system of government and would remain virtually unchanged until Victorian times. It survived dynastic upheaval, a civil war, the union with Scotland and the acquisition and loss of the American colonies – though the latter event hastened its eventual demise.

One area that had not been changed to anything like the same extent was tax collection. After the windfall provided by the sale of monastic lands, shortage of money continually hampered the Tudor and Stuart governments, and contributed to the final collapse of Stuart rule. During the Commonwealth period of Oliver Cromwell, some reforms were introduced, but these were mainly achieved by a plethora of committees that simply sidestepped the Exchequer, and the reforms disappeared with the restoration of King Charles II.

In many ways the problems of the Stuart monarchs, both before and after the Commonwealth era, were not much different from those experienced by Edward III when he had struggled to prise money from the Exchequer in order to fight wars in Scotland and Wales. Major reform was not achieved quickly, but the groundwork for change was initiated with the appointment to the post of Secretary to the Treasury of a man who later became a property speculator responsible for the most famous door in Britain: Sir George Downing.

Downing had spent some time as ambassador to the Dutch Republic and had been greatly impressed with the Dutch government's ability to raise huge sums of money with ease. He also studied the Dutch approach to taxation, and sought to introduce similar changes in England; a process that was made easier by the later accession of William of Orange. Downing was particularly keen on excise duties as opposed to customs duties, which he saw as hindering the development of trade. But his major coup was the 1665 Additional Aid Act, which created a new form of reliable credit in which Parliament effectively oversaw the orderly repayment of government debts and established the concept of paying fixed interest on government borrowing.

More importantly, the Act gave Parliament the ability to finance the government. There were moments when the new systems were in danger of collapse. The government repudiated its debts in 1672, but the basis of sound finances was eventually established and the founding of the Bank of England in 1694 set the seal of more robust management of the government's finances. The process was greatly helped by the quality of the secretaries who succeeded Downing, most importantly William Lowndes, who held the post from 1695 to 1721. It was Lowndes who effectively created the system of annual Budgets. In all, Lowndes worked in the Treasury for some fifty years, and development of state financing continued into the next century. In 1751, the Consolidating Act introduced 'consols' – the major mechanism for government funding until the First World War, and the forerunner of modern government bonds. It was these developments in state finances that enabled Britain to raise the funds needed to pay for the wars against Napoleon. A key change that Downing had introduced, and which underpinned his work and that of his successors, was the institution of far more rigorous statistical record-keeping at the Treasury; he wanted to know where the money came from and where it went. He was in good company at the Navy Board, where, as administrator, Samuel Pepys introduced similar efficient housekeeping, and at the War Office, where Sir William Blathwayt did the same. All three had been influenced by Sir William Petty, who had written a book extolling the virtues of 'political arithmetick', by which he meant not only using intellectual argument as a basis of policy-making, but backing it up with quantified analysis; a battle that has yet to be won in Whitehall.

However, despite these crucial developments in state finances, one thing had not changed. The office holders who worked so diligently summarising correspondence, suggesting draft replies and raising money to finance wars, just like their predecessors had done, held their appointments direct from the Crown under letters patent or a royal warrant. Their salaries, if any, were paid out of the revenue from the Crown estates. In many cases, there was no salary at all and the value of the office lay in the fact that it gave the office holder the right (often for life) to the fees of the office and any other perquisites. These could be extensive, particularly when the office involved the collection of taxes or customs duties. Those engaged in such work had an extra benefit because usually no clear distinction was enforced between an office holder's income from his office and any other income he might have. It was, for example, common for those responsible for collecting taxes to use some of the revenue raised to defray their own expenses in collection and to earn interest on such revenue as was left until they passed the money to the Exchequer. When major office holders died, it could take decades for the reckoning to be sorted out; in the meantime, their heirs enjoyed the use of the money.

The terms of these royal appointments often allowed the office holder to find a deputy to do the work, and even where it did not, the strength of the office holder's position as a Crown appointee meant that there was, in practice, no guarantee that the post holder would do any work or even attend the office. The people who really did the work might also be office holders, but increasingly, as the volume of business grew, they tended to be clerks paid by the office holder out of his perks. There were, in addition, defunct offices which had no duties at all but which carried a salary or a right to some perk, and which were awarded for services rendered to the government as honours are today. The service might be a particularly heroic act on the battlefield, a neat piece of diplomacy or simply helping the monarch avoid financial embarrassment.

There was always a strong demand for these offices, and although in theory all office holders were appointed by the monarch, the offices were mainly in the gift of other office holders. The most important jobs went to the King's top supporters, but they in turn decided who got the posts lower down, and some of these lower-level office holders had the gift of subordinate offices. In addition, those who had a right to have their work carried out by a deputy were responsible for finding someone to do it. To a great extent, the jobs went to those who were related to the person in whose gift the office lay, or to those to whom he (occasionally she) was indebted in one way or another. An accommodating trades-man who did not press too hard for debts to be paid off might thus get his son a job in his customer's office, or someone who had got his office through a well-connected relative might, in turn, be expected to provide for another nephew or cousin. And, of course, it wasn't only monarchs with money problems who provided an office in return for a cash payment. The system created a huge multi-layered network of clients and patrons and associated obli-gations and loyalties.

Although it did not always happen, the legal requirement was that only those capable of doing the work should be appointed to public offices. The concept that office holders should actually be able to do the job dated back at least to the reign of Richard II, and it was one to which would-be reformers of the system (and their opponents) would consistently refer. Even where office holders had a right under their letters patent to appoint a deputy to do the real work, the wording required the deputies to be 'suf-ficient'; they too had to be up to the work.

The combination of purchase and patronage did not necessar-ily usher in too many duffers, and it did produce some excellent administrators. Thomas Cromwell became a member of Cardinal Wolsey's staff because one of Wolsey's men was impressed by Cromwell's skill in conveyancing and recommended him to the cardinal as a potential recruit. Geoffrey Chaucer, author of *The Canterbury Tales*, entered royal service through family connec-tions, as did the diarist Samuel Pepys and the novelist Anthony Trollope. All three proved to be good administrators as well as good writers; the two characteristics are closely related.

Although the machinery of government established during the Tudor period had wrested control of the country's finances from the royal household, most of the household offices survived together with their incumbents. In addition, although procedures had been modernised in the state offices, many of the old redundant offices remained, and the relics of medieval management occupying them still clung to their posts and their perks. As the post holders died they were replaced, their offices having become sinecures with which those dispensing patronage might reward their clients. Offices that had ceased to have any function before the Spanish Armada sailed in 1588 were still being occupied as Napoleon planned his invasion of Britain more than 200 years later! The last Exchequer Pipe Rolls were compiled in 1832. The patent rolls are still compiled today and may be read at the National Archive at Kew.

# CHAPTER 2

# JOBS FOR THE BOYS

Although the number of offices increased over the years, the basic pattern of administration did not vary greatly (other than reflecting the competence or otherwise of the office holders). The outbreak of the English Civil War in 1642, Oliver Cromwell's assumption of the role of Lord Protector in 1653 and the restoration of the monarchy in 1660 created problems for office holders as their patrons came to grief or changed sides, but in the main the clerks put their heads down, got on with their work and hoped for the best. Since all governments required taxes to be levied and the army and navy to be kitted out, there was never any shortage of work. And the work continued to be carried out just as it had been in Tudor times – and the office holders continued to treat their offices as personal property.

Because the officers held their appointments directly from the Crown, there was precious little anyone could do to stop even flagrant abuse. In 1760, however, the precarious state of the royal finances forced King George III, on succeeding to the throne, to make a deal with Parliament. The Exchequer received the revenue from the Crown Estates and the King was granted an annual sum of money by Parliament – the Civil List – from which all payments of salaries to office holders were made; the arrangement still stands as regards the royal household. This deal would in time become a potent instrument for reform, for it gave Parliament a direct financial interest in how the King's money was spent, and, even more importantly, a means of getting its own way by threatening to limit or cut off the Civil List. Eventually, King George III would push his luck too far and Parliament would retaliate by attacking the patronage system, but in the meantime the arrangement flourished – and so did the abuses.

One of the most obvious abuses was the sale of offices. Although the exercise of patronage remained extensively an issue of knowing the right people, offices, once acquired, could be bought and sold. It was actually unlawful to sell offices, and had been so since the reign of Edward VI, but it is clear that the practice became widespread during the eighteenth century, increasingly facilitated by the growth of newspapers. In April 1793, for example, seven separate advertisements appeared in *The Times*, mostly seeking jobs, but in one case selling an office.

To be disposed of, a genteel Place under government: present salary £100 with the chance of rising and other advantages: the next rise will be a considerable one: any young Gentleman who can command from £500 to £1,000 will be treated with; and by addressing a line to AG Batson's Coffee-house, with real name and place of abode, will be informed of further Particulars. NB: No Brokers will be attended to.

The comment about brokers was common to all the advertisements, and suggests there was quite a thriving job-placement industry. In May of the same year, one of the brokers advertised his services thus:

Army Commission and Half Pay Agency Office No 17 Crown-street Westminster.

SMALE, many years in an Agent's House of the first Respectability, begs leave to acquaint Gentlemen of the Army etc. that he transacts all business (at his Office as above) relative to buying and selling or exchanging, Commissions, receipt of Prize Money, and Officers Half Pay, for the Army, Navy, Marines and the East India Company, on liberal terms.

The advertisers were clearly segregated by wealth, with some offering several hundred pounds for what must have been junior jobs, while others were clearly setting their sights much higher.

Place Under government. A Gentleman of Education and genteel Family is ready to advance Two or Three Thousand Pounds, or more, to any Gentleman who has interest to procure him a Place of respectability, and an adequate income, in any of the Public Offices. Letters to be addressed to AM at Mr Beckett's, Bookseller, Pall-mall. No Agent or Broker will be attended to.

The blatant sale of offices was accepted by society because the grant of an office was usually for life, which effectively made the office the property of the office holder. Owners of the office thus felt free to sell if it were in their own interests. As demonstrated by Mr Smales's business, the practice of buying and selling posts applied also to the army, and, in April 1793, *The Times* carried an advert for a cornetcy 'in an old and most respectable Regiment of Light Dragoons'. The purchaser would 'have the advantage of the refusal of purchasing a Lieutenancy in the same Regiment immediately'. The Church also joined in, and in the same month a living was sought in Essex or Kent by a clergyman from 'a living in the North of England worth 340*l* per Annum'. In May, an army chaplaincy was for sale, and in June 'a situation under the Corporation of the City of London' was available.

Those who obtained public offices, whether by patronage or purchase, shared one characteristic that was to provoke pressure for reform from non-parliamentary forces: they were all Anglicans. By virtue of the Test Act, which had been passed in 1673, all government office holders had to have received the sacrament according to the forms of the Church of England. They were also required to take oaths of supremacy and allegiance, as well as another oath against transubstantiation. Although mainly directed against Catholics, the Act effectively excluded Dissenters and Jews from public office too. They were also excluded from local authorities (by the Corporations Act) and from the universities of Oxford and Cambridge. The Test Act was not repealed until 1828, when Daniel O'Connell was elected for the Clare constituency in Ireland but barred from taking his seat at Westminster by the Act. Sir Robert Peel, the Prime Minister and a hitherto staunch opponent of Catholic emancipation, feared that if O'Connell was not allowed to take his seat, civil war might break out in Ireland. Peel tempered his convictions accordingly:

> I have for years attempted to maintain the exclusion of Roman Catholics from Parliament and the high offices of State. I do not think it was an unnatural or an unreasonable struggle. I resign it, in consequence of the conviction that it can no longer be advantageously maintained, from believing that there are not adequate materials or sufficient instruments for its effectual and permanent continuance. I yield, therefore, to a MORAL NECESSITY which I cannot control, unwilling to push resistance to a point which might endanger the establishments I wish to defend.

Catholics, Jews and Dissenters were now free to seek office, but Jews were still excluded from Parliament by the form of the oath taken by new MPs. Jewish disabilities were not removed until 1858, when Lord Rothschild was finally permitted to take his seat in Parliament, becoming the first unconverted Jew to do so, eleven years after his first election. The universities of Oxford and Cambridge clung on to their bigotry until 1871.

A consequence of religious discrimination was that many of those excluded from Oxford and Cambridge attended university in

Scotland and on the Continent, or studied at their own denominational educational establishments. These people tended to end up running businesses like Wedgwood, Boulton and Watt, and effectively powered the industrial revolution. These businessmen, whether captains of industry or just the owners of the local linen drapers or grocery stores, came to resent not only their exclusion from office, but the way Anglican toffs awarded themselves sinecures paid for out of taxes levied on thrifty, non-conformist businessmen, and the fact that those office holders who had a real job of work to do did not always run an efficient operation. For though many office holders were 'sufficient', the system (if it can be graced with such a name) was not really up to the task of running a country in transition from a rural economy to the leading nation of the industrial revolution. Indeed, during the latter part of the eighteenth century there was increasing criticism of both the waste and the inefficiency that were so deeply embedded in the administration of the country.

Despite their exclusion from Parliament, the disgruntled Dissenters were a powerful force for change in the late eighteenth century. One of them, the son of a Quaker who owned a woollen mill, would have a long-lasting influence on change in Britain. Born in 1805 in Hawick, James Wilson was educated at the Quaker school at Ackworth in Yorkshire. After a brief spell at teaching ('I would rather be the most menial servant in my father's mill than be a teacher'), James and his brother William established a hat factory in London. The factory proved successful, so when James became interested in the campaign to abolish Britain's Corn Laws he had both the money and the time to become thoroughly involved. He wrote a book, *Influences of the Corn Laws, as Affecting All Classes of the Community, and Particularly the Landed Interests*, which had a considerable impact in political circles, and which led eventually to a political career that impacted on civil service reform. Wilson's lasting influence, however, was that his interest in spreading his views on the political issues of the moment precipitated his founding of *The Economist* newspaper.

The pressure for reform by Dissenters might not have succeeded had it not been echoed by Members of Parliament, spurred on by the loss of the American colonies. Parliamentarians pressed for reform, but not because they sympathised with Dissenters or other victims of bigotry. Parliamentarians wanted to curb the power of the King – whom they judged to have mishandled the colonists' grievances – in order to maintain the political and religious settlement that had been reached in 1689 when William of Orange ascended to the throne.

A key element of the 1689 settlement had been the 'constitutional' role of the monarch, but it was a role which held no attraction for George III and one that he sought to circumvent. Patronage was a useful weapon in George's armoury, but it was a weapon that was viewed by Parliament as a symbol of his ambition. In 1780, John Dunning, later Baron Ashburton, succeeded in putting through the House of Commons a motion that 'the influence of the Crown has increased, is increasing, and ought to be diminished'. It was the harbinger of a sustained attack upon waste in public offices. Under intense parliamentary pressure, Lord North's administration conceded the need for a little light to be shed on the workings of departments of state. An Act was passed appointing commissioners to examine officers of the departments under oath, and to make recommendations for changing matters in the interests of better government.

The Act establishing the commission expired at the end of 1780, but was continued from year to year until the commissioners were satisfied they had completed their work. It was the work of these parliamentary commissioners that exposed the blatant abuses that had developed over the years, and the way in which such abuses were taken for granted and indeed regarded as appropriate and proper. In their first report, the commissioners examined the differences between the collection of land tax and excise. They found that the receivers of land tax, who were allowed to keep two pence in every pound they collected as a salary, found this insufficient to 'answer the trouble, risk, and expense attending his office'. The commissioners calculated the loss to the government at about £133,000 a year.

In contrast to the receivers of land tax, the collectors of excise were paid an annual salary of £120 and were allowed perquisites to add about £100 more. They did not keep any of the money they collected and were required to hand it over by a specified date depending on their distance from London. The commissioners were in no doubt which system they preferred. The government's growing need for money to finance war with France meant that the system of rewarding officials with a percentage of taxes (to give them a vested interest in efficient collection) had spiralled out of control.

When the commissioners examined the offices in Whitehall, they discovered the same problems existed, but on a much grander scale. The Auditor of the Receipts of His Majesty's Exchequer took nearly £17,000 a year in fees, allowances and gratuities; he cleared £14,000 after the expenses of office. In evidence to the commission, the auditor's first clerk stated that profits had been greatly inflated by the costs of financing the war against Napoleon; the clerk claimed that in peacetime profits did not exceed £7,000 a year. As the commissioners noted, 'In its first establishment, the revenue of the kingdom was not considerable, and the profits of the poundage exceeded not the earnings of the officer; but in these later times, the necessities of the state have required revenue far beyond the imagination of our ancestors.'

The commissioners said that it could not go on.

The exigencies of the age having converted what was designed to be the reward of industry, into a means of rendering some offices lucrative to an excess and of supporting others that are useless to the public ... and therefore we are of the opinion, that all poundage fees, of every kind should be suppressed and totally abolished.

The commissioners worked their way through the departments, finding cans of worms everywhere. When they investigated the office of the Treasurer of the Navy, they found that Viscount Falkland's final account for £27,611. 6s. 5¼d. (about £1 million in today's money) dating from 1689 was still outstanding; sensibly they decided this was a lost cause. But the accounts of more recent treasurers, which together also totalled some £27,000, had been outstanding for somewhere between nineteen and ten years. Unsurprisingly, the commissioners discovered that the navy's accounts were twenty-two years in arrears with the auditors. The affairs of the army were in no better state.

The commissioners got even more worked up over those who obtained fees and did nothing. The Clerk of the Pells cleared nearly £8,000 in 1779/80, but he was allowed to have his duties performed by a deputy. 'In consequence of this privilege it has not been usual for many years for the Clerk of the Pells to execute any part of the business himself.' In his evidence to the commissioners, Edward Roberts, the Deputy Clerk of the Pells, revealed that the practice of non-attendance had been in place 'ever since the beginning of the century'.

Some of the information which had enabled the commissioners to get their teeth into these abuses had been supplied by the Office of the Auditors of the Imprest. In 1784, the commission finally got round to examining the office's financial affairs. They were told by John Bray, a deputy to Mr Aislabie, one of the two auditors, that he did not 'recollect that Mr Aislabie ever executed any part of the business of the office' in the period between 1745, when Bray first joined the office, and 1781, when Aislabie died – a period of thirty-six years!

The commissioners noted that 'the present auditors have paid an attention beyond their predecessors, by regulating the public accounts, and bringing up the arrears'. The commission's increased attention to the work of the Office of the Auditors of the Imprest had proved highly effective. In the four years prior to 1782, the two auditors each netted some £6,000 a year (the equivalent of about £200,000 today). In 1782, when the new men had begun to take an interest in their work, income had soared to £16,565 for one auditor and £10,331 for the other. In 1783, both netted a cool £16,000, apparently by getting their clerks to chase up arrears.

The commissioners noted that 'the service of the presiding officer bears no proportion to the magnitude of his profits'. They also pointed out that 'the whole of the business is properly the labour of clerks only'. The public, the commissioners stated, 'cannot afford to maintain officers of any description at such expense'. They pointed out that the profits of the auditors had risen in proportion to the increase in the national debt, and concluded that 'the Public Good requires that all Fees and Gratuities in the Office of the Auditors of the Imprest should be forthwith abolished; that the Profit of the Auditors themselves should be reduced to a reasonable Standard'. The commissioners said that 'no right is vested in the auditor, either by the letters patent by which he holds his office, or by usage, that can be opposed to this reduction and regulation'.

The commissioners were clearly extremely concerned about the national debt, and they noted that in order to reduce it, revenue must exceed expenditure. While accepting that some aspects of the economy were beyond governmental control, the commissioners pointed out that

> frugality in the management of the revenue, the object to which the act by which we are constituted has pointed our attention, is within the reach of every government. It needs no concurrence or assistance from without: it possesses in itself full, absolute, and uncontrouled powers, to regulate the management of every article of its revenue: it can quicken the passage of a tax or duty into the public coffers: it can direct it from thence, without delay, to the purpose for which it is intended: it can abolish useless offices; cut off superfluous and unnecessary expences; and reduce those that are necessary within certain and reasonable limits; it can call its officers to account; and reclaim the sums of public money, either

detained in their hands, or converted to their own use it can correct every abuse, and infuse a spirit of œconomy through every branch of the receipt and expenditure of the revenue.

It was a forceful and compelling statement – one that modern governments would do well to ponder. The commissioners returned to the issue in their fourteenth report, issued on 30 December 1785, which concluded with a clarion call for action:

It is no mark of wisdom, even in an opulent nation, to lavish the public treasure in expenses unprofitable to the state: but where the subject is grievously oppressed by the burthen of an enormous debt, the reduction of which is essential to the justice, the credit, and security of the state, and that reduction cannot without difficulty be accomplished, even by the united exertions of wisdom and œconomy; in a nation under such circumstances, a duty presses upon the government and subject of no common obligation. The one is bound, in the administration of the revenue, to cut off every unnecessary and redundant expense; to suppress every useless and superfluous office; to correct every abuse in the public receipt and expenditure; and religiously to apply to the service of the state the produce of every branch of the revenue. The subject is bound, cheerfully and liberally, every one in proportion to the extent of his abilities, to contribute, without evasion, his share to the support, defence and security of the state, and to the relief of the necessities of his country.

It was a call to which Parliament responded, with reformers such as Edmund Burke inveighing against 'corrupt influence, which is itself the perennial spring of all prodigality, and of all disorder; which loads us, more than millions of debt; which takes away vigour from our arms, wisdom from our councils, and every shadow of authority and credit from the most venerable parts of our constitution'. By legislation, and by requiring returns about staffing, which exposed those whose work was carried out by deputies, Parliament gradually forced change on a reluctant bureaucracy and an equally reluctant set of ministers. A significant effect was produced by the establishment in 1785 of the 'Commissioners for Enquiring into Fees, Perquisites, and Emoluments which are or have lately been received in the several Public Offices'. This commission effectively took over where the previous one had left off, and produced more damming evidence.

In their first report, these commissioners looked at the Home and Foreign departments. They found that 'The Offices of Gazette Writer, Keeper of the State Papers, Collector and Transmitter of the State Papers, and the Secretary for the Latin Language, though they each had a Duty originally annexed to them, obvious from their respective titles, are in their present State entirely Sinecures.'

They also found that the 'Necessary Woman, Elizabeth Emmet, executes her Office by Deputy, to whom she allows twenty-eight guineas a year and the Benefit of the Perquisites'. The salary in question was £40 a year and the perquisites amounted to £20 17s 6d.

When they came to look at the Treasury, they found that 'The Office of one of the Solicitors, Hugh Valence Jones, Esquire, is at present and has been for these Forty Years past, a Sinecure, no Duty or attendance having ever been required either of him or his Predecessor.'

The sinecure was worth £200 a year (compared to the £1,426 paid to what the commissioners described as 'the efficient solicitor'). They proposed abolition of the post, but recommended that Jones receive £200 a year for the rest of his life. This was rather more generous than the amount they suggested for the housekeeper at the Admiralty, who received £40 a year 'without any duty being required of her, she being the widow of one of the former messengers, and this office being considered a kind of pension from the Admiralty on that account'. The commission proposed abolition, but thought 'some allowance should be made to the housekeeper during her life, considering the reasonableness of her claim to a pension from the office'.

Sometimes the commissioners hooked a fish that proved too big to land. The Treasurer of the Navy, they found, 'does not appear to execute the duties of his office in person but delegates powers for that purpose to the paymaster'. For this he received £4,000 a year, free stationery and a house. The commissioners flagged up what they found but made no recommendations, pointing out that 'the Treasurer of the Navy being always a Privy Councillor, may possibly be usefully employed in the service of the state'; a definite cop out.

Despite such obstacles, progress was made. But it proved to be slow work. Because Parliament was made up of property owners, and administered on behalf of property owners, there was great reluctance to upset the principle of property rights in public offices. The right to private property was seen as 'sacred' and one to 'be preserved inviolate'. Accordingly, when Parliament sought to abolish sinecures, the general rule was that office holders should receive compensation (a pension) for loss of office or be allowed to continue to enjoy the office for the remainder of their lives. Those with a clear legal right to perks of office got, more or less, what they were currently entitled to while the less fortunate received whatever the Treasury thought was 'equitable and just'. Naturally, this resulted in a rather long-drawn-out sunset for sinecures, with some office holders still going strong into the 1850s.

The odd thing to modern eyes is that it was all done in such piecemeal fashion. Acts abolished sinecures in one office but not in another; fees were replaced by salaries, but only in specific offices and sometimes just to a certain extent, with some fee income remaining enhanced by payments out of the Civil List or the Consolidated Fund, the government's general bank account at the Bank of England. It was not until 1849–50 that legislation finally provided that all fee income should be paid to the Exchequer, and it took another four years to reach the point where virtually all the costs of the civil service were included in the annual estimates.

Part of the reason for such slow progress was the perceived need to cope with the property rights of office holders, but another important factor was that the public offices were simply not seen as a collective monolithic entity. It was not, for example, until 1875 that the idea of paying similar salaries to similar grades in different departments was first mooted. It is also noticeable that the emphasis was on money; that officers should actually do the work if they wanted the pay; that they should not sell their offices, and that they should not keep money destined for the Exchequer. Little or no attention was given to what office holders did or how they did it, or to how departments were organised. In particular, although Parliament gained an increasingly firm grip on salaries and pensions, no change was made in the legal status of officers as servants of the Crown, a status which remains unaltered to this day.

Old habits die hard. In 1855, people were still seeking to purchase places. In the *Civil Service Gazette* of 17 February of that year, a man straight out of a Rider Haggard novel placed the following advertisement:

> A splendid nugget of pure gold weighing upwards of 24 ounces will be given by the advertiser to any lady or gentleman who will legally procure for him A PERMANENT SITUATION under government upon a railway or otherwise, bringing in about £150 a year, where trust and confidence may be relied upon and not much writing required. Has been a non-commissioned officer of cavalry.

The brokers seemed still to be around; every issue of the *Gazette* carried at least one advertisement in a standard format offering a 'Doucer' for any opportunity for a place. An enterprising publisher, Mr Mitchell of Red Lion Square, offered *Gazette* readers a 'guide to government situations; showing the extent, nature, and value of the civil service patronage at home and abroad; with the manner of disposal; and how to proceed in obtaining a government appointment'. These advertisements provoked the head of the Treasury, Sir Charles Trevelyan, to write to the editor of *The Times*, John Delane (with whom he was a frequent correspondent):

> I send another batch of these shameful advertisements cut out of the same part of today's Civil Service Gazette, and you will see from the note from our Assistant Solicitor that I have not appealed to public opinion through you before I had Ascertained that there was no legal remedy against publications so disgraceful to our country and corruptive of public morality. The Civil Service Gazette Office appears to have opened a shop for the brokerage of such transactions, and such is the impression produced by their weekly recurrence that I know even honest high minded Public Servants who have been insulted by the offer of bribes for appointments, and when they have expressed their disgust, they have been met with an expression of the notoriety of the practice. See the large sums of £800 or £1,000 for the higher situations down to £200 or £300 for a common Clerkship and £30 for a Messengers' Situation. If I recollect right it came out in the Irish Committee of the Session before last that £30 was the established price for an inferior class of situation in the Customs.

Despite Trevelyan's concerns, the advertisements continued to appear; two years later Trevelyan was writing to the Lord Chancellor of Ireland about a Mr O'Keefe who was suspected of selling his office: 'Before you accept a resignation you are clearly entitled to satisfy yourself that no consideration has been accepted for resigning.' The practice did gradually die out, but there was one case as late as 1866. In September 1865, the *Daily Telegraph* carried the following advertisement: 'Forty pounds will be paid to any person who can procure for the advertiser, an intelligent and educated young man of twenty years of age, a permanent appointment from

80*l* to 100*l* per annum. First rate references etc. Address, in confidence to SWR, Post-Office, St Austell Cornwall.'

The advertiser, Mathew John Thomas, who according to census records was almost certainly only eighteen and not twenty, had not specified any particular employment. But he received a reply from a William Girling Balls, who lived off Jermyn Street in London, asserting that a place in government could be found.

Thomas asked about posts in the Revenue or Customs, but Balls responded that he might have difficulty with those departments. However, Balls asserted that he could probably arrange something in the Post Office – and at £60 a year rather than the £80 to £100 Thomas had sought. What was needed, Balls explained, was a letter from Thomas addressed to Balls as though he were an old friend, asking Balls to use his contacts to secure him a post. It would also help, Balls added, if Thomas could persuade someone to write a reference for him, including a request for assistance in finding a post as a favour to his parents.

By October, Balls was ready to move. Using a false identity, he wrote to Robert Crawford, the MP for the City of London, asking Crawford to help procure a situation for Thomas as a sorter or clerk at the Post Office. Balls and Thomas then met with Crawford and, on 31 October, Crawford made an application to Lord Stanley of Alderley, the Postmaster General, to place Mathew Thomas on the list of applicants for a position as a sorter or clerk. Lord Stanley duly obliged, and Thomas joined the Post Office's circulation department as a temporary extra clerk at a wage of five shillings a day. He must have done well there, because he was transferred to the registered letters department where the staff were regarded as having superior intelligence and probity.

Although things seemed to be going well for Thomas at work, his relationship with Balls was not. Thomas had given Balls a promissory note for £10, and had already made some payments on this note, when Balls suddenly claimed to have lost it. Balls extracted another promissory note from Thomas, for £30 this time, but again, after some payments had been made, he claimed to have lost that note too. He got a third promissory note for £25, but after Thomas had paid £7 of this, Balls sold the note to someone else – without declaring that the £7 had already been paid.

All told, Thomas reckoned he had paid Balls some £50. In order to make ends meet and honour his promissory notes, Thomas started to open registered letters and remove valuables, which he then converted into cash, resealing the opened letters and putting them back in the system. In March 1867, the Post Office caught him, and on 11 April he appeared before the Recorder of the City of London. Thomas pleaded guilty, and although the Recorder seemed to have some sympathy for the young man, he said the law left him no alternative but to sentence Thomas to five years' imprisonment. It looks from the census records as though Thomas survived his ordeal and returned to Cornwall, where he became a tin miner.

Balls appeared before the Recorder in June, charged with trafficking in public situations. He pleaded guilty, but claimed he had acted in ignorance of the statute. The Recorder said that Balls had induced Mathew Thomas, whom he referred to as 'the lad', to rob his employers in order to pay Balls his fee. He sentenced Balls, who was aged forty-one, to nine months' hard labour.

It was not just the sale of offices that persisted. As late as 1877, the subpoena clerks in the Joint Stock Companies Registration Office were still demanding a guinea before they would hand over documents they were by law bound to produce for the courts. They split up this fund among themselves each year at Christmas. When one of them, Mr M. A. Creighton, was transferred to other duties at the Board of Trade, he asked for a pay increase to compensate for the loss of his share of the fund. In response, the Lords Commissioners of the Treasury expressed themselves in forthright terms: 'If their Lordships' attention had at any time been called to the existence of a practice by which a public office appears to have made a profit out of a private transaction for the benefit of its employees they would at once have directed its discontinuance.'

It is not surprising that the Lords Commissioners did not consider that the clerk in question, who happened to be my great-grandfather, had any claim to receive an addition to his salary. However, the file in the Public Record Office which contains the correspondence carries a note that the subpoena clerks were to keep their fees!

The parliamentary drive for reform initially focused upon bureaucracy in Britain. After the successful conclusion of the Napoleonic Wars, the focus began to turn towards India. The change was brought about by the rather odd arrangement under which the East India Company ran British India as a contracted-out service for the British government.

# CHAPTER 3

# THE COMPANY MEN

By the close of the eighteenth century the East India Company, which had begun existence as a trading operation, was finding itself increasingly responsible for administering a land area and a population vastly greater than that of Britain. The Company's workforce numbered about 800 and, like British holders of public office, many company men acquired their jobs by patronage and purchase. In the case of the East India Company, it was its court of directors who doled out jobs (and, it was alleged, took fees for doing so). It was an initiative to end this power of patronage which was to have a decisive long-term impact on the British civil service.

The term civil servant was originally used by the East India Company to describe commercial staff who were sent to India to conduct the trade for which the British government had granted the Company a monopoly on 31 December 1600. The first traders were known as 'factors' and the trading stations where they worked were known as 'factories'. The factors eventually felt the need for junior support for the routine business. In 1665, the Company's men at Surat in the state of Gujarat wrote to the court of directors asking them 'to send us half a dozen youths of meane parentage, who shall write good hands and shall be willing to be employed upon all occasions without murmuring'.

The directors agreed to this request. Young men were sent out to deal with the clerical work, and gradually the practice spread. Ten years later, in 1675, the Company, which throughout its existence was highly bureaucratic, established a grading system for its staff (like many of the Company's systems it was modelled on a practice established by the Dutch East India Company). On the lowest rung of the career ladder were apprentices who served for seven years, earning £5 a year for their first five years and £10 a year for the last two. After successfully completing their apprenticeship (many failed to do so as the mortality rate was high), they could become writers. After five years, writers then had the chance of being promoted to factors. Above the factors were merchants and senior merchants, while on the top rung of the ladder stood a president who was assisted by a council made up of senior merchants; the area they managed was called a presidency. There were three presidencies – Bengal, Madras and Bombay.

In Madras and Bombay the Company owned little more than its factory, but in Bengal it had acquired territory, so Company staff had to perform administrative duties. In 1675, the civil servants were also required to gain an understanding of military matters to provide additional resources to deal with unexpected attacks; some took to military skills very well and became commissioned officers. The most famous writer to follow this course was Robert Clive, who, having become a colonel in the Company's service, then found himself fighting a full-scale war against the French-backed Nawab Siraj-ud-Daulah. The Nawab was defeated at the Battle of Plassey in 1757 following his attack on Calcutta (where his supporters incarcerated the Company's men and their families in the notorious 'Black Hole'). The defeat marked the beginning of the decline of French influence in India. It initiated the establishment of a firm British influence over the subcontinent and set the Company (and Britain) on the road to empire.

The practice of employing apprentices ended in 1694, and thereafter the lowest grade was that of writer. The only requirement for becoming a writer, who had to 'weigh tea, count bales and measure muslin', was youth and proof of baptism (there was a long-standing concern that exposure to the religions of the East might sap moral strength) and, from 1682, a rudimentary knowledge of accounts. In 1749, Anthony Chester petitioned the court of directors to obtain a writership. He produced his baptismal certificate and a testimonial that he had 'learned the Rules of Three and Practice, with Merchant Accompts'; his petition was accepted. Warren Hastings, who was to become Governor-General of Bengal, was packed off as a writer by his guardian (who was anxious to rid himself of the burden of guardianship); the only preparation he had was to be placed for a few months at a commercial academy to study arithmetic and bookkeeping. A few days after his seventeenth birthday, Hastings sailed for Bengal.

Acceptance as a writer was dependent upon nomination by a director, and the directors did extremely well out of this. In the 1770s, nominating young men for writerships could earn directors between £2,000 and £3,000. But while the directors did well, it was the policy of the Company to pay staff meanly; as late as 1744 at Dacca writers received only £5 a year, factors £15, merchants £30 and senior merchants £40. The Company had initially engaged older men to become factors, but in 1699 it decided to send out only young men or youths who could be trained in the ways of the business. The main motivation was probably economic, since the services of young men could be procured for less pay (a line of thinking that was later followed in respect of the British civil service). The consequence was widespread corruption and staff trading on their own account, which was strictly forbidden at first, although eventually the Company realised that it had to allow this if it did not want to pay proper salaries.

It was the opportunity to make money in this way that gave rise to the high price of purchasing nominations. The problems posed by poor pay were exacerbated by the Company's dependence on local brokers called Banyans. The Banyans were able to make a considerable amount of money at the Company's expense, not least because writers, factors and merchants usually had no knowledge of local languages. The Banyans also defrauded native traders, forcing them to sell their goods at less than the market price.

After Clive's victory at Plassey, the weak government of the Nawab of Bengal was forced to concede three districts to the Company in order to help it defray the costs of defending the area. The task of revenue collection thus became the Company's responsibility, and later it also took over the administration of justice. The Company's civil servants became more heavily engaged in administration. But the Nawab who succeeded Siraj-ud-Daula gradually lost his last vestiges of control over Bengal, and the area fell into near anarchy. There was rampant extortion and smuggling, something both civil and military servants became involved in. In his biographical essay on Warren Hastings, the historian Thomas Macaulay wrote:

> The business of a servant of the company was simply to wring out of the natives a hundred or two hundred thousand pounds as quickly as possible, that he might return home before his constitution had suffered from the heat, to marry a peer's daughter, to buy rotten boroughs in Cornwall, and to give balls in St. James's Square.

It was not only the Company's men who were piling in. A later Governor of Bengal, Harry Verelst, provided a vivid description of what was going on:

> All who were disposed to plunder, assumed the authority of our name, usurped the seats of justice, and carried on what they called trade by violence and oppression. The Nabob's officers fled before them or, joining the invaders, divided the spoil. Mahomeden, Portuguese and Armenian alike, nay, every illiterate mariner who could escape from a ship, erected our flag and acted as lord of the district around him.

The Bengal Presidency was now a significant size and in a significant mess. In 1765, Clive, who had been in England basking in the glory of being a national hero, while at the same time causing difficulties for the Company by his intrigues with the opposition in Parliament, was sent out with a select committee of four members on a clean-up operation. A number of senior men were dismissed or resigned (one committed suicide), and Clive brought in fresh blood from the Madras Presidency. The free merchants were deported, and the civil servants were recalled from their trading stations in the interior and put under proper supervision. Clive realised, as others had done, that the key to progress was to pay decent wages. In the absence of any such move by the Company, Clive devised a scheme of recompense based on a monopoly of the inland trade of salt, betel and tobacco, the profits from which were divided up among factors and more senior servants – military and civil according to their rank. The writers were not included!

The directors of the Company would not officially agree to the scheme, but despite this it lasted for the next two years. Relations between Clive and the Company remained difficult – his skills as a general being excelled by his rapacity and lust for power – and eventually the Company was forced to seek help from the British government. The resulting Regulating Act of 1773 provided for a Governor-General to be appointed, together with a council of four others from outside the Company; the appointees had to be approved by the British Cabinet as well as by the directors of the Company. The role of the Governor-General was to administer Bengal, but he also had some degree of authority over the other presidencies.

Like all administrative arrangements, the Regulating Act was only as good as the people who implemented it. There was often much dissension between the council and the Governor-General. In 1781, a parliamentary committee was established in Westminster to examine the legal system in Bengal, and Edmund Burke, the great parliamentary proponent of liberty and rational government, became a member. Burke became hugely interested in Indian affairs and eventually found an opportunity to establish greater parliamentary control over the East India Company, and to also take a swipe at King George III's power of patronage. In 1783, Burke, together with prominent Whig Foreign Secretary Charles James Fox, introduced a Bill into Parliament that would establish a board of control for India, based in London and with members appointed by Parliament rather than by the King.

George III, who held a deep dislike for Fox, was not prepared to see his powers limited in this way and used his influence in the House of Lords to kill the Bill. The King's move brought an end to Fox's political ambitions and established the long premiership of William Pitt the Younger, who subsequently introduced a very similar Bill that was passed in 1784. Pitt's Bill outlined a board of control for India, but with members appointed by the King. Parliamentary control was established, but regal *amour propre* was safeguarded. It marked the beginning of a process that would lead to the eventual assumption of power in India by the British government. Paradoxically, the effect of Pitt's India Act was, according to the British politician George Cornewall Lewis, writing some sixty years later, to remove Indian matters from parliamentary conflict.

> So far as India itself is concerned, its Govt. is merely a colonial govt. on a larger and more elaborate and more self-supporting scale, but instead of having a colonial office at Downing St., it has a Court of Directors in Leadenhall St., who are only controlled by a department of the executive. Now it is true that this control is *legally* pretty absolute; but *practically*, everything that is done in England is done by the Court, unless the Board think fit to interfere.

One of the ways the board did see fit to interfere concerned the matter of patronage. The privilege of nominating candidates for writerships was extended by the Act to members of the board of control, and Pitt's great friend Henry Dundas pitched in on a considerable scale. As Cornewall Lewis put it, 'Being so many years at the head of the India board, and Scotland being managed by him, the Indian civil service has for many years been very Scotch.' On this latter point, Cornewall Lewis offered the thought that 'they (the Scots) are moreover an enterprising, thriving race and transplant well'.

The work Clive had undertaken in improving the administrative machine was followed up by his successor, Warren Hastings, who did much to eliminate corruption from the administration of justice and improved the efficiency of the revenue collection (though Hastings's own actions were far from being above reproach and would eventually lead to his impeachment by Parliament). In 1786, Lord (Charles) Cornwallis became Governor-General, but only after insisting that legislation should provide for the Governor-General to be independent of the council and have sufficient powers to face down local officials. These powers were granted and he continued implementing administrative reforms. Part of the problem was that there had been an eighteen-month interregnum following Warren Hastings's return to England, and the man who held office temporarily seems to have been complicit in the corruption of his juniors. As Cornwallis wrote to Pitt and Dundas, 'I ... will not conceal from you that the late government had no authority, and the grossest frauds were daily committed before their face; their whole conduct and all their pretensions to economy ... was a scene of delusion.'

Cornwallis perceived, as Clive had done, that only by providing proper salaries and abolishing all perquisites and other emoluments could permanent reforms be achieved. Clive had failed in his efforts because the court of directors was not interested. As Cornwallis put it, 'Few had any personal knowledge of the country, most were only anxious to promote their personal objectives; all, it may be said, revelled in jobs.' Cornwallis had better luck than Clive because the government had a vested interest in maximising the

Indian revenues and minimising the costs of running the country. In 1793, the Act renewing the Company's charter established the civil service in the modern sense of the word. All vacancies in the civil offices below the council were reserved for civil servants of the Company belonging to the Presidency in which the vacancy occurred; promotion was to be by seniority; the duties of the different departments were defined; and fixed salaries proportionate to the responsibilities were specified. Perquisites and allowances were abolished, as were sinecures. A civil auditor was appointed to check all civil expenditure. Officials could be brought before the courts for any action in their official capacity.

The 1793 Act also required the directors of the Company to take an oath that they would not accept any fees for nominations to writerships. As a result, nominations began to be obtained on the basis of political support and family connections. One director is alleged to have obtained appointments for most of his nineteen children! But the buying and selling of writerships continued, and at the instigation of one of their number, Charles Grant, the court of directors established a committee in 1798 to investigate. This committee found evidence of the trade, and the following year the court required each petitioner for a writership to include a signed declaration that no corrupt practices had taken place. Still the practice continued, and in 1809 Grant persuaded Parliament to investigate. A select committee was set up and it exposed the purchase of some two dozen posts.

A Dickensian story was exposed of writerships being dealt in by a solicitor, Mr Talhoudin, and the wonderfully named Mr Emperor J. A. Woodford. The latter was first cousin to one of the members of the East India Company's court of directors, Mr Woodford Thellusson, and engaged in a dispute with him in Chancery over Thellusson's inheritance, of which he was a trustee. Despite or perhaps because of the dispute, Thellusson obtained nominations to writerships in 1806, 1807 and 1808. All of these were given to Woodford, who then sold them for £3,500 each through the agency of Talhoudin, who picked up £100 or so for his pains. No action was taken against those involved in the trade, but the luckless purchasers were for the high jump. As the select committee put it:

> The immediate consequence of the information contained in this Report, must be that a certain number of persons in the service of the Company will be instantly deprived of their employments, recalled from India and declared incapable of again receiving any appointment under the Company. The money improperly given for procuring these situations will be absolutely lost without any possibility of recovery.

It is unlikely that the trade died out completely, but exposure did tend to reduce corruption and make its practitioners more cautious.

As British control of Indian states expanded, the additions were incorporated into the Bengal Presidency. Under the energetic command of the Marquess Wellesley, expansion was significant. Wellesley, rather like Clive, put much effort into military activity and played down the commercial interests of the Company. Expansion increased the demands made upon the administrative skills of the Company's men; concerns began to be voiced about their qualifications. Wellesley wrote to the directors in 1800, stressing the need to provide training for those who were to be entrusted with important administrative duties. Civil servants, he wrote, were 'appointed without any test of their possession of the requisite qualifications for their posts'.

Not bothering to wait for action from England, Wellesley proceeded to establish his own college in Bengal. His idea was that all new entrants to the service should be taught relevant local languages, as well as law (English and Indian) and political economy. The directors of the Company were unhappy about the costs of the college and proposed its closure.

At about the same time, the Company's factor in Canton wrote to the directors and suggested that the climate in China was unsuitable for fifteen-year-old boys. The factor argued that the minimum age for postings abroad should be nineteen, and that the years between fifteen and nineteen could be usefully devoted to suitable training. This struck a chord with Charles Grant, the director of the Company who had been so concerned about corruption. He worried that if boys of fifteen went to college in India they might succumb to 'the disease of Indianisation'. The letter from Canton encouraged the directors to consider the provision of education for its staff in England which would thus cut back the costs of Wellesley's college. A committee was appointed to consider the issue. Its conclusion was:

> As the Company's Civil Servants are to be employed in all the different branches of the Administration of extended dominions ... they should receive an Education which comprehends not only the usual course of classical learning, but the elements of such other parts of knowledge as may be more particularly applicable to the stations they have to fill.

They had accepted Wellesley's ideas of training a professional civil service for India, but they wanted to be in charge and hoped to keep down costs. After some threats on both sides, a compromise was reached under which Wellesley scaled down his ambitious scheme in India to a college for instruction in local languages, and the directors, reverting to an idea that had been canvassed in 1796, founded the East India College, initially at Hertford Castle and then at Haileybury.

As the prospectus for the new college explained:

> The object of the establishment is, to provide a supply of persons duly qualified to discharge the various and important duties required from the Civil Servants of the Company, in administering the government of India.

> Within the last thirty or forty years, a great change has taken place in the state of the Company's affairs in that country: the extension of empire has been followed by a great increase of power and authority; and persons of the same description, who, before, had acted in the capacity of Factors and Merchants, are now called upon to administer, throughout their respective districts, an extensive System of Finance: and fill the important offices of magistrates, ambassadors, and provincial governors.

The prospectus gave a reasonable description of the change that had taken place. It was not one that the Company had ever sought, for it saddled it with costs that it is doubtful it ever recouped. Coupled with the growth of the British cotton industry, military expansion placed the Company in a more difficult financial situation; between 1810 and 1812 it was forced to borrow £4 million from the government, thus further diminishing its independence and increasingly making it a tool of the British government. But whether the directors liked it or not, as a result of Wellesley's ambitions that was where the Company now was. It was perceptive of the Company's men that they saw the need to provide a relevant education for those who were to become administrators of great tracts of India.

It was not a perception that seemed to be shared by anyone in respect of the administration of Britain. Students at Haileybury were taught oriental literature, maths and natural philosophy, classical and general literature, law, history and political economy. Oxbridge professors, including Thomas Malthus, were brought in to teach the students; Malthus taught political economy. It was an extremely impressive and ambitious scheme, well ahead of its time; the Company directors had made a reasonably good effort to respond to Wellesley's criticisms, and many of those who passed through the college, which opened in 1806, went on to establish considerable reputations as administrators, not only in India, but in other parts of the empire. Among those who attended the college was Charles Trevelyan, who returned to England from service in India in 1840 at the invitation of the Chancellor of the Exchequer to become assistant secretary to the Treasury, from which vantage point Trevelyan sought to play a role in the reform of the British civil service.

The college was particularly valuable in providing prospective Indian civil servants with an understanding of India and its culture – a subject of almost total ignorance among the British population. In 1839, a young undergraduate at Balliol College, Oxford, Monier Monier-Williams, was notified that he had been nominated for a place at Haileybury (he claimed to be unaware that his name had been put forward). He knew nothing of India, so he asked fellow undergraduates what they knew; he found they understood nothing more of the East 'beyond what was to be gained from a perusal of such stories as Hajji Baba or Aladdin and his wonderful lamp'. For reasons that will become apparent, it is worth noting that one of these undergraduates was a clever classicist named Benjamin Jowett.

Monier-Williams then tried his tutors and also drew a blank, though one of them, the future Archbishop of Canterbury, Archibald Tait, had the wit to suggest that Monier-Williams should talk to the recently appointed professor of Sanskrit, Horace Hayman Wilson, who was 'the sole representative of Indian studies at the ancient universities'. The chair of Sanskrit had been financed by a bequest from a former soldier and Company man, Colonel Boden, whose will made it clear that the object of his bequest was to promote the translation of scripture into Sanskrit in order 'to enable his countrymen to proceed in the conversion of the natives of India to the Christian religion'. The degree of interest in this aspiration can be judged by the fact that, when more than one candidate sought the chair, a ballot in which some 4,000 graduates were entitled to participate (of whom the majority were Anglican clergymen) produced only 400 votes. After consulting Professor Wilson, Monier-Williams decided to go to Haileybury, though for family reasons he later withdrew and returned to Oxford; he eventually became professor of Sanskrit at Haileybury.

Although the opening of Haileybury represented an enormous step forward in terms of establishing a professional civil service for India, the fact that entry to the college was still obtained by patronage provoked criticism. In 1813, during the passage of the Act, which prohibited any person being sent to India as a writer unless he had spent four terms at Haileybury, Lord Grenville made a speech in which he advocated that entry into employment by the East India Company should be by competitive examination open to those from 'the great schools and universities'. But his proposal found no favour with Parliament, perhaps because he also thought candidates for the exam should not be 'the choice of any man', but be selected 'by some fixed course of succession from the families of those who had fallen in the public service'. It was not clear if this related only to military service or extended to bureaucrats who died in office. Lord Grenville saw his suggestion as encouraging 'valour, learning and religion', but did not explain how it did so. Whatever his intentions, nothing came of it, but pressure continued, not least because the government of India by the Company was never made permanent and periodically had to be extended by Parliament, thus providing opportunities to press for change.

In 1833, Thomas Macaulay, who was Secretary to the Board of Control for India, took up the baton and helped the government of the day to put through legislation renewing the Company's charter, but making two important changes to its constitution. The government had decided that commercial activity and administration were not compatible and the Company was prohibited from trading activity; henceforward it was solely an administrative body. The other change was to require admission to Haileybury to be by competitive examination. This scheme provided only limited competition, however, for the Act required that for every vacancy four candidates should be named (i.e. put forward by patrons) and the best candidate selected by examination. In advocating this proposal in the Commons, Macaulay directly confronted the argument that was to dog the issue of selection for the civil service for the next 150 years. 'It is said, I know, that examinations in Latin, in Greek and in mathematics are no tests of what men will prove to be in life. I am perfectly aware that they are not infallible tests; but that they are tests I confidently maintain.'

Macaulay then got rather carried away by his own eloquence into a long diatribe on the importance of being best in any subject. He was on relatively safe ground in claiming that 'if instead of learning Greek, we learned the Cherokee, the man who understood Cherokee best, who made the most correct and melodious Cherokee verses – who comprehended most accurately the effect of the Cherokee particles – would generally be a superior man to him who was destitute of these accomplishments.' But Macaulay was perhaps pushing his luck suggesting that 'if astrology were taught at our Universities, the young man who cast nativities best would generally turn out a superior man'; and he was definitely overdoing it in arguing that 'if alchymy were taught, the young man who showed the most activity in the pursuit of the philosopher's stone, would generally turn out a superior man'! But this was a theme dear to Macaulay's heart and was one he would return to.

The Act was passed in 1833, but the following year saw a change of government. Macaulay went off to a job in India and Lord Ellenborough became President of the Board of Control. As will be seen later, Lord Ellenborough had considerable reservations about competition (and civil servants too) and made no effort to put the new scheme into effect. This suited the court of directors, who valued their powers of patronage and were not prepared to accept even this quite modest change. When Lord Ellenborough was replaced as President of the Board of Control by Lord Broughton, the directors managed to use their influence to get the measure repealed. In 1837, Lord Broughton agreed to introduce amending legislation. An Act was passed enabling the directors to suspend and review the system. They suspended it, but somehow never got round to reviewing it.

Although each presidency had its own civil service, the members were known collectively as the 'covenanted civil service of India'. This reflected the fact that the office holders, before they left England, had to sign a covenant agreeing to subscribe to the pension fund, and not to accept presents or act corruptly. The uncovenanted civil service was mainly made up of Indian staff recruited locally, who were not required to execute a covenant. The covenanted civil service thus comprised an elite body that provided the top layers of management; day-to-day work was carried out by native civil servants who stood little chance of joining the covenanted service. The parliamentary committee that inquired into the administration of India prior to the renewal of the Company's charter in 1833 noted that:

> At present natives are employed in subordinate positions in the revenue, judicial and military departments. They are said to be alive to the grievance of being excluded from a larger share in the executive government. It is amply borne out by the evidence that such exclusion is not warranted on the score of incapacity for business or the want of application or trustworthiness; while it is contended that their admission, under European control, into the higher offices would strengthen their attachment to British dominion, would conduce to better administration of justice and would be productive of a great saving in the expenses of Indian government.

The government accepted the point and the 1833 Act required that 'no native of the British territories in India, nor any natural-born subject of His Majesty resident therein, should, by reason only of his religion, place of birth, descent, colour or any of them be disabled from holding any place, office or employment under the Company'. The directors acquiesced in this enlightened provision, confident in the knowledge that they possessed the power of patronage and had no intention of using it on behalf of natives whose intellectual heritage was, they believed, inherently inferior to that of the Europeans. They would have shared the view of George Cornewall Lewis:

> The great problem to be solved is whether there is such a capacity for improvement, intellectual and moral, in the Hindu race, as will within any assignable period enable us to take them into partnership to some considerable extent in the government of their own country, or must we reckon upon always keeping them, like children, in a state of tutelage?

Even those who had supported the drafting of the Act took the same view. Less than two years after he had spoken warmly in support of this provision, Macaulay, who had left Parliament to take up a post in the Indian civil service, became embroiled in a row over the teaching of native students. He took issue with those who thought native students in higher education should be taught in their own language. He favoured teaching in English, which would 'convey the findings of a more advanced culture and so the money would be more usefully spent'. His idea was that native Indians should be educated so as to make a class 'Indian in blood and colour, but English in taste, in opinion, in morals and in intellect'. Macaulay was warmly supported by his recently acquired brother-in-law, Charles Trevelyan, who was also in the Indian civil service: they won the battle. Macaulay proved consistent in his views. Ten years later, in his essay on Warren Hastings, Macaulay suggested that Hastings's 'fondness for Persian literature may have tended to corrupt his taste'.

The Company never did appoint an Indian to the covenanted civil service. It would be another thirty years, and two years after the British government assumed direct control of British India, before the first Indian, Satyendranath Tagore (elder brother of the Nobel Prize-winning poet and writer Rabindranath Tagore), was appointed as an assistant magistrate and tax collector at Ahmedabad, and another seven years before more Indians joined him as covenanted civil servants.

# CHAPTER 4

# THE BALLIOL CONSPIRACY

While the East India Company's directors were fighting their rearguard action in defence of patronage, a series of events occurred at Oxford University that would have a fundamental impact on the Indian and British civil services, particularly on the use of competitive examinations as a means of ending patronage.

In 1836, Benjamin Jowett, the son of a failed businessman, went up to Balliol on the back of a precocious aptitude for Latin and Greek. He became a fellow in 1838 before he had even taken his degree, and by 1842 had been appointed a tutor. He was, after much personal frustration, to become Master of Balliol. He also became a close friend of Florence Nightingale (Jowett claimed to have proposed marriage to her) and many other important Victorians – in particular those with political influence. He used such connections to place his protégés in positions of power. As Jowett once wrote to Florence Nightingale, he aspired to govern the world through his pupils. He was, perhaps, merely boasting, but he did manage to get many Balliol men into government jobs, and he also played a major role in the reforms of both the Indian and the British civil services.

Jowett's role was not fully understood until the early 1960s, when research by the historian R. J. Moore revealed the part that Jowett had played, a part that has certainly not been widely appreciated. What motivated Jowett, apart from wanting to impress Miss Nightingale, was a desire to find jobs for his students, many of whom were unwilling to enter the Church or join the Bar (traditional occupations for graduates with no independent means). The key to his success was the arrival in Balliol of two other Greek scholars, Stafford Northcote and Ralph Lingen, who both became close friends of Jowett.

Northcote, who came from a landed family in Devon that could trace its roots back to the twelfth century, arrived in Balliol at the same time as Jowett; Lingen, the son of a Birmingham businessman, became a fellow of the college in 1841. Jowett's good fortune was that both Northcote and Lingen obtained important posts in the government at critical times for civil service reform. In 1842, William Gladstone, who was then vice-president of the Board of Trade, wrote to Eton housemaster Edward Coleridge, asking him to recommend a former pupil to become his private secretary. Northcote was one of three names that Coleridge put forward; he got the job and kept it until 1850, when ill health forced him to give up work for several years. By the time Northcote's health had improved and he was able to resume work, his boss Gladstone had become Chancellor of the Exchequer. Northcote was thus able to be of crucial help to Jowett.

Lingen got his break in 1846, when the powerful Whig politician Lord Lansdowne appointed him to a commission of inquiry into Welsh education. He must have made the right impression because, in 1847, Lansdowne appointed him to the newly created post of chief examiner in the Education department; Lingen became the department's Permanent Secretary two years later. It is not clear whether Jowett had any hand in securing Lingen's appointment, but he soon made good use of it.

Balliol men began to get jobs in the Education department. First off was poet and literary critic Matthew Arnold, who became Lord Lansdowne's private secretary; then Francis Sandford, who would later become and Under-Secretary of State for Education;

followed by poet A. H. Clough. Future Archbishop of Canterbury Frederick Temple was appointed to Kneller College as its principal, while poet Francis Palgrave became vice-principal. Although the link between Lingen and Jowett was proving fruitful, it would be another twenty-five years before Jowett reaped the full rewards of this friendship. In the meantime, Lingen's role at the committee of education helped Jowett in quite an unexpected way to find an outlet for his protégés.

The East India Company's charter was up for renewal in 1854, and in order to help the Secretary to the Board of Control, Sir Charles Wood, deal with the impending legislative burden, the Prime Minister, Lord Aberdeen, appointed Robert Lowe as Joint Secretary to the Board of Control: effectively a junior minister. Lowe was a rather bizarre character; he had been born into a clergyman's family but aspired to become a member of the ruling class. Lacking the means necessary to achieve this lofty ambition, he ventured to Australia where he made, if not a fortune, then at least a competence as a lawyer and politician.

Lowe was a man of a certain ability (yet another Greek scholar!), but even more importantly a man with a biting tongue and no tact. When he left Australia after eight years, one of his few remaining acquaintances commented that 'no man ever made so many bitter foes in so short a time or acquired such little influence with such commanding abilities'. Lowe didn't mellow over the coming years; in fact, he got worse. Lowe's abiding neurosis was a fear of democracy, and he endeavoured by all available means to forward his own ascension into the ruling class, as well as to prevent those whom he deemed less worthy from following him there.

In June 1853, the government's India Bill was brought forward. It included a clause to re-establish a competitive examination for entry to the East India College at Haileybury, giving the Board of Control for India the power to determine which subjects prospective students were to be examined on and to appoint the examiners. It would be, asserted Sir Charles Wood, 'a great experiment which would justify itself by securing intellectual superiority, while affording as good a chance as then existed of obtaining in successful candidates those qualities which no examination can test'.

Macaulay, now back in Parliament after his spell in India, and anxious to undo this reversal, gave his full support to the Bill and brought his customary oratorical flights of fancy into play. Suggestions had been made that patronage should continue, but be exercised by the Governor-General rather than the court of directors. Macaulay rose to the challenge in the House on 25 June. He told MPs that 'every Governor-General would, in such case, carry out with him, or would soon be followed by, a crowd of relatives, nephews, first and second cousins, friends and sons of friends' all seeking jobs. He witheringly asked proponents of the idea whether they had been 'so completely successful in extirpating nepotism and jobbing at your own door, and in excluding all abuses from Whitehall and Somerset House, that you should fancy you could establish purity in countries the situation of which you do not know and the names of which you cannot pronounce'. When Macaulay got into his stride few people were eager to face him down; the opposition made no headway.

Macaulay again received support from his brother-in-law Charles Trevelyan. The latter's job at the top of the Treasury, coupled with his experience of Haileybury and work in India, meant his support had added value. Trevelyan appeared before the House of Lords Select Committee on Indian Affairs and gave Haileybury significant praise: 'I have a very high opinion of the course of study at Haileybury. The Company has thoroughly done its duty in that respect. It has provided a course of instruction well adapted to the special exigencies of India, and taught by the best instructors possible.'

Trevelyan did qualify his praise slightly. He thought 'a great deal too much attention has been given to Oriental studies', and that the college's function as a probation had not been properly carried into effect:

It will be quite as necessary to attend to this under the proposed new mode of selecting the young civilians as under the old system; because, although a competing examination is the best test of intellectual proficiency, and every practicable guarantee of good conduct will no doubt be obtained, yet it is impossible to judge the habitual character and conduct of young men from testimonials.

Trevelyan was explicitly pressed on the potential value of Oxford and Cambridge as training grounds for the Indian civil service, and specifically on whether it would be possible to run Haileybury courses at the two universities. His view was an emphatic one: 'The two cannot be united, and this may be proved by a single instance. Attention is already given to legal instruction at Haileybury, and an increased attention must be given there to Anglo-Indian law, which could not be expected at the University.' He was asked if he thought 'Cambridge had ever exhibited at the same time a collection of men so distinguished in the special branches of instruction given at Haileybury as Malthus, Empson, Professor Jones and others'; predictably he did not. He went on to suggest that during every term some 20 per cent of Haileybury's young men were 'really distinguished and remarkable'. He suggested that their lordships would be able to judge if the same held true for Cambridge. Asked whether having chosen such eminent men was to the East India Company's credit, Trevelyan agreed that it was, and then could not resist a small flourish on his own trumpet: 'Had it not been for the very admirable and interesting lectures of Mr Malthus, and the attention which I paid them, it would never have entered my head to work out the abolition of the Indian transit and town duties. If you read my report upon that system, you will find in it the spirit, and a great deal of the letter, of the notes which I took from Malthus's lectures, which enabled me to carry off his prize.'

The Bill made good progress, but despite Macaulay's fiery oratory, the clause on competition was not without critics. In a debate in the Lords on 13 July, the Earl of Ellenborough waxed lyrical on the virtues of the existing Indian civil servants and on the perils of introducing exams. This was slightly insincere of him, since in a brief spell as Governor-General of India between 1842 and 1844 the earl had been contemptuous of those self-same Indian civil servants, and had appointed army men to civil posts whenever he could legally do so. His relations with the civil service became so bad that the Prime Minister, Sir Robert Peel, was forced to recall him (though he got a step up in the peerage and the Grand Cross of the Order of the Bath as consolation prizes). The earl later had a number of spells as President of the Board of Control for India, in which position, it was alleged by staff at Haileybury, he sought to close the college.

In the House that July, however, the earl was full of praise, declaring that he knew 'not whether by any possible examination you could acquire that great advantage. Depend upon it, there is nothing in the government of India so important as to preserve the tone of both [exams also were proposed for the military] services'. The noble lord explained that he had

> seen with very great pain that the Minister for India expressed his satisfaction that under the proposed system the son of a horse dealer would, in future, be able to obtain admission to the Indian service, and I think you could not do worse than introduce into that country the morality and feeling of the horse yard.

For good measure, he raised in a slightly different form the same issue that Macaulay had raised in 1833: were tests any use in the first place? 'But it is said these persons are to be admitted on merit. What is the merit in being "crammed anyway?"' queried the earl.

His question was a prescient one. So also was a point made by Lord Stanley, who remarked that 'while the old system could not have been permanent, the present plan would not be felt as an abuse in this country, whatever it might be in India, and it would therefore be allowed to continue without improvement'.

Despite criticisms, Charles Wood safely steered the competition clause through the committee stage. Wood said that proposals had been made to retain patronage, and to reserve half the places at the college for exam candidates and the other half for patronage, but he was having none of it; the clause would stand. In the subsequent debate the advocates of full and half patronage had their say, but there were also two speeches in favour of the clause which raised an issue that would achieve considerable prominence over the next few weeks. Sir Thomas Herbert Maddock favoured opening the Indian civil service to competition, not just entrance to the college. He said that when once they should have thrown open the civil service to all the country, he could not conceive the necessity there would be for retaining Haileybury as a separate establishment. Lord Stanley supported exams for the civil service and not the college, but believed 'it was important that the competition was not set too early in life' when young men might be less inclined to diligence; he preferred twenty or twenty-one rather than seventeen or eighteen.

Wood wound up the debate, yielding no ground at all. His brief speech concluded: 'With regard to education he thought the only place where an education could be acquired that would fit a person for employment in India was Haileybury.' Ministers and their top officials had put their weight fully and publicly in favour of the desirability of providing an education that fitted people for the task of administering India. Even as Wood spoke, however, the first moves were taking place that would lead, in little over a year, to the decision to close Haileybury and end the concept of training prospective civil servants in relevant areas of study.

I have found no evidence as to how Jowett first became involved in the India Bill, but since he now had well-placed contacts in the administration it would be quite reasonable for him to have been aware of its progress. In 1847, for example, soon after being appointed private secretary to the 2nd Marquess of Lansdowne, Matthew Arnold had passed on to Jowett Lansdowne's accurate prediction of the final death toll in the Irish famine. It is unlikely that Jowett's network would have failed to relay the latest news from Whitehall on a subject that had possible implications for the universities. His interest might also have been engaged by reading the report in *The Times* of the House of Lords' 13 July debate on the India Bill. The first evidence of Jowett's involvement is provided by a letter that Trevelyan wrote to the headmaster of Harrow, the Rev. Dr Charles Vaughan, on 19 July 1853.

> Sir Stafford Northcote, Mr Lingen and myself are engaged in an inquiry into the establishment of the Committee of Council for Education, one vital point of which is to secure the services for the headquarters office of young men equal in education and ability to the best who are annually turned out by the universities. We do not know where we would go for advice better than to you and Mr Jowett who we believe to be now at Harrow.

There was nothing untoward in schoolmasters being asked to nominate potential civil servants – that was how Northcote had been recruited by Gladstone – but the request for this meeting was odd. First and foremost, it was not necessary; of all the departments that Trevelyan investigated, the Education department was the only one that had in place arrangements to recruit as many Greek scholars as Balliol could provide and which the department could absorb. Yet this was the only instance of such a meeting being proposed. Secondly, Northcote and Lingen were both close friends of Jowett and hardly needed a formal meeting to exchange ideas on recruitment.

One might also wonder what had prompted Trevelyan to write to that particular headmaster at a time when Jowett was on a visit (or indeed how he knew that Jowett was visiting). The timing was also a bit odd, as Trevelyan suggested that he and his colleagues should pay their visit the very next day; a bit of an imposition if the letter actually had come out of the blue. It seems rather unlikely that Trevelyan, who was up to his ears in difficulties with the commissariat (of which he was in charge) and its inability to supply troops in Crimea, would have dreamed this up of his own accord. There is a strong temptation to suggest that Trevelyan was 'set up' by the Balliol mafia to provide Jowett with an opportunity to nobble him, but there is no evidence and so it must be left as an open question.

It is not known for certain that the meeting did take place, but there is no reason to believe it did not. The implication is that there was a meeting, and that in the course of conversation the subject of the India Bill came up, and a discussion about the competition proposals ensued. What is not in dispute is that the events that followed were dramatic and effective, or that they were orchestrated by Jowett, who by 23 July had penned his first letter on the subject.

Jowett was a dab hand at intrigue, and having got the bit between his teeth he quickly organised a coup involving Trevelyan, Macaulay, Vaughan, Lowe and Henry Liddell, the headmaster of Westminster School. Key politicians were harangued both in correspondence and in meetings about the importance of allowing Oxbridge graduates a share of the posts in the Indian civil service. In his opening salvo of 23 July to Gladstone, who as Chancellor of the Exchequer was Trevelyan's boss and one of Oxford University's two MPs, Jowett suggested that everybody, including Dissenters, should be free to take the exam for entry to Haileybury. The change, he suggested, was 'slight, not one of principle', and so it would have been if that had been all that was intended.

Three days later Jowett was due to have a meeting with Wood. But Wood was detained in the House, so instead Jowett met Robert Lowe and found Lowe, so he reported later, 'strongly favourable' to his ideas. This is credible. Lowe would have been particularly happy to leap on anything that he thought might keep the sons of tradesmen, let alone horse dealers, from becoming administrators. During 1855, the incompetence of the Crimean campaign caused the Administrative Reform Association to gain widespread public support for its idea that government departments could do with an infusion of business ability. The idea that the sons of butchers and bakers and candlestick makers might grasp the levers of power drove Lowe to distraction.

Having failed to meet Wood, but secure in the knowledge that Lowe was now enthusiastically on his side, Jowett wrote to Wood and again to Gladstone, enclosing with both of these letters one written by Vaughan to Trevelyan which raised strong objections to the proposals for Haileybury. Jowett urged Gladstone to 'stir up' Wood, but in his letter to Wood Jowett simply suggested that all he wanted was for the Board of Control to keep the power to determine how many Indian appointments were reserved for Haileybury. Jowett knew how to make a point persuasively. Gladstone was soon converted (as an MP for Oxford University he had a direct interest), though with his own top civil servant lobbying at one end and Jowett blasting away at the other, Gladstone stood little chance.

Trevelyan, reverting to his customary role as a provider of advice, suggested to Jowett that he should next nobble Lord Granville, who was due to introduce the Bill into the Lords on 8 August. This Jowett did, catching the luckless Granville in an academic pincer movement. Jowett passed on a copy of the Vaughan–Trevelyan letter to Henry Liddell. Liddell then obligingly wrote to Lord Granville on 27 July, suggesting that the right thing to do would be to have competitive exams not for admission to Haileybury but to the Indian civil service itself, and of course to make these exams open to all.

Armed with the knowledge of Liddell's support, Jowett sought a meeting with Granville. By this time Wood must have been feeling slightly beleaguered, since the Prime Minister, Lord Aberdeen, was nagging him too. Gladstone, perhaps at the suggestion of Trevelyan as a good way of complying with Jowett's request to 'stir up' Wood, had left his recent correspondence from Jowett with the Prime Minister, and Aberdeen dutifully wrote to Wood, also on

27 July, in support of Vaughan. The Prime Minister supposed it would be possible for Wood to retain the power advocated by Vaughan, adding that 'at all events it can do no harm to be so armed'; Lord Aberdeen had also swallowed the line that all that was being advocated was a power to act, not a commitment to do so. He had also clearly taken the point about helping to reform the universities, for he added that 'it would be a misfortune if our liberal intentions with respect to education should practically be defeated'.

Among the Wood and Granville collections of papers at the British Library are identical notes written in Jowett's hand, undated and addressed 'care of R Lingen Privy Council Office to be forwarded'. They set out precisely how the Bill should be amended – 'that the Board of Control should reserve to itself the right of regulating these appointments ... and not confine them by the words of the Act of Parliament to Haileybury'. The notes also emphasise the benefit of the change to the universities, 'to which ... a greater stimulus would be given than by the creation of ten new colleges', and take a swipe at Haileybury, claiming that 'no college like Haileybury can bring the same moral and social influences to bear on the character'. It is likely that this was a briefing note intended to be held by Jowett's protégé, Lingen, until he found a useful moment to deploy it. Such notes are the hallmark of the prudent campaigner (bureaucratic or academic) who understands the crucial importance of having to hand a text that can be slapped down on the table at a moment of crisis.

Jowett had won his battle. In a little over two weeks he had bounced the Prime Minister and the Chancellor of the Exchequer into supporting his line, and had converted Lowe into a friend for life. Granville and Wood duly rolled over and the Bill was amended in the Lords. The relevant clause no longer contained any reference to examining students leaving the college, but simply to examining 'candidates for appointment to the civil service ... of the said Company in India'.

Given the speed with which Jowett had staged his coup, it is not surprising that Granville, Wood and even Gladstone failed to understand that they (and the college) had been positioned neatly at the top of a greasy slope. It is clear from comments made in letters, as well as in Parliament, that Jowett's proposal was regarded as no more than an enabling power, and that ministers (and no doubt the Company) envisaged the majority of candidates for the Indian civil service continuing to come from Haileybury.

But although he had done well, Jowett realised that winning one battle was not the same as winning an entire campaign; more work needed to be done. But by now he and Trevelyan were working together, and Trevelyan was also almost ready to start drafting his report on the reform of the British civil service. Jowett must have begun to realise that he could achieve a prize far greater than any he had at first perhaps imagined. He set to on working out the finer details of his plan.

The India Act, which received the royal assent on 20 August 1853, provided for a committee to work out the details of the examination that candidates for the Indian civil service would have to take. During the next few months, Trevelyan worked on Wood to get Macaulay made chairman of the committee and for Jowett to become a member. On 11 November, Trevelyan wrote to Wood:

I have again asked Macaulay what his feeling is about serving on a committee for the purpose of launching the Selection of Writers Competition, and his answer was that he would do anything rather than it should fail a second time [a reference to the failure to introduce competition in 1833]. He also said he thought no time should be lost as it would take time to commence, meet with the persons proposed to be members and to prepare for and arrange a meeting – and he thought it should be a Royal Commission, and not a mere Committee appointed by the Board of Control – both to give weight to it and to guard against any improbable accident of a change of Ministry.

Trevelyan returned to the charge on 25 November.

I have asked Dr Vaughan who he would recommend as the representatives of Oxford and Cambridge in your commission – and after a few moments reflection he answered in a decided manner: Thompson (Regius Professor of Greek) for Cambridge and Jowett for Oxford; and he added that they have the confidence and respect of the younger and more active portion of the Universities at the same time that they would be acceptable to the Dons. With Macaulay and Northcote the work would be certain to be satisfactorily done, and the rest of the Commission might be freely constituted on the principle of representation.

In February, Trevelyan was still banging away. But he was now seeking to limit membership.

After the fullest consideration, I cannot see that any advantage will be obtained by having a fourth person on the committee. Jowett will represent Oxford, J. S. Lefevre Cambridge and London Universities, and, incidentally the Dissenters: while Macaulay being an universal genius will represent all the world. It is important that the Committee should communicate freely on the subject with selected persons of several classes and they will be able to do this all the better for being few.

Lefevre, the clerk of the House of Commons, had been introduced as a substitute for Professor Thompson, but it is not evident why the change was made. In the end Wood stuck to his guns and added the principal of Haileybury, the Rev. Henry Melville, and also Lord Ashburton.

Jowett and Macaulay now worked closely together to ensure the committee produced the intended results, with Jowett supplying the ideas and Macaulay the chairmanship skills to ensure that other members accepted Jowett's proposals, which he had pretty well sketched out by the end of 1853.

Unsurprisingly, Jowett envisaged a system of open exams

designed to test the skills of those who had fared best at Oxford and Cambridge. He suggested that Haileybury might train students to compete with university graduates (having carefully designed the exams in a way that Haileybury's current syllabus would not address). But for the first time, Jowett now also suggested that Haileybury might be closed. He believed that a fine classical education coupled with an opportunity to make the right social connections, which was what the universities provided, was what really fitted men for high office. An insight into Jowett's thinking is provided by a letter he wrote some thirty years later to yet another Balliol man, the 5th Marquess of Lansdowne, when Lansdowne became Under-Secretary of State for War. 'Administration', Jowett wrote, 'is much alike in all offices when you have got up some technical details'.

If this had been true, then Jowett's idea that all administrators needed was a classical education and the right connections would have been valid. But it was not true, and Jowett's view was becoming increasingly invalid as the nineteenth century progressed. But it was a view that seemed to be shared by those who sought to reform the public offices, and one that was bitterly criticised by those whom the reformers sought to regiment into one-size-fits-all solutions.

Macaulay had shown in the past that he was against such practices as teaching Indians in their own languages. Jowett, however, was not so prejudiced. In 1883, he spoke at the opening of the Indian Institute at Oxford. Commenting on Sanskrit, Arabic and Persian studies, Jowett said that such studies 'can hardly be made the basis of education in the same way as the classics, nor can they enter into our religious life as the Hebrew scriptures do, yet they have a surpassing interest; they take us back to the beginning of civilisation'.

He also suggested that it was not possible to 'govern a people without understanding it ... and an understanding of it must be gained through a knowledge of its languages'. Trevelyan's position is not entirely clear. Although he had supported Macaulay in his successful efforts to ensure Indians were taught in English, Trevelyan had told the India Bill Committee that it was 'especially desirable' that British officials heading for India 'should all go out with some knowledge of the vernacular languages'. By June 1854, Trevelyan seemed to have reversed his view on teaching in the vernacular languages. He wrote to Sir Charles Wood:

> To read and write them readily, to converse in them and to translate out of them should be established as the most indispensable and honoured part of the system of instruction in every school and college throughout the country; and good books in them should be encouraged by being extensively produced as class books or for school and college libraries.

While Jowett schemed with Macaulay to kill off Haileybury, he continued to work on Trevelyan, not least because he wanted to keep abreast of Trevelyan's work on the future of the British civil service; Jowett was keen to ensure the top posts were made available exclusively to Oxbridge graduates. On 27 November 1853, Jowett wrote to Trevelyan and explained that he envisioned three possible futures for Haileybury. The first of these was that the college be retained solely for the probationary period before successful candidates were sent to India, while the second envisioned closure of the college; older professors would be pensioned off and younger ones transferred to the universities.

Jowett's third proposal was to turn Haileybury into a public school. Rather archly he denied his remarks were 'an attack upon Haileybury', though he qualified this by noting that 'it is in general doubtful policy to retain under an entirely new system an institution adapted to an old one. Trevelyan replied a few days later, telling Jowett that a copy of his letter had been sent to Charles Wood, and enclosing a copy of the 'general report which Northcote and I have submitted to Mr Gladstone on the civil establishments in this country'. As Gladstone was the only person to whom the report had been given, Jowett was certainly succeeding in getting himself into a privileged position. Trevelyan expressed caution about Haileybury: 'I will not give any opinion at present upon your observations upon Haileybury beyond a suggestion that your proposed recast of Haileybury might with much advantage be also applied to some colleges at Oxford.'

Jowett was probably untroubled by any doubts Trevelyan might have, for he now had Macaulay firmly on board, and where Macaulay went, his brother-in-law was sure to follow. Macaulay had written the report of the committee charged with devising an exam system for the Indian civil service and had done so with considerable skill – he would, after all, be remembered chiefly as a writer. He did not ostensibly seek to kill off Haileybury directly, but undermined its purpose by pointing out the contradictions of maintaining a college that would not be appropriate for university graduates to attend (not least because they would be older than those joining the college from schools) and whose non-graduate leavers would be unlikely to be able to compete with those 'who have obtained the highest honours of Oxford and Cambridge'. In an echo of his speech of 1833, Macaulay offered up the thought that 'the youth who does best what all the ablest and most ambitious youths about him are trying to do well will generally prove a superior man'.

Macaulay wrote:

It is undoubtedly desirable that the civil servants of the Company should enter on his duties whilst still young; but it is also desirable that he should have received the best, the most liberal, the most fruitful education that his native country affords. Such an education has been proved by experience to be the best preparation for every calling which requires the exercise of the higher powers of the mind. We think it desirable that a considerable number of the civil servants of the Company should be men who have taken a first degree in arts at Oxford or Cambridge.

Consistent with his views on the education of Indians, Macaulay added:

> It therefore seems to us quite clear that those vernacular Indian languages which are of no value except for the purpose of communicating with the natives of India ought not to be the subjects of examination. But we are inclined, though with much distrust of our judgement, to think that a distinction might be made between the vernacular languages and the two languages which may be called the classical languages of India, the Sanscrit and the Arabic.

Macaulay's breathtaking dismissal of languages that might prove useful to Indian civil servants was entirely consistent with the efforts to destroy Haileybury, but his half-hearted support for Sanskrit sat unhappily with espousal of academic performance. While disdain for native Indian culture was widespread among the British, the similarity of Sanskrit and European languages had been noted in the sixteenth century, and by the middle of the nineteenth century the existence of a common source for Indo-European languages had been established. Sanskrit was in no way an inferior language, and some academics thought it superior to Latin and Greek. On the other hand, it suited Macaulay's plan to play upon British prejudices; this would help undermine Haileybury, where Indian languages were taught.

In a final section of his report, Macaulay pointed out that if Haileybury were to be retained then the system of regulation, the accommodation and the standard of instruction would have to be changed to meet the needs of Oxbridge graduates.

That Macaulay's drafting was accepted by the headmaster of the East India College suggests his end game was still not obvious to everyone, and this is reinforced by the fact that Gladstone and Wood were still making it clear they envisioned Haileybury retaining its existing role. In January 1854, in a long letter to the Prime Minister, Gladstone urged support for reform of the

British civil service and mentioned the public's approval of 'the new Haileybury plan'. In August of the same year, Wood told the House of Commons that he had 'requested a number of gentlemen, most of them friends of my own, who felt an interest in this subject [competitive exams] to take it into their consideration'. He then listed the members of the committee and said, 'As soon as I am informed of the results of their deliberations, I shall be able to promulgate the regulations which may be necessary with respect to admission to Haileybury, and next summer admission will probably take place by competition.'

Between August and November, Wood was clearly worked on. It might be that he was persuaded simply by Macaulay's elegant prose, but it is much more likely, given the way such issues were decided then (and just as they are now), that the Balliol mafia simply outargued him. Some historians have been somewhat dismissive of Wood's abilities, suggesting his opinions were lightly held and equally lightly changed, though others have praised him as possessing great knowledge, patience and judgement. The two views are not necessarily incompatible, but even if Wood had been an average performer, the Balliol mafia would still have made mincemeat of him. Jowett, Macaulay and Lowe were extremely clever men, and what Trevelyan lacked in brains he made up for with bombast. Like Trevelyan before him, Wood was shifted from a position where he had declared that only Haileybury could provide the right people for the Indian civil service, to one in which the college appeared to him 'altogether unsuitable for the instruction of gentlemen, any of whom may have passed through the full course of education at one or other of the universities'.

This was the Jowett–Macaulay argument. But Wood went even further by adding, 'Nor does it appear to me that any change in the constitution of Haileybury would render it possible that gentlemen residing there would have the opportunity of acquiring the knowledge which it is most desirable that all the civil servants of the East India Company should possess.'

In a single sentence, Wood had thrown away everything that had been achieved by the Marquess Wellesley and the more enlightened directors of the East India Company in ensuring potential recruits were taught relevant subjects. He had thrown away nearly fifty years' practical experience of delivering that education. He had thrown away also the sense of *esprit de corps* which had been noted by those who had passed through Haileybury. Wood's volte-face had major implications for the British civil service as well as the Indian, and it is also possible that it played a significant part in the development of the British education system's long-standing aversion to vocational training. The government had turned its back on professional administrators; the way had been paved for the reign of the gifted amateur.

Not content with destroying Haileybury's *raison d'être*, Wood then proceeded to close the college. A short Act was passed in July 1855, relieving the East India Company of its obligation to maintain the college. Time had to be allowed for existing students to finish their courses, and the college finally closed in December 1857. The site was sold in 1861. It was then purchased by a group of locals (led ironically by one of those tradesmen so despised by Lowe) and in 1862 the Haileybury School opened – an accidental fulfilment of Jowett's third option of 1854.

Jowett and his friends had won a crushing victory. In May 1855, the first competition under the new regulations took place. Of the candidates selected for the Indian civil service, eight were graduates of Oxford colleges; five came from Cambridge; two from London; one from Edinburgh; and two from Queen's College in Ireland. But though Jowett's group had won the battle, they failed to win the war. Although at first Oxbridge scooped the pool, over the next two decades jobs in India went not to Jowett's graduates in search of a meal ticket, but to the products of the reformed or newly founded public schools, and even to those of big state schools in Irish and Scottish cities. Graduates from Oxford and Cambridge simply did not seem interested in the Indian civil service as a career, which caused concern to Sir Charles Wood. He worried that too many successful candidates were coming from middle-class (or worse) backgrounds. 'Nothing', he complained, 'can keep out a clever fellow, though he may not be up to the mark in manners and conversation.' Whether from school or university, those who took the exams were increasingly 'crammed'. The pages of the *Civil Service Gazette* carried advertisements for these services: 'Indian Telegraph, Works, Forests, Woolwich, Home Civil Service and Army. Mr W Lupton (Author of 'English History and Arithmetic') assisted by a gentleman of the War Office and other qualified Tutors, prepares Candidates for all departments.'

The gloomy forebodings of the Earl of Ellenborough had been realised. Sir Charles Wood complained to Trevelyan about the success of 'well-crammed youths from Irish universities or commercial schools'. What Wood wanted was 'university men who are gentlemen', and he told Trevelyan that 'we have added more marks for Greek and Latin by way of giving them a turn'.

But it was all in vain. Jowett's meddling had achieved the worst of all worlds: the benefits of educating candidates for the Indian civil service in a specially designated college had been lost, and the service was not obtaining the supposed compensation of graduates with a classical education who had shared their education with like-minded, well-connected young men. There was considerable disquiet. Just as Lord Ellenborough had done, people deplored the loss of tone. Dr G. Bradward of the Bombay Medical Service wrote, 'In India efficiency is quite of secondary importance; it indeed bores the natives desperately. But a high tone, down to the drummer-boy, is everything, at least to the stability of the British government in the country.'

It might be that a factor contributing to the lack of interest of Oxbridge graduates was the mortality rate of those who went out to India – it was certainly still a factor fifty years later when my father-in-law's mother insisted that for health reasons her son should not go to India but instead seek a position in the British civil service (which he did). It might also have been related to the demise of the East India Company. In 1858, hard on the heels of the Indian Mutiny, Lord Palmerston's government introduced a Bill to abolish the Company and vest the government of India in the Crown. The Company fought back using the skills of one of their most senior officials, the economist and philosopher John Stuart Mill, to draft a petition to Parliament. But parliamentary sentiment was against the Company. On 1 November 1858, Lord Canning, now viceroy as well as Governor-General, issued a proclamation at Allahabad establishing that all future Acts relating to the government of India would be effected in the name of the sovereign.

Whatever the reason, the civil service commissioners who had taken over responsibility for running the exams from the India Office were finding it increasingly difficult to find adequate candidates for the Indian civil service. Changes in the age limits for the exam were made in 1865 – when the maximum age for competing for places in the Indian civil service was set at twenty-one – and again the following year, when the minimum age was reduced to seventeen.

Both changes were explicitly directed at attracting 'from the principal public schools many distinguished youths who have not yet taken the first step towards a university or professional career at home'. The civil service commissioners had no choice; they had been saddled with a system designed to test the brightest and best of Oxbridge, but the brightest and best weren't applying to take the exam. After 1861, Oxbridge never accounted for more than 25 per cent of candidates, and by the 1870s the figure had fallen to 7 per cent. The public schools, burgeoning under the reforming zeal of headmasters such as Steuart Adolphus Pears at Repton and George Cotton at Marlborough, made up 50 per cent of candidates. Even those candidates from Oxbridge who did apply were not notably successful, with under 20 per cent of applicants accepted into the service.

In 1874, the Conservatives gained power and Lord Salisbury, Secretary of State for India, wrote to the civil service commissioners complaining about the arrangements for selecting candidates for the Indian civil service. Salisbury made a number of suggestions for improving matters. Among the ideas he put forward was the establishment of a special college, or the creation of a scholarship that would enable selected candidates to reside at a college at Oxford or Cambridge for two years.

The secretary to the Civil Service Commission was another Jowett protégé, Theodore Walrond, who according to Jowett's biographers 'lost no time in discussing the matter with Jowett'. Jowett pondered how he might use this new opportunity to claw back what had been lost. In December, he wrote to Lord Salisbury and outlined his ideas for making selected candidates attend university – but only such colleges or universities that offered special instruction and superintendence, and possibly the awarding of a degree.

This time, however, Jowett had moved too slowly. In October, a committee had been formed in Oxford to consider the matter and in November the chairman, Dean Liddell, had written to Lord Salisbury suggesting the maximum age for candidates for the Indian civil service should be set at nineteen. Thus candidates could earn a degree in the normal way, or at a college established for the purpose. Liddell pointed out that the University of Oxford already had readerships in Urdu and Indian law and history, and would do more if it were appropriate. The dean's ideas prevailed and, in 1878, the first competition was held.

Jowett tried hard to get the candidates to Balliol, and here he achieved greater success, as more than half of the candidates resided at the college. Over the next decade there continued to be some concerns that candidates were too young to gain the full benefits of tuition and in 1892, after the matter had been considered by a commission, the maximum age was raised to twenty-three. This meant that candidates who had already obtained a degree could now compete. From that point onwards the recruits to the Indian civil service came almost exclusively from Oxbridge and Trinity College Dublin. Jowett had finally achieved his aim.

It might have been thought that Jowett would be pleased that the Indian civil service had at last been securely delivered into the hands of Oxbridge graduates. He was not. Jowett had a new game to play, which involved getting the India Office to finance the development of the school of oriental studies that had been recently established. But the India Office would not be moved. The best that Jowett could manage was to persuade the Office to pay half the money needed to provide teachers of subjects required by the Indian civil service to any university or college that guaranteed to pay the other half. It was Jowett's final throw of the dice on India; within a year he was dead. But if he failed to achieve success with his last particular ploy, he had nevertheless lived to witness the triumph of the plan he and Macaulay had hatched nearly forty years earlier. Jowett could also console himself with the knowledge that he and his friends had ensured that the top jobs in the British civil service were increasingly becoming the domain of Oxbridge graduates. Patronage was dead, but, far more importantly, so was professionalism.

# CHAPTER 5

# THE NORTHCOTE-
# TREVELYAN REPORT

While Jowett was sending his protégés to the Education department and its satellites, over at the Treasury Charles Trevelyan was becoming concerned at the prevalence of what he saw as incompetent civil servants and antiquated procedures. Trevelyan grew interested in civil service reform. His particular hobby horse was that work should be divided so that low-grade tasks, which he termed 'mechanical', should not be carried out by 'intellectuals'. It may well be that Trevelyan had been shocked by the contrast between India, where the covenanted civil service formed an intellectual elite who left the skivvying to the native Indians, and the English system, where there was, in theory, a single organisation and promotion was determined by seniority. His view would also have been affected by the work of the Treasury, much of which was of a routine nature, and where some procedures left a great deal to be desired.

Whatever the origin of his idea, Trevelyan had a point. But it was not as important a point as he imagined, and it was one that was to become outdated fairly quickly as the work of the civil service changed over the course of the century. It was a point upon which Trevelyan would make little progress himself, but which others would adopt for quite different purposes, and make a cornerstone of the British civil service.

Charles Trevelyan came from a Cornish family and saw himself as belonging 'to the class of reformed Cornish Celts, who by long habits of intercourse with the Anglo-Saxons have learned at last to be practical men'. The evidence of his own letters and the opinions of his contemporaries strongly suggests that Trevelyan was anything but practical; however he was extremely good at advertising his opinions – he frequently wrote to John Delane, editor of *The Times*, to solicit support for his ideas and policies, and had the good fortune to be written up as a very worthy administrator by historians who never read his letters.

The views of Trevelyan's contemporaries and the evidence of his own letters are strongly supported by his record as a public servant. He compounded the impact of the Irish famine, made a hash of supplying troops in the Crimea and failed to achieve reform of the civil service. He was also hauled back from the governorship of Madras after causing a furore by leaking official taxation papers to the press. It was not a terribly impressive record.

Trevelyan's early career in the Indian civil service had been marked by a number of rows, but he had emerged unscathed. Lord Bentinck, the Governor-General of India, told Trevelyan's brother-in-law, Macaulay, that Trevelyan was 'almost always on the right side in every question, and it is as well that he is so, for he gives a most confounded deal of trouble when he happens to take the wrong one'. Trevelyan managed to make a good impression on British politician Sir Francis Thornhill Baring. When Baring became Chancellor of the Exchequer, he invited Trevelyan to take the post of assistant secretary to the Treasury, which Trevelyan duly took up in 1840; he would remain at the Treasury for the next nineteen years.

Whatever criticisms may be levelled against the quality of Trevelyan's work, there can be no doubting his effort; he worked long hours and seldom took leave. It may well have been his energy that induced Baring to appoint him, since Trevelyan's two immediate predecessors had retired on health grounds as a result of the pressures of work. Trevelyan not only laboured hard himself; he drove his subordinates with corresponding vigour. He would not allow staff working in Ireland to return to England except on official business, and many of them were kept at work even when they fell ill; a number of his Treasury subordinates had their health broken by the demands Trevelyan made on them. He wrote to one of his staff who suffered from ill health, informing the man that if he mentioned this fact in any letters it would be 'inconsistent with the propriety of official correspondence'.

Trevelyan's first public articulation of his ideas for reforming the civil service took place in March 1848, when he appeared before the Parliamentary Select Committee on Miscellaneous Expenditure and was quizzed about the operations of the Treasury. The inquisition was wide-ranging and covered the organisation and workload of the department, as well as the handsome bonus (a year's salary of £2,500) that Trevelyan had received for his work on Irish famine relief.

It was probably because he knew questions would be asked about this bonus that he laid it on about the volume of work he and other senior officials undertook. Being in charge of famine relief was, Trevelyan said, 'the most laborious work I ever had in my life'. In response to questions from the committee, he said no extra assistance had been provided 'expressly for that purpose' (which suggests that extra assistance was provided, but that he thought it would sound better if he could imply the opposite). 'Many officers of the Treasury were kept in day after day late at night,' Trevelyan stated. 'There were six or eight of us who never went home before half-past seven or eight, and we often stayed till nine or ten; sometimes we saw daylight before we left the Treasury.'

In response to further probing he said normal hours of work were from ten till four, 'but it is considered sufficient if everybody is present at half-past ten'. Some indication of the extent of the uselessness of much of what went on in the Treasury was revealed as committee members chipped away. Trevelyan was asked to explain how business was conducted. His explanation was one Thomas Cromwell would have been familiar with. Incoming post went to the registry, where it was briefly summarised, registered numerically and details placed in an alphabetical book under relevant headings. Post was then assigned to the relevant person by the principal clerk at the registry. If it was an ordinary matter coming under some established rule, that person would prepare a minute on the action needed. More complex issues were referred to the secretary (Trevelyan) or the Chancellor for a decision.

Whatever the route, the end product was a minute suggesting action, which would be read out at one of two weekly meetings of the board of the Treasury. On average, Trevelyan and four other officials each spent five hours a week taking part in this pantomime. When pressed, Trevelyan admitted that the Lords of the Treasury, to whom the minutes were read, added little value, and that they were not in any sense responsible for actions taken in their name. The sheer futility of the exercise was finally prised out of Trevelyan when he revealed that no note of these meetings had been taken since 1809!

In the context of explaining about the heavy burden placed on senior staff, Trevelyan was able to introduce his idea that low-grade work should be done by specially hired clerks. He wanted senior staff to be recruited directly, rather than as was currently the more general practice, of employing young men at a junior level and having them work their way up the career ladder. He was asked if the five divisions of clerks who carried out the Treasury's executive work were as overworked as the senior men. Trevelyan thought not.

There can be little doubt that this portion of the Treasury is overpaid compared with the nature of the business done by them. The business is principally of a mechanical kind, such as copying the minutes, letters and warrants, which would be more properly done by the class of extra clerks ... who are trained to this kind of work and to whom a much lower rate of remuneration affords a sufficient motive for exertion.

It was not just a matter of economy, Trevelyan told the committee. 'A young man comes from a public school full of energy and excited hopes, but after two or three years' incessant copying he becomes disappointed and disgusted. Feeling that he is employed on work of an inferior kind he learns to do it in a mechanical manner.'

What was particularly interesting in view of what happened later was Trevelyan's view that instead of 'young men whose education is unfinished, and of whose qualifications we have no experience', he would take men 'who had completed their education at the universities or elsewhere'. He said that in particular cases he would even go beyond that, and take young men 'who have had some experience and success in life; for I conceive that no test of fitness for the public service is equal to that of a person having succeeded in some other line'. It was perhaps a tad inconsistent to bemoan the fate of energetic and excited public school boys, and then, only a few sentences later, dump the public schools as a source of recruitment. But consistency was never one of Trevelyan's strong points.

Other witnesses were quizzed about Trevelyan's proposal. Sir Alexander Spearman, who had been assistant secretary to the Treasury from 1836 until 1840, when ill health forced him to resign, said his opinion was 'in entire disaccordance' with Trevelyan's. Spearman thought that if the Treasury recruited senior staff from outside the Treasury and employed junior copy clerks from the law stationers, no one would gain any understanding of the work of the office.

To enable those officers properly to execute those functions requires, of course, a thorough knowledge of the Treasury, and that knowledge I think they acquire very satisfactorily by the system under which they rise gradually from a junior clerkship, through the assistantship, to be senior and to be chief ... whereas if they were selected, as I understand from Mr Trevelyan's evidence he proposed they should be, from other walks of life, having no previous acquaintance whatever with the duties of the Treasury, or with the regulations by which the Treasury is governed in its relation to other departments of state, they must come in igno-rant upon such subjects, however able men they may be in other respects, and therefore they must themselves depend in very great degree, and for a long time, upon assistance from others; and which it does not seem to me they ever could get from persons in the situation of mere law stationers' clerks.

Spearman was supported by George Boyd, the chief clerk of the second division, who said, 'The first years I was in the office I did not understand what I was doing ... By degrees I began to under-stand it and enter into the importance of the duties ... which by degrees made me competent.'

In its report, the committee said it was not prepared 'to express an opinion favourable to the suggestion submitted by Sir Charles Trevelyan for an alteration to the Establishment of the Treasury'. Committee members noted that senior staff at the Treasury had criticised it, and also made the point that if it was appropriate for the Treasury then it should be applied to all public offices.

Although he made no progress with the committee, Trevelyan continued to beaver away (despite his pressing workload), initi-ating a series of inquiries into major government departments such as the Home Office, some Irish departments, the Foreign Office and the War Office. On the whole, he was not particular-ly successful in propagating his ideas among other departments, with the War Office, Foreign Office and Home Office seeing him off reasonably comprehensively. Both the War Office and the Home Office accused him of failing to understand their work.

The Foreign Office, much to Trevelyan's chagrin, simply ignored him. In the Treasury, and also in the Colonial Office, there was movement towards instituting a distinction between 'intellectual' and 'mechanical' work, but the Financial Secretary to the Treasury, James Wilson, blocked Trevelyan's efforts to widen the divide between the intellectual and the mechanical to the point of divorcing policy-making from policy implementation.

The relationship between Trevelyan and Wilson was a poor one, and would worsen later. Wilson was a man with a habit of 'always beginning with the facts, always arguing from the facts and always ending with the result applicable to the facts'. Trevelyan was seldom interested in anything other than his own opinions, which might have some factual input, but just as likely would be no more than prejudice without any basis in fact. Trevelyan was one of the few people for whom Wilson, a notably amiable man, conceived an intense dislike.

Trevelyan enjoyed more luck with his inquiry at the Board of Trade. He had been joined in this inquiry by Sir Stafford Northcote, who as well as being private secretary to Gladstone had been a highly regarded legal advisor at the Board of Trade, before resigning on the advice of his doctors, who told him that he suffered from a 'very decided disease of the heart' and needed perhaps two years' rest. In late 1852, feeling much recovered, he was in correspondence with Gladstone about the possibility of a job. Northcote wanted a seat in Parliament but had no immediate hopes of selection, so he said he would accept a job under the Liberal government despite being 'a rather stiff Conservative' (when Gladstone sought his opinion in 1853, Northcote said he opposed opening the universities to Dissenters). In December, Northcote wrote to tell Gladstone he was 'free of the doctors', and on Christmas Day he wrote again: 'I have heard of a piece of work going on which, if it is to be continued, would suit me exactly. It would keep me in sight and in occupation without placing me in any difficulty.'

The work was to take up the spare place on Trevelyan's Board of Trade inquiry team. Northcote did not say how he had heard of this work, but the most likely source was Thomas Farrer, the recently appointed assistant secretary at the board's marine department. Farrer had been a friend of Northcote at Eton and both had gone to Balliol. More recently, Northcote had married Farrer's sister. Having no doubt heard of some of the difficulties other departments had encountered with Trevelyan's inquiries, the Board of Trade officials might well have been hoping to use Northcote as a knowledgeable balance against Trevelyan.

Whatever the reason, Northcote got the job, and Trevelyan subsequently developed a high opinion of him. As a result of the inquiry, which Trevelyan regarded as his masterpiece, a special department was formed to do the mechanical work (a practice the Department of Trade and Industry revived in the late noughties). However, following Trevelyan's return to India in 1859, to become the Governor of Madras, the Board of Trade reverted to a single class of clerks because pressures of business had made Trevelyan's system unworkable. For the time being, though, Trevelyan could relish some progress, and no doubt Northcote benefited as a consequence. At any rate, he was invited to help Trevelyan in another inquiry at the Board of Control for India, just at a time when Northcote's friend Benjamin Jowett was about to get his opportunity to subvert the India Bill.

Jowett, while working hard on the India Bill, kept a close watch on Trevelyan's work on the public departments in England. Although Trevelyan had not been particularly successful in foisting his ideas on government departments, he had managed to persuade Gladstone that his work could have implications for the civil service generally. In April 1853, a Treasury minute was issued requesting Trevelyan to undertake a review of the public establishments in order to 'place them on the footing best calculated for the efficient discharge of their important functions, according to the actual circumstances of the present time'. There is evidence that Trevelyan had a hand in the drafting of the minute for, among other topics, the review was to consider 'establishing a proper distinction between intellectual and mechanical labour', and to ensure that only those in good health were appointed.

By the late summer of 1853, Trevelyan had completed nearly all his reports on individual departments. On 13 September, he wrote to Gladstone to inform him about progress on the few outstanding inquiries and enclosing copies of all inquiry reports, except those (at the Home Office, Foreign Office and War Office) which had been rejected, and about which Trevelyan was silent. The final paragraph of the letter addressed the outstanding remit to produce a wider-ranging report.

> But by far the most important work which we have before us is the general report to which our attention was called by the second paragraph of the Treasury minute of 12 April last, the object of which will be to suggest the improvements applicable to the whole of the departments and especially those which are required to secure proper qualification of young men appointed to them, and their subsequent promotion according to merit so as to provide a future supply of able senior officers for the public service.

The letter indicates the extent to which Trevelyan had a clear idea of what he wanted to achieve. This is not surprising given the amount of work that he had done on the reports on individual departments; he would later describe the general report as bringing 'to fruition the result of fourteen years continual labour'.

Shortly after writing this letter, Trevelyan took a month's leave, but by 23 November he had delivered the completed report to Gladstone. It is highly likely that he drafted it while on holiday. He managed to produce it so quickly, Trevelyan said, because it was simply the distillation of inquiries he had carried out in the departments over the previous few years. The reality is that he wrote it quickly partly because the report was short – twenty-three pages – and partly because it consisted of little more than a rant against alleged abuses (for which he produced no evidence) followed by a prescription (equally devoid of supporting evidence) to put things right.

For a report that aimed to revolutionise Whitehall and place the public services on a statutory footing for the first time, it was lamentably lacking in substance and, as originally drafted, fatally flawed in terms of appealing to Trevelyan's colleagues in other departments. He wrote that admission to the civil service was eagerly sought after, 'but it is for the unambitious and the indolent or incapable that it is chiefly desired'. Those men 'whose abilities do not warrant an expectation that they will succeed in the open professions … and those whose indolence of temperament or physical infirmities make them unfit for active exertions' were placed in the civil service. Trevelyan chose to ignore the excellent work done in public health by Edwin Chadwick, and in education by James Kay-Shuttleworth. He also ignored the supervision of Britain's exceptional economic growth by the Board of Trade, and the factory inspectorate's alleviation of working conditions caused by that growth. It is perhaps relevant that Trevelyan considered such activities a waste of public money.

He elaborated his concerns about employing those with disabilities, noting 'in particular that the comparative lightness of the work, and the certainty of provision in the case of retirement owing to bodily incapacity, furnish strong inducements to the parents and friends of sickly youths to endeavour to obtain for them employment in the service of the government'. The civil service would cherish for many years a bias against disabled people; it became almost impossible for them to join the service. When I became a civil servant in 1963, I was scandalised to learn that a colleague who suffered from chronic myopia was 'permanent but unestablished' – he could never get a pension. Even today only some 4 per cent of civil servants are disabled, and many of them acquired their disability after joining.

The report raised the issue about whether youths or more mature adults should be recruited. Trevelyan believed 'it was decidedly best' to train youths as 'the superior docility of young men renders it much easier to make valuable public servants of them'. Docility is still highly valued by the civil service; in 2003 a candidate was failed for being too forthright and confident in his own abilities. He joined a major UK retailer where his talents were quickly recognised. Within three years he was promoted to just below director level. The retail company is highly successful, perhaps because it has no hang-ups about employing confident or forthright staff.

Trevelyan also worried about the important issue of costs.

A young man who has not made trial of any of the other professions will be induced to enter the civil service by a much more modest remuneration than would suffice to attract him a few years later from the pursuit of one in which he had overcome the first difficulties and begun to achieve success; while to attempt to fill the ranks of the civil service with those who had failed elsewhere, and were on that account willing to accept a moderate salary, would be simply to bring it into discredit.

The report's key recommendations were that work in departments should be divided between intellectual and mechanical activity, and that promotion be based on merit. The report also recommended that staff be subjected to regular reporting procedures, and be moved around regularly to gain a breadth of experience. It also wanted top posts in a specific department to be open to staff across the service. Apart from Trevelyan's pet theory about splitting intellectual and mechanical work, these recommendations were potentially useful. And although he made no significant attempt to justify them, such a case could have been made. Even the division of work could have been justified in some circumstances, though these were few and declining in number.

What is surprising is that, as originally drafted, the report contained only the most meagre proposals for establishing entry to the civil service via a competitive literary exam – one for intellectuals and one for the mechanicals. There was such a proposal but it did not extend to departments subordinate to the Treasury – i.e. some 90 per cent of the civil service who worked in the Revenue departments and the Post Office. It was, in many ways, illustrative of Trevelyan's limited abilities that he should think it possible to ram competitive exams down the throats of other departments while preserving for the Treasury the power of patronage.

As drafted, the report reflected Trevelyan's practice of seeking to place friends and relatives in government jobs without much concern about their abilities. Shortly after publication of the report he wrote to Benjamin Hawes at the War Office, soliciting a post for a Macaulay relative 'not with any view of asking a favour, but to indicate an eligible candidate for employment'. It was possible, though, to strain Trevelyan's willingness to use his patronage: 'I twice obtained probationary appointments for your nephew, and twice he was removed for misconduct. I cannot consistently with my duty to the public ask for a third trial for him'.

There was also, in the original draft of the report, a suggestion harking back to Lord Grenville's ideas of 1813 that there should be a separate competition for the sons of 'deserving public servants'. Trevelyan regularly used patronage as an appropriate reward for colleagues he thought deserving: 'Mr Wild is an officer of the highest merit, and would according to our common practice be entitled to an appointment for his son'. On another occasion he explained that

The person who attends to the binding of books at the Treasury, J. M. Parker, is anxious to get a son of his employed in the coast-guard service. I do not in the least wish to press him upon your notice, but as Parker has earned a good character in the public service, it is due to him to submit his request for your consideration.

Most bizarrely of all, in a report that was supposed to be an assault upon patronage, there was a recommendation that candidates for clerkships in the highest offices be selected by the First Lord of the Treasury, and that in making this selection he give due weight to the recommendations of his colleagues and parliamentary supporters. In effect, Trevelyan was proposing to put patronage on a statutory footing!

Gladstone must have been amazed; he put pen to paper and wrote at considerable length and with considerable vigour. Although it had been Trevelyan who had submitted the draft report to Gladstone, and indeed he who had written it, Gladstone sent his response to Northcote; Gladstone warmly supported other aspects of the report but criticised its limited attack on patronage.

Gladstone was 'keenly anxious to strike a blow at parliamentary patronage … aimed at its seat of life'. He was equally concerned to avoid the proposal 'failing through the reciprocal jealousy of departments'. Gladstone thought that if this happened the proposal would 'not only be unsuccessful but discredited, as the whole discussion will assume the character of a selfish squabble, strongly flavoured with hypocrisy'. Excluding the Treasury from competition would be 'viewed as a device for the aggrandisement of the functionaries of the Treasury at the expense, it may be said by the plunder, of other departments'. Gladstone added the further thought that it was precisely the Treasury departments where the worst appointments were made. He wanted the principle of competition 'sanctioned in its full breadth', and applied to the Treasury 'with unsparing vigour'. Of the proposal that MPs should lobby for candidates for the highest offices, he said it should 'disappear'; otherwise patronage would have a 'standing ground from which it would wriggle itself once more into possession of all the spaces from which it had been ejected'.

There was clearly a meeting of minds, as three days later Gladstone dropped a note to Northcote to say he was 'very glad to find that we are so unequivocally in harmony' and suggesting that the proceedings 'ought to be kept closely to ourselves for the present'. Gladstone's latter point was no doubt intended to try to head off Trevelyan's propensity to write to *The Times*; it failed!

On the contents of the report, Gladstone was successful. Within a few weeks, Northcote was able to inform Gladstone that common sense had prevailed. It is not clear how he won the point, but he did, and when the amended report was published nearly a year later it proposed to apply the competitive principle to all departments. Following discussions with Gladstone, as well as adverse comments from Jowett, Trevelyan also dropped his proposal for special treatment for the sons of deserving public servants. On 28 January 1854, Trevelyan wrote to Northcote:

> I have in some degree matured my ideas and have talked them over with Gladstone and I now propose to give you the result.
>
> I think that the Act should be confined 1st To laying down the principle in the most carefully selected words we can employ, that those persons should be appointed to the public offices who are most eligible in points of character, health, ability and education.
>
> 2nd To appoint a Board of Examiners to carry that principle into effect.
>
> 3rd To directing that the rules under which the examinations are to be conducted should be determined from time to time by Order in Council.
>
> 4th To prescribing that the reasons for every promotion shall be recorded in each department and that a copy of this record shall be forwarded to the Board of Examiners.
>
> I ought to have mentioned at an earlier period of my letter that I was agreeably surprised to find that not only is our principle to be applied without dilution, but we are to be at liberty to apply it to every case of first appointment.
>
> Great doubts were, however, entertained of the felicity of giving any advantage to the sons of public servants. It was stated that when everybody else gave up their patronage, public officers ought

to do so too, and Gladstone justly remarked that from their more perfect knowledge of what was required to pass the examinations they would have an advantage over other people in getting appointments for their sons.

You will see what Jowett says about it in one of the accompanying letters. My conclusion is we shall have to give it up at last and that we had therefore better do so at first before we have weakened our cause by the odium it would bring upon us.

On the same day, Trevelyan wrote to Jowett that he would be 'glad to know that you are not the only person opposed to the special position for the sons of public servants'. Trevelyan had clearly taken on board Gladstone's point, and on 31 January he wrote to tell Gladstone he was 'now quite convinced that the paragraph ... ought to be omitted' and that he had 'persuaded Northcote accordingly'. But if Trevelyan had lost this point, he seemed to have won the main argument, and to have the Chancellor's blessing for legislation to implement it. His first instinct was to get some publicity. There is an unfinished draft of a letter to Delane at *The Times*, dated 4 February:

My friend and colleague Mr Jowett writes to me from Oxford that one of the objections made to the plan for throwing open the public service is the suddenness with which it has broken upon the public, and he suggests that the public should be prepared for it by articles exposing patronage and showing the bearing of the system upon the election.

The draft letter is crossed out, and it is not clear if it was sent. It is possible that Trevelyan remembered how in January Gladstone had choked him off for leaking to the press. He replied on 18 January: 'I will immediately take the most effectual steps in my power to prevent any further discussion of the plan in the newspapers, and I shall be disappointed if I cannot do it effectually.' In theory,

Trevelyan could guarantee to be effectual as he was probably the only source of the leaks. But he was so uncontrollable that barely a fortnight later, on 6 February, Trevelyan did write to Delane at *The Times*: 'The high aristocracy have been accustomed to employ the civil establishment as a means of providing for the waifs and strays of their families – a sort of foundling hospital.' The letter went on to accuse successive dukes of Norfolk of having a tradition of using the civil service to provide for illegitimate sons. But although Trevelyan wrote in lurid terms to Delane, he was capable of taking a different line if it suited his purpose. On 14 March, he wrote reassuringly to a correspondent about those who might enter the service by examination: 'The arbiters of their official fate, remember, under the political heads of departments, will be the gentlemen appointed under the old system. Experience and ability, and long faithful and useful service, which exist in large proportion in every office will always be respected by young men.'

Trevelyan was equally capable of representing the report as a form of social engineering, rather than a means of increasing efficiency, claiming that 'the irresistible tendency of the times is to bring into activity the political power of the lower classes of society'. He believed that with good schooling, inherent superiority would enable the ruling class to maintain its ascendancy, and 'we must prepare for the trial by cultivating to the utmost the superior morality and intelligence which comprise our real strength'. The key to achieving this was to make entry to the civil service conditional on passing a competitive exam. Trevelyan reasoned that the ruling class would always come out on top. In commenting to Gladstone on a paper written by Captain H. D. O'Brien, private secretary to the First Lord of the Admiralty, Trevelyan wrote:

The tendency of the measure [the report] will, I am confident, be distinctly aristocratic, but it will be so in a good sense by securing for the public service those who are, in a true sense, worthy. At present a mixed multitude is sent up, a large proportion of whom, owing to the operation of political and personal patronage, are of an inferior rank of society.

The words 'a mixed multitude' are slightly out of the ordinary; the phrase was used by the Greek historian Thucydides to describe people in the city of Amphipolis, some of whom could not be relied upon to support the Athenian cause. Trevelyan's use of the phrase might well have carried pejorative significance for his colleagues with a good knowledge of the Greek classics (there is evidence that Trevelyan was reading Thucydides's *History of the Peloponnesian Wars* during this period).

While he extolled the aristocratic effects of his proposals to Gladstone, Trevelyan was equally happy to assure others that the proposals would not discriminate against 'inferior ranks'. In January 1855, he wrote to Sir A. Y. Spearman (Comptroller of the National Debt Office):

> I enclose a paragraph cut out of Northcote's and my answer to the Lords of the Treasury in which we disclaim any intention of proposing that the supplementary clerks should not be eligible for higher appointments. Such an idea never occurred to us ... Any person ... who shows that he possesses qualifications for higher employment should be removed to a higher sphere of employment, and the tenor of all our remarks and recommendations is to favour such promotions.

Irrespective of what Trevelyan really thought, his comments about the superiority of the upper classes could have come from the pen of any of those engaged in the Victorian reforms of the public schools and universities, or from existing members of the political establishment. Journalist and essayist Walter Bagehot, for example, thought that 'the highest classes must, as such, have more political ability than the lower classes', while Gladstone offered the view that 'the aristocracy in this country are even superior in natural gifts, on the average, to the mass'. Since the latter point was made in a letter to the Prime Minister, Lord John Russell, who had erupted in a fit of noble rage over Trevelyan's report, it is possible that Gladstone, who was to exhibit some duplicity over the implementation of reform, was simply following his rival Disraeli's advice, and 'laying it on with a trowel' in order to win the PM's backing for civil service reform.

The ructions with Lord John Russell underline how the Victorian reform movements were highly polarised. At one end there was an attempt (supported by writers such as Thackeray and Dickens) to widen the franchise, send the ruling class packing and bring business skills into the process of government. At the other end there was a concerted effort by the ruling class to produce a system that drew the country's greatest scions effortlessly through public school, university and a civil service career with a pension to follow – a cradle-to-grave reward for keeping the lower classes in order!

The upper classes in Britain had been rattled by Europe's 'Year of Revolutions' in 1848 and tended to see anything that did not buttress the existing order as rank republicanism. Early in 1854, Lord John Russell wrote to Gladstone to say he hoped Gladstone was 'not thinking seriously of the plan of throwing open to competition the whole civil service of this country'. The Prime Minister regarded the plan as an attempt 'to substitute talent and cramming for character' in a civil service made up of men of 'unquestionable fidelity, average ability and persevering industry'. It was not a view that Gladstone shared. In his reply, Gladstone took a line not all that different from Trevelyan, although Gladstone's tone was rather more measured.

> I fear the fidelity of the service, which is not to be doubted, is generally negative – it consists in abstinence from doing what is positively wrong. Although there are many able men in the service, yet there are so many who are placed there mainly for their

inability, inability that is to make way in an independent career, that the aggregate, I fear, can scarcely reach the average – in persevering industry I hold them to be chiefly deficient – a relaxed and relaxing tone seems to me the inevitable consequence of seniority under which promotions are usually made, and which is again intimately connected with the system of appointment by patronage.

It was a formidable indictment, but Gladstone was not destined to carry the day.

Although Trevelyan and his Balliol minders were convinced of the need to introduce the new system, they still faced considerable opposition, not only from the Prime Minister, but from those who dispensed patronage lower down the food chain – men such as the Permanent Secretary of the Home Office Horatio Waddington, who did not think 'the system by which appointments are made by the head of the office capable of improvement'. He claimed exams could do nothing to test candidates' integrity, and pointed out that the work of departments was varied; thus departments needed to be able to tailor their recruitment process to their own needs.

In effect, such critics were making the very points Trevelyan himself had made in 1848 and 1853 in respect of selecting staff for the Indian civil service. Most probably, the major issue was the one Gladstone had warned Northcote about: a reluctance to concede power to a central authority that departmental heads probably viewed, rightly, as being an extension of the Treasury and hence of the Treasury's ability to meddle in their affairs. In addition, departmental heads knew that resolute opposition had enabled the Home Office and War Office to see off Trevelyan's earlier proposals for organisational change (and the Foreign Office to ignore his report on its work altogether). Trevelyan had also probably done himself no favours by habitually and gratuitously offering advice to those about whose business he knew little, and understood less.

Trevelyan's biggest mistake, however, had been the inclusion in the report of rude and unsubstantiated comments about civil servants. There seems little doubt that he had some duffers on his books at the Treasury, but his letters reveal only a few cases.

> Has not sufficient time elapsed to enable you to arrive at a clear opinion on Mr Drugan's case? We cannot submit to the scandal of a person being contained in the ranks of the Department who has rendered himself unfit for the performance of its duties – but if, on the other hand, he has overcome the destructive and beastly habit, and is effective and hard-working, it ought to be so stated. In any case the matter should be made the subject of an official report.

One can only speculate as to the nature of Mr Drugan's 'destructive and beastly habit'. Other cases were clearer.

> Your application for leave of absence is such as I cannot approve of. I have often warned you against making your duties at the Treasury secondary to your zeal and supposed interest in connection with your invention; and it is now quite time that you should choose between them. If you can only give a divided and unsettled attention to the business of the Treasury, you ought in common honesty to resign your situation here. I must entirely decline giving any countenance to your proposal to remain absent from the Treasury for a month on the plea of ill health, but with the real object of exerting yourself in various ways in forwarding your private interests. The medical certificate which you have sent states that the rheumatic gout having attacked your left ankle, you are at present incapacitated from walking. If at the end of a week you are still unable to come to the Treasury, I must desire that you will send me another medical certificate to that effect. Else I shall submit our correspondence to the Board, with a statement of the case.

Trevelyan understood that people often put up with a sub-standard service (as they do now) because of the effort involved in getting rid of staff. But the key point about Trevelyan's adverse comments on civil servants was not whether they could be justified, but that they caused unnecessary opposition to the report – a point he himself came to recognise eventually. In October 1855, Trevelyan wrote that 'people do not easily forgive what they esteem an attack on the character of the body to which they belong', but by then it was too late.

Early in 1854, the revised report, together with Jowett's proposals for a competitive exam, was circulated to a number of academics and senior bureaucrats. The academics' comments tended to concentrate on Jowett's proposals, and were mainly supportive – though Jowett's co-conspirator over Haileybury, Dr Vaughan, wondered whether Jowett had been too prescriptive. But the bureaucrats went for Trevelyan's attack on the civil servants and rubbished him. Reading their replies, you can sense that they relished the opportunity.

From the Home Office, Horatio Waddington wrote:

> The assertion that a large proportion of the civil servants of this country are men unambitious, indolent or incapable; men whose abilities do not warrant an expectation that they will succeed in the open professions; men whose indolence of temperament or physical infirmities unfit them for active exertion; sickly youths who retire upon pensions, owing to bodily incapacity, or absent themselves from their duties on the grounds of ill health, so as to burden the public to an extent hardly to be credited – are, as far as my experience and information extend, entirely without foundation.

Sir Thomas Francis Fremantle, chairman of the Board of Customs, was equally trenchant:

> I feel called upon, so far as my own experience goes, to deny the accuracy of those conclusions. I believe that the clerks and

officers of the civil departments generally are faithful, diligent and competent; that the public business of those departments is well conducted; and that their efficiency would not suffer by comparison with that of the army, the navy or any other service in the state; or with public companies or large establishments, under the management of private individuals.

Mr Arbuthnot, the auditor of the Civil List, referred to a contemporary article in *The Times* that was couched in similar terms to the offending paragraphs of the report, which, Arbuthnot wrote, 'created a strong feeling of indignation in the minds of the civil servants, which has been confirmed and strengthened since they found the same opinion ventilated in a public and formal document'.

The article that Arbuthnot referred to was probably the one printed in *The Times* on 12 January 1854.

The clerk in a government office is generally looked upon as a person not to do more than he can help – as one whose unambitious youth preferred a small certainty and the routine duties of an office to the enterprise and perseverance which have led his schoolfellows and acquaintances to prosperity ... the service is sought after rather by the indolent and inefficient than by a more desirable class ... at present it is notorious that in this country the public service is hardly ever thought of by those who have a chance of succeeding in any other walk of life.

Trevelyan, on behalf of himself and Northcote, wrote to the Lords Commissioners of the Treasury (effectively to his boss, Gladstone):

We admit that, looking to the effect which the publication of our remarks was likely to have upon the minds of persons less well acquainted with the civil service than Your Lordships, it was an error on our part that we did not more distinctly express the sense we entertain of its merits.

As apologies go, it was about as mealy-mouthed as he could make it. Concerning the report in *The Times*, Trevelyan blandly claimed to be 'wholly ignorant of the authorship of the article', which was a bit rich given that he'd been writing incessantly to the editor. The leaks caused Gladstone some difficulty with the Prime Minister, Lord John Russell.

The departmental heads, in their responses to the draft report, also criticised the thinking underlying the proposals for change; as ever it was the concept of 'one size fits all' that they objected to most. Oddly, none of them pointed out that the Treasury minute commissioning the report had required Trevelyan to frame his recommendation 'according to the actual circumstances of the present time'; he had certainly not done so, and though they didn't pick up on his failure to comply with his remit, they certainly made their feelings clear. As the Rt Hon. H. U. Addington, Under-Secretary of State at the Foreign Office, put it, 'The Foreign Office and the Excise Office, for instance, are equally component parts of the civil service, and yet they are so totally dissimilar in all essential points that the same rules touching qualifications, and consequently touching examination, cannot possibly apply to both.'

Benjamin Hawes, Under-Secretary of State for War, who had already seen off Trevelyan's inquiry into the War Office, attacked the criticisms of the civil service and then proceeded to tweak Trevelyan's tail: 'I should, therefore, reverse the recommendation of the report and confine the duties of the examiners to determining who is not to be admitted to the public service, not who is to be employed; in fact, to putting simply a negative upon the appointment of incompetent candidates.'

One of the most considered comments came from Rowland Hill at the Post Office. Hill was technically subordinate to Trevelyan, but he was not noted for keeping his opinions to himself.

Examination, indeed, so far as relates to such qualifications as are necessary for the service in view, would undoubtedly be of great use; but a competition by which appointments would be given mechanically to such non-disqualified candidates as display the greatest amount of literary attainment would, I fear, place admission and exclusion on an unsound basis.

I am of the opinion that all ends might be tolerably well attained by an arrangement which should provide for the examination of all such candidates as might be nominated by the heads of the respective offices, and should limit appointments to those who after satisfying the examiners as to their age, health and moral fitness, should demonstrate their possession of such knowledge, and, so far as it can be ascertained, such intelligence as are required for that grade in the service to which they have been nominated. Further security being taken by a probation which I think should last for at least a year.

In a nutshell, Hill had reasserted the concept of the East India Company: relevant knowledge and a probationary period.

Similar points to those made by the heads of departments were made by Lord Monteagle in a debate that he initiated in the House of Lords on 13 March. He referred to a leak to the press that had resulted in a 9 February newspaper article which quoted verbatim from the report; Monteagle deplored the fact the press should be given a sight of official papers before the House had read them. He also deplored the 'most insulting expressions to the civil service, which is described as characterised by its incapacity, its indifference, and its idleness; as owing its origin chiefly to private interest, or to political venality, and remarkable for neglected duties and for a supercilious demeanour'.

Monteagle vigorously attacked such views, citing civil servants whom he had worked with, and pointing out that no evidence had been produced to support the criticisms. He noted that while the overall report had been published, together with reports of investigations into specific departments where Trevelyan's proposals had been accepted, those reports that had failed to win acceptance had not been published. Monteagle argued, as did other lords, that Parliament was being asked to legislate on evidence that was 'not only incomplete, but partial and *ex parte*'. He pointed out, at some length, that the only precedent for appointing civil servants by competitive literary exams was that of the Chinese government. In the fifth century BC, after the end of feudalism in China, officials had grown increasingly interested in a literary style based heavily on certain old books; admission to the civil service became dependent on examinations geared almost exclusively to literary style and a knowledge of antiquity.

Monteagle did not consider the Chinese model a good one to follow and, in a parody of Macaulay's 1833 speech, he argued that elegant writing had become an end in itself, and the stultifying effect of this on the Chinese civil service had contributed in no small measure to China's failure to develop its early lead over Western civilisations. Monteagle moved 'that there be laid before this House, a copy of the instructions given to the commissioners who have reported on the state of the civil service, and of the evidence taken before them'.

Replying for the government, Lord Granville pointed out that it had yet to decide what action to take on reform of the civil service and had not asked Parliament to agree to anything. Granville managed to sidestep the issue of the non-existent evidence by blandly stating it was not the practice to take down evidence in shorthand, which implied that evidence had been taken without involving the noble lord in an outright lie. He refused to answer detailed criticism concerning Trevelyan's diatribe against civil servants, but did offer the thought that 'both gentlemen and persons of lower class found their way into the service, and that the latter owed their preferment not to any exertion or merit of their own'. Granville went further: 'With respect, too, to the other class, it might be said, without disrespect to the service, that, of the class of gentlemen, under the present system, the best persons in the family did not seek to go into the public services.' As a lordly put-down it could hardly be bettered, but it would have done nothing to help Trevelyan's chances of getting any action.

It was not only the top men who held strong views on the subject. Anthony Trollope, who was still working for the Post Office as well as writing his novels, had obtained his original clerkship because one of his mother's friends was the daughter-in-law of the secretary of the Post Office. After something of a lackadaisical start, Trollope proved to be hard-working and highly inventive (he is credited with introducing the pillar box to the UK). Trollope had grown highly attached to the existing system and became so enraged by the Trevelyan proposals that he wrote a book, *The Three Clerks*, about the evils of promotion on merit.

One letter writer to the *Civil Service Gazette*, who signed off as 'An Ex-official', took up Lord Monteagle's example of the Chinese system, arguing that 'we do not want mandarin ministers, nor is it the English habit to confound pedantry with talent'. The *Civil Service Gazette*, which enjoyed a wide circulation, probably reflected the majority view when it took a swipe at Jowett, whose paper, titled 'Organisation of the Permanent Civil Service', was bound with the Northcote–Trevelyan Report for presentation to Parliament.

We cannot but regret the publication of [Jowett's note] as exceedingly ill-advised as, whatever credit the public and the government offices may allow to those two distinguished civilians for an important desire to raise the standard of talent in the several departments of the state service, will be greatly detracted from when it is found that a cut and dried plan of examinations by a university tutor is apparently made part of the scheme, which bears all the appearance of an arrangement for enabling gentlemen who have attained but limited honours at the universities to successfully compete with the steady-going, efficient, but non-classically educated men to be found in the majority of our public offices.

The *Gazette* had a point. Jowett had worked his way into a

controlling position. In later correspondence with Robert Lowe, Gladstone commented that all Trevelyan needed was 'a strong man over him'; it seems likely that Jowett provided such strength.

Trevelyan realised that he was in trouble, but he was not aware of the extent of his problem. On 27 February, he wrote to Jowett:

> Now that the report and letters have been published, the nature of the opposition to the plan has begun to appear. It is mainly to be expected from classes of persons interested in the continuation of the present system. The corps of civil servants do not like it because the introduction of well-educated, active men appointed on a different principle will force them to bestir themselves, and because they cannot hope to get their own ill-educated sons appointed under the new system. The old established political families habitually batten on the public patronage – their sons legitimate and illegitimate, their relations and dependants of every degree are provided for by the score. Besides the adventuring disreputable class of MPs who make God knows what use of the patronage, a large number of borough Members are mainly dependent upon it for their seats. What, for instance, are the Members to do who have been sent down by the Patronage Secretary to contest the boroughs in the interest of the government and who are pledged twenty deep to their constituents?

It was a fair assessment of the forces ranged against him, though Trevelyan's comments about MPs and patronage sit oddly with his original proposal in the draft report to give them a statutory role in appointments to higher offices. On 14 March, he wrote to a colleague, 'The struggle will be sharp because we are here in London in the midst of a community composed of patrons and clients: but if the unpatronised masses understand and accept the proposed boon, it will be short.' It is a bit difficult to see quite what this 'boon' for the masses was, since Trevelyan had said the effect of the change would be 'distinctly aristocratic'. In any event, what really mattered was what the top bureaucrats thought – and what they said to their chums in the London clubs. And the weight of such opinion was clear; the Northcote–Trevelyan Report was dead in the water.

Trevelyan had done himself no favours by seeking to canvass support for his ideas in the press, which annoyed his political masters as well as his colleagues in Whitehall. Had he not been so tactless he might have proved more successful. He did have some valid points, and it is probably fair to say that at least some of the anger vented against him was the rage of Caliban seeing his face in the mirror. But the one lesson that Trevelyan seemed quite incapable of learning was that the civil service was not homogenous; the Foreign Office Under-Secretary had been right: a single prescription would never work. The *Civil Service Gazette* weighed in on this point:

> That clerks in the Treasury, Board of Trade and Foreign Office might advantageously possess an elementary acquaintance with political economy, modern history, international law and modern languages, we think will on all hands be admitted, but that the Post Office clerks would send letters more effectively to their destinations, or Customs or Revenue officers perform their duties with greater benefit to the public, if they were learned in classical literature, natural science or moral philosophy, we think no one would be bold enough to assert.

Trevelyan sensed that his report had placed too little emphasis on the lower ranks of the civil service, and on the career opportunities it could provide for the sons of middle-class families. He wrote to Professor Thompson at Cambridge University:

> After our plan was promulgated the great body of public officers and the middle classes generally complained that the Oxford and Cambridge men would carry off all the prizes and of the two they have most reason on their side. We must take care that the plan

of the examinations is formed to encourage <u>every</u> <u>good</u> system of examination.

In order to get publicity for his new insight, Trevelyan wrote an anonymous letter to the *Civil Service Gazette* in March 1854 using the sign-off 'A Civil Servant'. In the letter, he suggested that what was proposed would involve tests for three levels of candidates: those from the universities; those with a good education; and those of good character and industry. He then proceeded to undermine completely the basis of Jowett's examination proposals. 'In order to prevent cramming it is proposed to have no fixed tests. The principle upon which the examination will be conducted will be to examine the young men in whatever happens to have been the subject matter of their education'.

It is not clear whether Trevelyan intended to change tack, or was simply writing whatever he thought might help to win support for the report. He followed up by writing to a range of people – including the Bishop of Manchester – drawing their attention to the letter in the *Gazette* and admitting authorship. The letter had been written, he explained,

> for the purpose of supplying a defect in Mr Jowett's explanation of the practical application of our plan. It is now obvious that there must be <u>three</u> classes of candidates and three descriptions of examinations, the middle one of which will comprehend the larger number of clerkships, and will act in a direct manner upon the education of the great middle class of society. Those who are unable to give their sons an expensive finished education will not now be discouraged by the prospect of having them brought into competition with highly educated young men from the universities who will have a suitable separate field appropriated to them.

It is not clear if this was Trevelyan's own initiative, or whether Jowett had seen a weakness in his proposals – or had them drawn to his attention by, for example, Dr Vaughan. In any event, it was all too late. In the face of opposition from top civil servants, and a distinct lack of enthusiasm on the part of most ministers – particularly the Prime Minister – Gladstone was not inclined to push the matter too hard. The idea of a central competitive exam was dropped, along with most of the other proposals.

Only one proposal was put into effect; in 1854, Gladstone having damped down the Prime Minister's fire, the Cabinet agreed to the creation of a central examining board. A year later the Civil Service Commission was established, and given the task of testing, according to fixed rules, candidates for junior situations. Candidates were to be nominated by departments which could also set their own entry requirements; the role of the commission was simply to apply those requirements fairly to the candidates put forward. In addition, departments could still appoint persons of mature age to those posts where age limits were not prescribed. Effectively, it was the Rowland Hill model that prevailed.

But even in defeat Jowett sought to gain what he could from the wreckage. He was asked by Gladstone whether he would chair the new Civil Service Commission at a salary of £1,000 a year. Jowett declined, and was then asked by Gladstone to suggest an alternative; Jowett recommended his Oxford colleague and long-term friend, Theodore Walrond.

> I have known Mr Walrond more or less all my life from boyhood: at school, at college, as Master in Rugby School – but chiefly and most intimately during a six month journey with him in the East … living continually for days together in the same boat or in the same tent.

In February 1855, Trevelyan wrote to Walrond offering him the job. For some reason, which I have not been able to establish, Walrond initially did not become a commissioner. But in 1863 he became the commission's secretary, and Jowett had managed to place one more friend in an important position. Walrond was to remain in the post for the next thirteen years, only giving it up to become one of the civil service commissioners – a post he held until 1887. For a quarter of a century, then, one of Jowett's closest friends was to hold a position where he could exert huge influence in the operation of the competition scheme Jowett had masterminded.

# CHAPTER 6

# NO TRADESMEN!

During the 1850s and 1860s, reform of the British civil service continued to inch along as the Treasury used financial means to achieve its ends; the Superannuation Act of 1859 made possession of a certificate from the Civil Service Commission a requirement for getting a pension. Increasingly, departments succumbed to pressure from the commission to nominate more than one candidate for posts, gradually establishing the principle of real competition, albeit that it was competition between departmental nominees.

Even this move could be circumvented by the determined. The Treasury Patronage Secretary, William Hayter, was alleged to keep two halfwits on the payroll (known as 'Hayter's idiots') whose only function was to 'compete' with the desired candidate, thus ensuring that the favoured man always secured the post. Despite such tricks, the new selection arrangements did seem to have an effect in terms of keeping out the totally unsuitable. In 1869, the commissioners produced a paper in which they reported that since 1855, a total of 8,261 nominated candidates had been rejected by the commission (they did not indicate to what extent this figure might include people who had attempted more than once – or stooge candidates such as Hayter's idiots). Some candidates were rejected because they were an unsuitable age, some for reasons of defective health and some for having a bad character, but nearly 6,000 candidates were rejected for being deficient in knowledge. These candidates had not been beaten by a stiff test; they had failed abjectly 'in writing, spelling, arithmetic and other elementary and practical subjects'.

Because the commission had succeeded in excluding outright duffers, the drive for wider reform waned in the years after 1855. James Wilson, the Financial Secretary at the Treasury, had noted the impact of 'the great number of rejections in consequence of inadequate knowledge ... acting as a stimulant to the lower classes in parliamentary boroughs to educate better', while Prime Ministers such as Palmerston were quite content with the new system; there was no one in a position of power to push the issue up the agenda again.

Macaulay died in 1859, and in that same year Trevelyan returned to India to become Governor of Madras (where he immediately caused a rumpus by leaking budget information to the press and had to be recalled). But though there was no one in power who wanted to stir the pot, Jowett and his friends Lowe and Lingen kept the flame alive. Lowe, ever fearful of the Administrative Reform Society's businessmen, remained anxious to find ways to exclude tradesmen's sons from the corridors of power. In 1859, Jowett wrote to Walter Bagehot that 'the passion for equality (the shallowest of all delusions) is so fixed that any attempt to create inequalities between classes in different places would fail'.

Despite his capacity for making enemies (including Queen Victoria), Lowe drifted in and out of office as the political tides ebbed and flowed. When out of office (and sometimes while in office), Lowe earned his keep as a leader writer for *The Times*, on whose pages he inveighed against the rising tide of democracy. It was as a result of his role as a leader writer and friend of Delane, the editor, that Lowe obtained his next important ministerial post. *The Times* cut a deal with Lord Palmerston and began to support the Crimean War; in return, Lowe was made vice-president of the Board of Trade. He thus found himself in his idea of heaven, surrounded by able administrators (for all that they had entered the service by unreformed means) who were disciples of Jeremy Bentham.

It was one of the interesting side effects of the patronage system that it enabled reformers, once they obtained office, to have a lasting impact by selecting young like-minded office holders who would remain in positions of influence for thirty or forty years. That is exactly what happened at the Board of Trade. William Huskisson had been president of the board from 1823 to 1827. A noted Benthamite, he used his powers of patronage to ensure that like-minded officials were appointed.

In 1821, the Political Economy Club was formed with the deliberate intention of propagating the theories of David Ricardo (one of Bentham's closest followers). Two of the businessmen elected to the club – W. B. Baring and Charles Poulett Thomson – would later serve at the Board of Trade, and they also gave their patronage to Benthamite nominees. It was the influence and the appointments made by all three men that turned the board into a great bastion of free trade. Lowe and the Benthamites quickly formed a mutual admiration society and spent long hours planning the reform of company law and shipping dues, and trying to avoid making the railways safer.

Such experiences reinforced Lowe's views about the need to recruit an intellectual elite to run the civil service. It perhaps did not occur to him that those he met at the Board of Trade were not necessarily entirely typical of the output of the universities. It was not just that the Benthamites selected like-minded recruits, but that those of a Benthamite disposition were attracted by those departments which affected the country's economy – the Board of Trade, the Factory Inspectorate, the Education department and the Poor Law Commission. The power of the Benthamites was increased by the fact that such departments were the ones that grew during the middle of the century, so significant numbers were recruited. Lowe's love affair with the board did not last long. In 1858, Palmerston's government fell and Lowe left the Board of Trade for the back benches of the House of Commons.

Lowe held other posts in government, most notably in the Education department, where he found Jowett's friend Ralph Lingen, the department's Permanent Secretary, to be the next best thing to a Board of Trade Benthamite. Together, the two men put back the cause of elementary education some thirty years; Lingen performed this task so well that he gained the rare privilege of becoming someone Lowe actually considered able. Lowe was to harness that ability in the cause of civil service reform, and his opportunity came when Gladstone formed his first ministry in 1868 and appointed Lowe as Chancellor of the Exchequer. Lowe brought Lingen with him as his Permanent Secretary. Jowett's friends were back in power.

Gladstone had suggested to Lowe that he might appoint Trevelyan following his recall from Madras, but Lowe had dismissed the idea out of hand:

> I am averse to the idea of bringing Trevelyan back to the public service. It would be very distasteful to the office. I think very meanly of his judgement. His conduct as regards the income tax in India was very discreditable to him. I know him well and have the strongest conviction that he neither possesses nor deserves further confidence.

It is worth recalling that his work on *The Times* meant Lowe would have had every opportunity to observe Trevelyan leaking like a sieve to try to get his own way. In addition, Lowe might have read Walter Bagehot's criticism of Trevelyan over the Indian budget leak which had appeared in *The Economist*. Bagehot was the brother-in-law of James Wilson, who as Financial Secretary to the Treasury had limited Trevelyan's reform of the Treasury. By chance, Wilson was in Madras when Trevelyan arrived.

Wilson had been invited by Charles Wood, Secretary of State for India, to sort out the finances in the wake of the Indian Mutiny, which had left India some £9 million in the red. The Indian Revenue and Finance departments were to be merged, and Wilson was to be given a new post similar to that of Britain's Chancellor of the Exchequer. Despite his age (he was fifty-four), Wilson had set out for India in October 1859. He made a thorough examination of the issues and, by mid-February 1860, he had produced a budget that covered the deficit and won universal plaudits – from Prince Albert and Robert Lowe in Britain, from the press in India and Britain and from the maharajahs in India. The budget had been a success, but Trevelyan disagreed with it. Without authority, Trevelyan published the minute of the budget meeting and a minute which he himself had written on the issue. His actions caused great embarrassment, both in India and at home, and Trevelyan was recalled. Bagehot duly put the boot in. On 12 May 1860, the front page of *The Economist* gave full details of what had happened and concluded with a damming paragraph:

> Sir Charles Trevelyan thinks there is danger in the course Mr Wilson has taken, but is there not a greater danger in his own course? He has told the natives of Madras that new taxes which are unjust and unnecessary are about to be levied upon them. He has used his authority as local governor to spread this doctrine. He has hinted that he expects the natives will rebel. Who will be to blame if they do rebel? Surely the ruler who was invested with an authority over 30,000,000 of people and who incited them to resistance.

Coming hard upon the heels of the Indian Mutiny, it was a severe stricture. The day before *The Economist* was published, Sir Charles Wood, who had made the decision to appoint Trevelyan, was forced to perform a parliamentary balancing act. Wood attempted to justify his original decision, while also defending Trevelyan's recall:

A more honest, upright and independent servant could not be. He was a loss to India, but there would be danger if he were allowed to remain, after having adopted a course so subversive of all authority, so fearfully tending to endanger our rule and so likely to provoke the people to insurrection against the central and responsible authority.

Later that year, Wilson wrote to Bagehot about the budget. His letter included a very revealing paragraph on Trevelyan:

From the first I anticipated trouble from him, and warned my colleagues of the danger, and our confidential despatch of 9 April was written by me as a consequence of my apprehensions. But it was all in vain. I expected trouble from him, but never that he would proceed to such extremities. I tell you confidentially, and I have told it to others years ago, that I consider poor Trevelyan scarcely accountable for his actions. He has so impulsive a mind, so ill balanced, with such overweening confidence in himself, no matter what the subject might be, equally to command a squadron, lead an army, or regenerate the civil government of a country: with a large smattering upon everything but profound in nothing; with a dull apprehension but with the most dogged obstinacy I ever saw: and with an inordinate vanity and love of notoriety to be gratified; without the slightest judgement or discretion or forethought, or calculation of consequences: all these characteristics lead a man so heedlessly into danger and control him so completely as to leave him hardly a responsible being.

It was a devastating critique, but one that is extensively borne out by Trevelyan's own letters (which fill sixty-eight volumes). There seems to have been a general rejoicing when Trevelyan was recalled to London – the Maharajah of Mysore ordered the firing of a forty-gun salute. Ironically, the death of James Wilson from dysentery shortly after Trevelyan's return to Britain created a vacancy which Sir Charles Wood, despite his criticisms, chose Trevelyan to fill. Trevelyan held the post for three years, implementing the very policies he had previously criticised. He spent the rest of his life seeking to take credit for the work of the man who really did change the civil service, Robert Lowe.

While budgets were Lowe's main concern, when he became Chancellor of the Exchequer it did not take him long to revert to the need for the introduction of open competition. Other ministers were, however, as loath to change the system as their predecessors had been during the previous fourteen years. Successive Prime Ministers in particular had expressed themselves content with the system of limited competition between nominated candidates. There was also little pressure in the country for change, though the matter was raised in the House of Commons in April 1869 in a resolution put forward by the MP for Brighton, Henry Fawcett, a member of the Political Economy Club who had taken a special interest in India.

Fawcett proposed that all posts in the civil and diplomatic services should be subject to open competition. He made the point that some MPs refused to nominate candidates because they thought it might be seen as undermining their independence, while others were only too happy to do so. He cited Sir William Hayter, who kept idiots on the Treasury payroll, who had boasted in a speech at Wells of securing no less than 300 places for his constituents (as with many other aspects of administration, there is nothing new in postcode lotteries).

Fawcett pointed out that tests could not address physical or moral attributes. He quoted a Dr Gull, who had physically examined 500 candidates for the Indian civil service, and who 'could not resist the conclusion that intellectual vigour and physical strength were necessary to success in open competitions'. Fawcett also quoted an unnamed Cambridge tutor who thought that all those who took distinguished degrees possessed a high moral tone.

Despite the fact that such an argument probably appealed to

him, Lowe had to oppose the resolution because the government was content with the existing system and had no intention of changing it. Lowe based his opposition not on the principle of competition, but on the basis that Fawcett's proposal applied across the board and took no account of the appointments that were made of mature men, who should not be subject to such indignity as an exam. Lowe took the opportunity to remind the House that 'since I have been in Parliament, I have always done everything in my power to promote [competition]. Indeed, I had the happiness to take my share in founding the system of Indian competition in 1854 when I was Secretary to the Board of Control.'

Though Lowe toed the party line, he still sought to change it. Lowe was driven by a desire to prevent tradesmen from attaining power and he won support from Jowett, soon to achieve his goal of becoming Master of Balliol. Jowett still sought careers for his graduates who did not fancy either the Church or the Bar, and he remained concerned that his attempts to open up the Indian civil service for this purpose had not fully succeeded. At Lowe's behest ('if we do not make the competitive examination more efficient we are in danger of reverting to the days of Hayter's idiots'), the issue was raised in the Cabinet three times during 1869, but it proved impossible to reach agreement. Gladstone was mildly supportive, but not in a mood to force the pace. He offered Lowe the suggestion that open competition might be introduced in those departments whose ministers were content for it to happen.

Lowe was at first reluctant to follow this half-hearted route. But during the autumn, when he would have had a chance to discuss the issue with Lingen and Jowett, he began to see the possibilities of staging another coup like that which had destroyed the East India College. In November Lowe wrote to Gladstone, saying that the more he thought about the latter's suggestion the more he saw the force of it.

In December 1869, the Cabinet reached a compromise

agreement; departments would be asked whether their minister wished to adopt open competition and if so the extent to which it would apply to posts in their department. In addition, departments would have the right to withdraw from the scheme or to modify it in particular instances. The position was clearly spelled out in the Treasury minutes of 8 December, which were sent to all departments together with a letter requesting 'on the part of their Lordships that you will give your consideration to the subject and that you will be good enough to let me know for their Lordships' information how far you may be disposed to render your co-operation in establishing in your department a system founded upon the principles set forth in this minute'.

The Home Office and the Foreign Office declined to play ball, in both instances citing special needs – the Home Office a need for secrecy and discretion and the Foreign Office the need for 'general intelligence, the habits of subordination and the moral character, that are essential to the well-working of a department like the Foreign Office'. Clarendon, the Foreign Secretary, had shown his draft reply to Gladstone and the latter had suggested some changes. Clarendon had been a friend of James Wilson and would have been aware of Wilson's opposition to Trevelyan's plans for the Treasury in 1854; Clarendon may have been apprehensive that Lowe was seeking to introduce the split between policy-making and implementation that Trevelyan had tried to introduce earlier.

Most other departments responded with cautious approval, but several made it clear that they wanted to keep open the option of nominated appointments to special posts. The reply from the War Office stated that:

Mr Cardwell [the Secretary of State] would, however, at the same time, observe that, for highly confidential situations, some qualities which lie outside the province of examination, are, in his opinion, indispensable; and he concludes that in framing a general scheme upon the subject, this consideration will not be overlooked but that proper safeguards will be provided for ensuring, as far as the nature of the case will admit, the maintenance of a high tone of honour by the selection of persons likely to maintain it.

The Admiralty was less verbose; it agreed to competition 'provided reservation is made of the unmistakeable right of HM's government to appoint otherwise'.

Lord Romilly at the Records Office did not consider the plan for competition

suitable for all the requirements of this office for which special qualifications are necessary. Industry, quickness of apprehension, docility, a disposition to make oneself generally useful in promoting the interests of the department, a correct judgement in ordering affairs (usually termed common sense) and regularity of conduct can never be ascertained by any competitive exam.

The Inland Revenue agreed with the general scheme for senior clerks, but wanted second- and third-class clerks to have a test administered which was adapted to the requirements of each office. Lord Granville at the Colonial Office was content so long as he could prescribe the test for his department, i.e. effectively maintain the existing system.

The writers of these caveats no doubt imagined that their concerns would be taken into account, and probably be the subject of further correspondence or discussion, as would normally be the case in Whitehall on an issue of such importance. But they had reckoned without Lowe and Lingen. Once the departments had committed themselves in principle, Lowen and Lingen began drafting an Order in Council. This order ignored all the special pleading by departments and was to be implemented in a way that effectively did what the Cabinet had specifically rejected: it gave the Treasury full control of recruitment into departments and allowed only the smallest number of exemptions from competitive exams.

There were three further comments from departments that are worth quoting, because they raised issues that would later become important. The Permanent Secretary at the Board of Trade was concerned by the idea to promote an 'inferior class of clerks'. 'In this class', Sir Thomas Farrer wrote, 'there will be men of real ability who ought to be able to rise out of it. Provision should be made to meet special cases'. This was, of course, the very thing that Lowe wished to prevent.

Two departments which clearly shared Lowe's aim of keeping out the lower orders were perceptive enough to see that what Lowe was doing actually jeopardised this aim. The Board of Manufacturing in Edinburgh opposed competition because it would let in those 'unfitted for the work of the department and be also liable to disturb those social relations and distinctions which now exist'. The Paymaster General's Office thought that competition 'would result in a mixture of persons of very various social positions' entering the department and that 'such a diversity of persons performing the same class of work must in various ways be prejudicial and cause friction in the passage of business'. These were exactly the points being made at this time by Sir Charles Wood and Dr Bradward about the consequences of introducing competitive exams for the Indian civil service fifteen years earlier. But no one seems to have made the link.

Lowe could not take on the big guns at the Home and Foreign Offices, but the caveats of the rest were ignored. The Order in Council of 4 June 1870 established the requirement that, for defined posts in the specified departments, entrance would be by examination only. But the order also handed over effective control of the examining process and the Civil Service Commission to the Treasury.

The cautious response of departments in 1854 was now vindicated. But during those intervening years the Treasury's control of departments' finances had grown, and Lowe and Lingen now had access to levers of financial power that enabled them to coerce most of the recalcitrant into line. Most departments concentrated on keeping as many posts as possible exempted from competition, but some dug in their heels and refused to budge. The Home Office, the Foreign Office and the Board of Education saw off the Treasury threat, and were able to do so because Lowe had gone well beyond the Cabinet's remit; but the rest, to a greater or lesser extent, went along with reform. In a period of six months, Lowe and Lingen had advanced from a position where the Treasury had no control over recruitment, to one in which it now not only controlled recruitment to most departments, but also effectively the Civil Service Commission and the examination process itself. The two men succeeded because they were both determined. They had separate drivers – for Lowe, it was an obsession with keeping the lower classes out of government (an obsession that grew with age); for Lingen, it was a desire to cut the costs of administration – but together they made a formidable team.

Gladstone was ambivalent. He supported the idea of competition, but, as we have seen, was quite happy to help his Foreign Secretary with advice as to how to keep Lowe at bay. Gladstone also helped his friend George Glyn, the Liberal Chief Whip, retain some powers of patronage for staff in customs and the census office; Glyn needed a way to reward Liberal MPs for their good conduct in close votes in the Commons. Though he had to put up with such setbacks, Lowe was not happy that any escaped his clutches. In December 1870 (by which time Lord Granville had become Foreign Secretary following the death of Clarendon), Lowe wrote to Gladstone:

> I have now before me the Foreign Office plan under the Order in Council of June 4. It withholds the appointment from competition – from Lord Clarendon I never expected anything else but Granville, who is very much identified with the principle, will do our scheme, us and himself much mischief if he withholds his department, for it will be said that we don't believe in our own measure

and have one rule for the rich and another for the poor. Will you try your influence with him on the point? I would neither have troubled him or you just now if the matter had not been brought officially before me and prepared for a decision. While I am on the subject, would you not try a remonstrance with Bruce on the same point? His office, as you know, is in a most unsatisfactory state; the complaints of the manner in which the work is done are endless and yet he stands out almost alone against competition, as if he wanted to draw attention to the fact that his office is just the one where the present system has most signally failed.

Lowe had perhaps forgotten that Granville's approval of competition, given when he was at the Colonial Office, was conditional upon the head of the department being able to prescribe the test. Like others, this caveat had been ignored. It is not clear what, if anything, Gladstone did about Lowe's letter, but in the Public Record Office is what appears to be a draft reply from Lord Granville putting his side of the case. The draft commences by highlighting Lowe's double-crossing of the Cabinet: 'When you introduced to the Cabinet the subject of a further extension of the system, it was on the clear understanding that different methods might apply to different offices, and the heads of most important offices were to judge for themselves.'

Granville then proceeded to point out that his predecessor Clarendon, 'after a very careful examination of the facts, with his long experience of the office came to the conclusion, upon special grounds, that it would be disadvantageous to the public service to make the change'. Granville said that in accepting the office, he had told Gladstone he did not wish to start off by making a decision 'which would be so unpalatable to the department'. Finally, Granville dismissed further debate, writing that 'since then I have been too busy to go into departmental questions'.

Lowe and Lingen did not always get their own way even with smaller departments. In August 1872, Lingen became involved in a dispute with Henry Stansfeld at the Local Government Board over the appointment of three legal advisors. Stansfeld said that he had been told by Lowe's private secretary, Rivers Wilson, that heads of departments could decide whom they would submit to competition and whom to withdraw. That was, of course, correct, but it was not the line that Lowe and Lingen followed. Lowe's response to this episode was to tell Lingen that 'when a new office is created, we can insist upon its being open to competition as a condition of appointment'. The Foreign Office and the Board of Education held out; they succumbed only in 1918! Henry Bruce at the Home Office also held out. But when Bruce was replaced as Home Secretary by Lowe in 1873, the Home Office rapidly came into line.

Lowe's action in double-crossing Cabinet colleagues was characteristic of him; he paid no attention to rules when they failed to suit his purpose, and he did not care about offending colleagues if he thought they were not up to his standards (and he thought very few of them were). Such characteristics were to prove Lowe's undoing as Chancellor a few years later, but in the meantime they enabled him to achieve what Trevelyan had failed to. In particular, the drafting of the Order in Council enabled Lowe to impose Trevelyan's scheme for dividing civil servants into intellectual and mechanical grades.

Trevelyan's motives in seeking such a division had been based on his (not necessarily valid) perception that most civil service work involved the drafting of letters and minutes on straightforward issues, the writing of fair copies after drafts had been approved, and supervising registries, paper rooms and copy rooms. It was monotonous work and offered a second-class clerk 'the prospect of passing his whole life at registry work, and of rising in his turn to headship of his room at a rate of pay which to those not occupying the social position of gentlemen is affluence'.

In contrast, intellectual work consisted of approving drafts and preparing instructions for drafts in complex cases and 'involved responsibility, discretion and the power to direct work and deal with the outside public in such a manner as to uphold the credit and efficiency of their departments'. This was a fair reflection of the work of some departments in mid-Victorian Britain, and had been for many years previously. Until the end of the nineteenth century, the Home Office handled incoming correspondence in exactly the same way as it had done since the time of Walsingham. In 1853, there were some 40,000 civil servants (the vast majority of whom worked in the Post Office and the Revenue departments) and government expenditure represented about 5 per cent of GDP. The departments in Whitehall, such as the Treasury, Foreign Office and Board of Trade, each employed only a few dozen staff.

Paintings by Georgian artist Thomas Rowlandson show government offices were like the interiors of exclusive London clubs. And the atmosphere that Trevelyan and his fellow intellectuals worked in also resembled that of a gentlemen's club. Ministers and 'intellectual' civil servants came from similar backgrounds; they had attended the same schools and universities; they shared a common mindset and moral code; and they happily engaged in philosophising at length on relatively few issues in considerable comfort. It was not just the House of Lords that 'did nothing in particular and did it rather well'. When all was said and done, there really wasn't that much to do. Trollope caught the atmosphere nicely in *Phineas Finn*, when he wrote that 'a fainéant government is not the worst government that England can have. It has been the great fault of our politicians that they have all wanted to do something.' This still rings true today!

Trevelyan took the view that getting clever people to do mechanical work would bore them witless, and he did not think it was a sensible use of their talents. He was right, but his assessment did not apply with equal force to all departments, and especially not to the newer and expanding departments where whole new areas of work were being undertaken. By the time Lowe came to ram the division down the throats of departments in 1870, the distinction was even less applicable, but Lowe had a different agenda: he didn't want to make the best use of the talent available, he wanted to keep the lower classes out of government. Lowe's aim was to keep the intellectual elite in power. He was happy for anyone with ability to aspire to do mechanical work, but was equally adamant that no one from the lower classes should aspire to join the ruling intellectual elite.

The device that Lowe and Ralph Lingen used to achieve this end was to draw up three separate levels of examination corresponding to three different levels of work – intellectual, mechanical and writing. Those seeking intellectual work basically needed a good Oxbridge education. While they could take papers on the language, literature and the history of France, Germany or Italy, they would earn in those papers only half the marks obtainable from similar papers relating to Greece or Rome. They could take papers on jurisprudence or political economy, but these too carried only half the marks obtainable from the classics. At the same time as departments were becoming increasingly involved in economic and social issues, Lowe and Lingen were ensuring that the top jobs in the civil service would be held by some of the best-educated classicists in the world.

The concept that those who ran departments should possess some really relevant knowledge, which had flowered briefly at Haileybury, was well and truly dead. For those who could not compete with Oxbridge classicists, there was a very basic set of papers covering handwriting, spelling, arithmetic, copying and similar tasks. Curiously, the mechanical workers could also take a geography paper, which was a treat not afforded to applicants for intellectual work.

The third level of examination was for writers, who were to be supplied to departments by the Civil Service Commission as the need arose. Each department had to agree with the Treasury which of its existing posts fell into the three categories. Lowe and Lingen were adamant that there should be absolute uniformity across departments, and they brooked no arguments about differ-ent needs for different departments. Any differences of opinion were resolved at meetings attended by Lingen and the secretary of the Civil Service Commission (Jowett's close friend Theodore Walrond) as well as representatives from the relevant department. As Lingen was reputedly even ruder and more abrasive than Lowe, the outcome would seldom have been in doubt, though no records of these meetings survive.

The *Civil Service Gazette*, which had proved so critical of Trev-elyan's proposals, was sceptical, but was prepared to wait and see how matters progressed. In particular, the newspaper had a view much more akin to Lowe's about examinations:

> It is well known that civil service employees are never called upon, in their official capacity, to display any knowledge in some of the subjects on which they have been examined by the civil service commissioners; but no one in his senses would recommend that examinations be curtailed on that account to the merely practi-cal knowledge that will be required in the future. The object is to obtain a class of well-educated officials.

It was a complete volte-face; the editors had bought into Lowe's class-based approach to government, and abandoned their prede-cessors' support for relevant learning and practical ability. What were needed now were gentlemen; it didn't matter if they were competent, just so long as they had class!

It would have been possible to offset some of the disadvantages of the reforms, if scope had been provided for those engaged in mechanical work to progress to intellectual work by demonstrat-ing their competence (as Farrar, the Permanent Secretary at the Board of Trade, had suggested, and Trevelyan had explicitly en-dorsed). But since the whole purpose of the reforms (at least as far as Lowe was concerned) was to keep top dogs on top, such a measure could not be contemplated.

Lowe ensured there would be no movement from the mechanical to the intellectual class. Pressed by the Playfair Committee in July 1873, Lowe had great intellectual difficulties in maintaining the justification for this stratification of the civil service, but he was not a man to yield to rational argument when bigoted class prejudice might win the day, and so he persevered. He thought that 'public schools and colleges and such things' endowed those educated in them 'with a sort of freemasonry among men which is not very easy to describe, but which everybody feels'. Lowe found this 'extremely desirable'. Some civil servants came into contact with the upper classes of the country, and such civil servants 'should be of that class, in order that they may hold their own on behalf of the government and not be overcrowed by other people'. Perhaps Lowe's finest effort was to suggest that if the wrong sort of people got important jobs they might drop their aitches 'or commit some similar solecism, which might be a most serious damage to a department in a case of negotiation'. The committee accepted his line.

There had been pressure from the junior clerks to allow movement from mechanical to intellectual work, but it was effectively killed off by the Playfair Report, which found that 'the mechanical and monotonous work on which the clerks must be employed so long and so continuously did not as a matter of course fit them for those higher posts', and that 'the character of the work in the inferior grades will be rarely calculated to develop superior capacities'. The position was set in concrete by an Order in Council of 12 February 1876 constituting the lower division of the civil service. Members of the lower division were not to be excluded from promotion to the higher division, but to get there they had to complete ten years' service. They also needed a special certificate, something they could only obtain after a recommendation by their head of department and the assent of the Treasury.

In time, the two divisions were renamed; the higher division became the first division and the lower division became the second division. As late as 1887, Home Office clerks were complaining to a royal commission that 'this insuperable barrier was unnecessary to prevent incompetent men rising ... was impolitic in stifling instead of stimulating effort', and that a scheme 'under which liberality is lavished exclusively upon one class and economy is practised rigidly and exclusively upon the other is fundamentally unjust'. In 1889, the government accepted that exceptional fitness might be recognised by promotion to the upper division after a minimum of eight years' service in the lower grade. But although promotion was theoretically possible, it rarely happened. It is indicative of the entrenched nature of the split between intellectuals and mechanicals that the trade union of the top civil servants is still called the First Division Association, though to spare people's blushes it is commonly known as the FDA.

What Jowett, Lingen and Lowe created was probably no better than what had gone before; it was (and still is) better than many other bureaucracies, but it is still not appropriate to the needs of governing Britain in the twenty-first century. Unfortunately, the Victorians built to last. The new public offices they erected in Parliament Street and the new civil service they put into them are both still there; but the offices have been completely refurbished.

# CHAPTER 7

# AND NO WOMEN EITHER!

J ust over a mile away from the new public offices stood another
major public office: the headquarters of the General Post Office.
This building, too, had recently been rebuilt, for it was to be the
engine room of a major communications revolution – the Penny
Post and the halfpenny postcard. The success of these two brilliant
Victorian innovations ensured that the Post Office dominated the
growth of the civil service for most of the nineteenth century.
But the Post Office was also responsible for an even greater social
revolution, one that would have a much longer-lasting impact: it
was the Post Office that introduced women into the civil service.

The driving force for this development was pressure from the
Victorian business world for better communications. Expanding
companies recognised the benefits of the recently introduced
telegraph system, but were unhappy with the difficulties posed
for them by the existence of competing private sector providers.
A royal commission, appointed to look into the issue, suggested
that users' difficulties would be met if the competing services were
taken over by the Post Office, and then rationalised and developed.

During the late 1860s, an assistant secretary at the Post Office,
Frank Scudamore (who had leapfrogged an infuriated Anthony
Trollope to get the position), was charged with organising the
nationalisation of the private telegraph companies. Once that had

been achieved early in 1870, Scudamore was tasked with developing a national telegraph network. He tackled the job with energy and enthusiasm and was able to show good results in short order. Unfortunately, to finance the expansion he engaged in some imaginative accounting with the funds of the Post Office Savings Bank and other Post Office revenue to the tune of over £500,000. He did so with the help of the Chancellor of the Exchequer, Robert Lowe, who allowed Scudamore to bypass proper channels, seeing this as a way of cutting through red tape. The resulting parliamentary scandal led to the resignations of Lowe and Postmaster General William Monsell; at one point the entire government seemed at risk. Scudamore, however, retained his office; the general view was that he had been guilty of nothing more than excessive zeal.

The key point about this operation in the context of the development of the civil service was that private telegraph companies had employed female workers for some time, so when the telegraph system was taken over by the Post Office, 3,300 women became civil servants. Strictly speaking they were not the first, since for many years departments such as the Home Office and the joint stock companies registration office had employed a 'necessary woman' to look after the housekeeping, but the telegraph women were certainly the first significant number of women to be engaged in the duties of a public office. More importantly, as a result of an initiative by the Society for Promoting the Training of Women, the telegraph operators had been carefully chosen and gave good service. Frank Scudamore proved to be as imaginative in his management role as he had been in his financial dealings; within a year he was able to report that the Post Office had considerably extended its use of women.

Scudamore had been quick to realise that women candidates for jobs would be better educated than men because of the absence of other female employment opportunities. When twelve female junior vacancies were advertised in 1873, a total of 1,200 applicants turned up and for a time blocked Cannon Row as they sought entry into the offices of the civil service commissioners. Scudamore also thought that the women would all get married 'as soon as they get the chance' and would never progress far up the salary scale, thereby keeping overall costs lower still. He also noted that when men and women were employed together, 'the female clerks will raise the tone of the whole staff'.

In allowing men and women to work side by side, Scudamore proved to be far ahead of his time. On the whole, the managers of these first female civil servants were well satisfied with their work, but the male clerks took a very different view, and theirs was to be the prevailing view of the civil service for a century; in some quarters it prevails still. When questioned by the Playfair Commission during 1875, Patrick Comyns from the Post Office's returned letter section said women could cope with simple tasks like copying an address, 'but at any time when tact, discrimination or judgement is required, I find that they are perfectly at a loss in the matter'. He was asked whether this might not be due to a lack of experience, but Comyns was having none of it: 'I think that generally where women perform official duties, their minds are wanting in that respect!'

Having accidentally acquired a toehold in the telegraph office, women moved into the postal service and then the savings bank, where they caused great surprise by taking their work seriously and adding up figures without making mistakes. This move had been strenuously opposed by male staff from the controller downwards, who feared 'the grievous dangers, moral and official, which are likely to follow the adoption of so extraordinary a course'. In the face of such views, the managers of the Post Office did well to press on. But press on they did, and the women continued to deliver the goods.

Women, however, were not allowed to compete for jobs in the open competition which had been introduced for men. Women could only be employed after being nominated to take their own exam, similar to the system of patronage and limited competition that had been introduced for men in 1855. This arrangement continued until Henry Fawcett became Postmaster General in 1880. Fawcett had moved the resolution in the Commons in 1869 that called for all posts to be open to competition, and, unsurprisingly, once he was in charge, appointment to women clerkships in the Post Office became the subject of open competition.

Gradually women began to take over more and more tasks, but still only within the confines of the rapidly expanding Post Office. The first breakout occurred in 1899 when the Board of Education asked the Post Office for some of its female staff. One of the early Post Office recruits, Maria Smith, had risen to the rank of 'Lady Superintendent' and was responsible for oversight of all female staff. Realising the opportunity that the request presented, she sent some of her best clerks over to the Education Board. Soon afterwards, the Registrar General's office made a similar request for female staff, and when the Office of the Public Trustee was set up in 1908 and the women's branch of the National Health Insurance Commission was established in 1912, Maria Smith came to the rescue again.

It was perhaps as a consequence of perceiving that the world had not totally collapsed into chaos after such developments that the committee appointed in 1877 to inquire into copying machines and departmental printing felt able to recommend that women typists should be employed since their wages would be not more than two-thirds the wages of male clerks.

The case clearly appealed to the Inland Revenue, who by 1888 were employing 'typewriting women' for all correspondence with the Treasury. This sort of reasoning also appealed to the Lords Commissioners of the Treasury, who in 1889 suggested in response to an enquiry from the Ridley Commission that the employment of female clerks might be extended 'under proper precautions'. The Lords Commissioners thought typewriting could be done better by women than men and hoped 'that before long typewriting will generally supersede hand copying in the civil service'.

The Foreign Office said that it had one female typist, and added that the innovation worked well. There were, of course, those who feared the worst. The Board of Agriculture's sole female typist was immured in the basement, and no male member of staff over the age of fifteen was allowed to enter her room.

Despite early concerns, typing did indeed take off in the last quarter of the nineteenth century, although for some years it was considered improper to type the Queen's name, so wherever it appeared a gap was left and her name written in later. The rate of growth in the number of typists, though, was initially slow. The Treasury had estimated that typists would never number more than 100, and while this prediction proved wide of the mark, there were still no more than 600 typists and shorthand writers by 1914. At first the 'type-writers' were hired along with their machines, but as they became more useful they pressed to be allowed to become civil servants (and receive a pension), and after the issue was raised in Parliament they did indeed achieve that status in 1894. In the Post Office and Inland Revenue, typists were admitted by open competition, but elsewhere they were nominated by departments. Patronage lived on.

While most jobs obtained by women in the civil service were relatively junior positions, certain women did begin to obtain jobs of some seniority. These women were few in number, and they usually got their jobs because a minister was appointed who championed female employment or because an issue was raised in Parliament and the relevant department had no real answer to offer for not appointing women.

In 1871, James Stansfeld became president of the Local Government Board and appointed a woman as inspector of girls' education at pauper schools. Unfortunately, the new inspector contracted a fatal disease and resigned in 1877; she was not replaced until Arthur Balfour appointed a woman in 1886 as an inspector of boarded-out children. She proved so successful that two more female inspectors were appointed who also had a positive impact, something that was favourably commented on in the press.

Steady progress was also made at the Board of Education. Progress proved slower at the Home Office, where as late as 1879 the Chief Inspector of Factories was able to state in his annual report that the 'duties of an inspector of factories would really be incompatible with the gentle and home-loving character of a woman'. Fortunately, the trade unions, as well as the more enlightened employers and Parliament, continued to press for the appointment of female inspectors at factories where most workers were women. It was a notorious groper, the then Home Secretary Herbert Asquith, who finally appointed the first woman factory inspectors in 1894. Within two years, Asquith was telling the House of Commons that a great many provisions of the Factory Act of 1895 could not be satisfactorily enforced except by female inspectors.

But it still required pressure from MPs to get the first woman inspector of prisons appointed. In 1907, the matter was raised in Parliament, where it was pointed out that there were 50,000 women prisoners, yet the members of the Prison Commission and inspectorate were all men. Home Secretary Herbert Gladstone (son of William) could not be persuaded to appoint a female prison commissioner, but somewhat grudgingly a woman doctor was appointed to the role of inspector (and also an inspector of inebriate reformatories).

There were, of course, still no women prison governors. The first, Dr Selina Fox, was appointed governor of Aylesbury Prison in 1916 – possibly helped by the pressure on numbers created by the war. Thereafter Aylesbury Prison (it became a borstal between the two world wars) was normally run by a female governor, but no other prison was until 1945, when Dr May Taylor became governor of Holloway Prison. It would be another thirty-four years before a woman was allowed to run a men's prison; Agnes Curran took control of Dungavel Prison in Scotland in 1979.

That so many women were in prison reflected, to some extent, the absence of women magistrates, which had a serious impact on the treatment of women charged with offences. In 1908, suffragette leader Emmeline Pankhurst commented on a case she had witnessed in which an unmarried mother appeared in court for neglecting her child. The magistrates were all men. They asked no questions about the father, such as whether he contributed to the child's upkeep, nor did they enquire about the woman's wages before jailing her for three months. Pankhurst suggested that if women had a hand in framing laws they would find ways to make fathers pay for the upkeep of their offspring. She implied that if women had been on the bench instead of 'colonels and landowners', more practical enquiries might have been made.

Better progress was made when new organisations were set up and there was no existing body of grumpy chauvinists to overcome. In 1910, the first labour exchanges were set up by the Board of Trade, which had already employed women successfully in its labour department. From the outset it was decided to recruit men and women, and female staff at the Post Office again made a significant contribution by transferring to the new service. The numbers employed in the new service were further augmented in 1911, when the administration of unemployment insurance became the responsibility of the labour exchanges.

The same Act that established unemployment insurance also created a National Health Insurance Commission. There were separate commissions for England, Scotland, Wales and Ireland, and one woman was appointed to each commission. Women were employed in all grades, though in England they were segregated from male workers and dealt only with women's issues; the more liberal Scots allowed males and females to work side by side and to deal with all work.

Women civil servants were far from accepting of their limited roles and pursued their administrative and political masters (though women still could not vote in general elections), pressing for wider opportunities. In 1912, a royal commission on the civil service was appointed and one of the issues it thought important was the 'conditions under which women should be employed in the service'. The evidence showed that while some men recognised prejudice for what it was, the dinosaurs were still in good voice. So while Viscount Haldane took the view that the exclusion of women was a 'result of superstition', the First Civil Service Commissioner Sir Stanley Leathes thought it would be 'very difficult to have men and women working side by side'. 'Is there', he asked, 'a room where we can put them by themselves? If you can do that, there is a lot of work they can do very well.' The Permanent Secretary to the Board of Education, while acknowledging the good work done by female staff, foresaw all sorts of problems connected with discipline, supervision and promotion if they were employed on an equal footing with men.

The commission produced both majority and minority reports, and there were two reservations in the majority report that affected women. The report concluded that 'the object should be, not to provide employment of women as such, but to secure for the state the advantages of the services of women wherever those services will best promote its interests.' Members of the commission did not feel it was right to recruit without taking account of gender because, they asserted, the evidence showed that 'in power of sustained work, in the continuity of service, and in adaptability to varying service conditions, the advantage lies with the men'.

The commission did agree that women had a role to play in matters relating to women and children, and thought them underrepresented at the boards of education and local government, as well as in the Home Office and the prison service. The commission thought women should be eligible for work in museums and libraries. In a daring move, the commission suggested that specially qualified women should be eligible for appointment to particular posts in the administrative grade, but these women would need to be chosen by special methods of selection and not via the competitive exams taken by men.

Members of the commission wondered why, if the Post Office

employed 3,000 female clerks, the rest of the civil service only employed 500; they recommended that the Treasury examine the situations in each department that might 'with advantage to the public service be filled by qualified women'. Some commission members expressed reservations about the value of the 'evidence' relating to the advantages of employing males, and thought that the administrative exam should be opened to women in time (and only for a limited number of places). The minority report favoured the extension of female employment in the upper ranks of the civil service (though to a lesser extent than in the lower ranks). But, somewhat oddly, the report thought that the middle reaches presented a field in which women could not usefully or conveniently be employed.

The royal commission presented its final reports in April 1914; within four months the First World War began, during the course of which all the comfortable assumptions of the establishment were to be overturned, among them the place of women at work. In the early stages of the 1914–18 war, the growth in the number of female civil servants was confined mainly to the clerical, typing and messenger grades, and recruitment was extensively on a temporary basis. There still existed a reluctance to allow women to take administrative posts. No doubt the mandarins thought the demands of a world war were met best by promoting men not considered adequate to the needs of a peacetime service, rather than recruiting their better qualified sisters.

The Federation of University Women made a list of qualified women available for work, but little use was made of it at first. As the country gradually became aware of the huge consequences of the war, attitudes began to change and women were appointed to all sorts of posts, albeit on a temporary basis. Women reached new heights, both literally and metaphorically. While female clerks in Whitehall found themselves taking responsible decisions for the first time, women working for the Post Office found themselves shinning up telegraph poles to maintain and repair the phone network. By 1919, there were 175,000 women civil servants, many of them employed in hitherto exclusively male departments, and before the war had ended the government was seeking to establish ground rules for employing women in the post-war world. Four committees were set up which had an input on this issue.

A committee on the machinery of government was appointed to look into the size and structure of post-war government operations. It was chaired by Lord Haldane. Unsurprisingly, the committee was 'strongly of the opinion that among the changes that should be made ... must certainly be included an extension of the range and variety of the duties entrusted to women in the civil service and in practically all departments.' The committee also commented that the experience of the past four years had demonstrated that women could do as good a job as men, and thought it in the public interest to open up all posts usually obtained by competition to women.

The second committee looked at recruitment for the civil service after the war and was chaired by Herbert Gladstone, who as Home Secretary had been unable to bring himself to appoint a female prison commissioner. Unsurprisingly, this committee took the view that very few women had been engaged in general administrative work, and it was generally agreed that women did not cope with sudden or prolonged strain as well as men. The committee members did not favour competition between the sexes, and thought there was insufficient evidence to suggest it would be conducive to efficiency to place men under the control of women (the ghost of John Knox was no doubt chuckling in his grave!). For good measure, the committee felt it would be unwise to regard women as interchangeable with men, and that the time had certainly not come for opening up competitive exams to women. The committee concluded that 'there is not sufficient proof that woman are at present capable of performing with equal efficiency the most responsible duties assigned to men, except in certain branches for which they are specially qualified'.

The third committee produced a report that had little impact on the role of women, though it clearly envisaged that they would be more extensively employed in departments after the war. This committee mainly looked at the role of women in industry, but one recommendation which suggested that its members were living in the real world was that separate grades and separate exams for women clerks should be abolished.

One development that affected the employment of women after the war was that they had finally got the vote, and therefore political leverage, but, as the Gladstone committee demonstrated, there were still whole armies of dinosaurs to overcome; there would be no quick female victory. The Labour Party introduced a Private Member's Bill to make women eligible for the whole civil service, but though it was passed by the Commons, the Bill was defeated in the Lords. Then the government introduced its own Bill, which was passed. This Bill provided that no person should be disqualified from any civil or judicial office by sex or marriage, but enabled the government to introduce regulations establishing rules for admitting women to the civil service and for reserving any jobs for men in both the home civil service and the foreign and colonial services. In other words, all was still to be fought for.

The next development was that an internal civil service committee was set up with both trade union and departmental members (including four women) to consider the organisation of the clerical classes of the civil service. The committee reported back in early 1920 (women had now been employed in the civil service for fifty years) and claimed it was not possible 'at this stage to attempt a final solution of the novel and complex problems involved in the employment of women side by side with men'. But the committee managed to recommend that the structure should be simplified and, most importantly, that women should be admitted to administrative and executive grades on the same basis as men; women should have access to the same work and be provided with opportunities to prove their administrative capabilities.

The departments still baulked at competitive exams, however, and although the trade unions wanted open competition, they agreed to selection boards for women on the basis that the arrangement would be reviewed after five years. In 1921, the appropriate regulations were drawn up, but later that year a resolution was moved in the Commons requiring the same procedures to apply to men as to women. Eventually, the government was forced into a compromise under which the proposals would stand, but after three years women would be admitted in the same way as men. In 1925, following post-war reconstruction, open competition for the administrative class was resumed. Eighty men and twenty-seven women sat the exam, and nineteen men and three women were appointed. By the 1930s, women were regularly taking a reasonable number of places and were also clocking up excellent scores. In 1936, Jenifer Williams came third out of 493 candidates, the highest position so far attained by a woman. Later, Williams left the civil service for an academic life and it was her research (as Jenifer Hart) that disclosed the link between Jowett and the work of Northcote and Trevelyan.

Jenifer Williams not only did well in the exams; she so impressed her bosses that when she married they let her keep her job (she became an academic because her husband moved to Oxford). But Hart was an exception in being allowed to retain her post after marriage. As far back as 1870, Frank Scudamore had noted that women would marry 'at the first chance' and so keep wages down. At first, however, the Post Office did not require women to resign after marriage and even encouraged married women to return to work. Gradually, though, a different view developed; one where it was not considered proper to allow a woman to decide for herself what she would do. It became the rule that marriage meant the end of paid employment. The issue became tied up with pension rights as women acquired established status and eventually, in 1894, the rule was made universal and linked to the payment of a marriage gratuity upon resignation.

The McDonnell Commission looked into the marriage bar in 1914 and concluded 'that the responsibilities of married life are normally incompatible with the devotion of a woman's whole time and unimpaired energy to the public service'. Eight commission members dissented, taking the sensible view that neither men nor women should devote their 'whole time and unimpaired energy to the public service'. The rule, which had hitherto been enforced by a Treasury minute, was made the subject of regulation in 1921. The dinosaurs were determined to keep women at bay.

The effect of the marriage bar in numerical terms was not too significant. In the 1930s, only some 4 per cent of women civil servants resigned each year for this reason. But if the number of married women leaving was not a particularly large one, the qualitative impact in terms of talent lost was possibly quite significant. The regulation did allow the rule to be waived in the interests of the public service, but such exceptions proved few and far between; in the four years before the outbreak of the Second World War, just eight women were retained after marriage (among their number was Jenifer Williams).

The resoundingly successful career of one of these women reveals the loss the civil service suffered by making retention after marriage so difficult. On 3 September 1907, Leonard and Frances Tostevin of Streatham Hill welcomed a daughter whom they named Elsie Myrtle. Leonard was a jeweller's clerk – just the sort of person to send shivers up the spine of Robert Lowe.

Elsie attended Clapham County Secondary School before winning a state scholarship to St Hugh's College, Oxford, where she gained a first-class degree in modern history in 1929, and then one in politics, philosophy and economics the following year. In 1930, she entered the civil service administrative class and joined the Post Office as its only assistant principal. It is unlikely that a man with similar qualifications would have been placed there.

In November 1933, Elsie applied to be retained after getting married. Her initial application was rejected, but she resubmitted the application in April 1934. The director-general of the Post Office wrote to the Treasury, asking whether her case could be considered within the rules; she did not possess 'special qualifications or special experience', but was 'undoubtedly a girl of great ability who has adapted well to the work and the conditions generally, and is well above the average level of the present members of her class in the Department'. The letter was sent to the director of women establishments, a formidable person called Hilda Martindale, who had been one of the earliest female factory inspectors and who now played a key role in promoting the cause of women civil servants across Whitehall.

Martindale made a persuasive case to Sir James Rae, the relevant under-secretary, pointing out that Elsie Tostevin was the only woman of administrative grade in the Post Office and that this fact meant that, in many ways, she possessed special experience. Sir James, however, was not to be moved by considerations of mere ability. He claimed that with only three-and-a-half years' experience 'she is still learning her duties'. Responding to Martindale's argument that the Post Office had no women of suitable quality to take Tostevin's place, Sir James said women in other departments might be appointed so that the Post Office could fill the gap 'without facing the probable inconvenience attached to the employment of a young married woman'. Tostevin was turned down again, but she refused to give up. She was promoted to principal in 1938, and applied again on 25 May of that year.

This time, the Treasury caved in. The case was discussed between Mr Peel, the private secretary to the director-general of the Post Office, and Miss Martindale's successor as director of women establishments, Myra Curtis. A manuscript note by Curtis records that, on 16 June 1938, she and Peel discussed the case. They agreed that there was no case under the provision relating to special experience, but that in respect of special qualifications and 'special requirements of the department', Elsie Tostevin had a case. The Post Office regarded her potential as well beyond that of most

members of her grade, which seemed to address the special qualifications factor. The Post Office also found it 'a definite advantage,
which they would be reluctant to forego, in having a woman available in a responsible administrative position for consultation on
staff questions'. This was, in effect, the same argument put forward
by Martindale four years earlier.

At any event, still on 16 June, Curtis passed a brief note to her
Treasury colleague Mr Parker (another assistant secretary and
deputy establishments officer), and he responded the same day
agreeing that the bar should be lifted. The letter to the Post Office
giving agreement (providing the would-be husband was British)
was sent the same day. A subsequent formal exchange took place
between the Post Office and the Treasury: the Treasury's formal
agreement was sent on 24 June by none other than Sir James Rae.

Elsie Tostevin speedily became Elsie Arnott and worked for the
Post Office throughout the Second World War; in 1946, she was
promoted to assistant secretary. The following year, Mrs Arnott,
now divorced, married a Mr Abbot (a Post Office colleague); she
was duly sent on loan to the Treasury, no doubt to ensure that
propriety was not rocked by having husband and wife working in
the same department.

In 1950, Elsie Abbot's move became permanent. In 1955, she
was promoted to the rank of under-secretary and, in 1957, she was
made a Commander of the British Empire. In 1961, she became the
Treasury's Establishments Officer at the level of Third Secretary;
colleagues at this level included the economist Alec Cairncross
and a clutch of future Permanent Secretaries. Elsie Abbot retired
in 1968, having been made a Dame Commander of the British
Empire in the New Year's Honours of 1966. The Post Office had
indeed spotted a high-flyer, but it was only Elsie Abbot's own
determination that had prevented her being sunk by the marriage
bar; others, less forceful or less fortunate, did sink, and the service
was all the poorer.

The marriage bar was not the only discriminatory policy: women still did not get equal pay for equal work. In the 1870s they had been paid about half the rate paid to men, and in the 1930s they still received less pay even though the unprejudiced knew they did the same work as men and did it just as well. Thanks to constant parliamentary pressure (a benefit of women having the vote), they were, by 1938, being paid at about 80 per cent of the male rate, but for most of the period up to then the majority of women earned about half what their male colleagues did.

As the country prepared for war, Whitehall was still securely in the hands of a bunch of men, most of whom could not bring themselves to accept the evidence of women's ability to hold their own in the workplace. These men in denial were, it must be remembered, the finest minds that Oxbridge could hone; the product of the Victorian reforms of the civil service; the heirs of Benjamin Jowett.

And there were still no women allowed in overseas posts in the foreign and colonial services. British women might tramp the Empty Quarter as explorers, convert or nurse the inhabitants of Africa, or serve foreign potentates as governesses to their children, but they couldn't serve their country abroad. A flavour of the mindset of the foreign and consular services is given by their response to Amy Johnson's flight to Australia; the consulate in Java thought women 'should not be permitted to venture alone upon such dangerous undertakings for purely selfish ends'.

Within the decade, women pilots, including Amy Johnson, were playing a vital wartime role in ferrying military aircraft to and from front-line airfields in Britain and later on the Continent as members of the Air Transport Auxiliary (ATA). That they did so was the result of a decision taken in the first weeks of the war by the Under-Secretary for Air, Captain Harold Harington Balfour, allowing women as well as men to be recruited. Balfour had been a private pilot for some years and knew there were many competent women aviators in the country. For the next six years 156 women, about one-fifth of the air-crew strength of the ATA, played a full part alongside male colleagues, flying phenomenal numbers of hours and making over 300,000 flights in aircraft as diverse as Mosquitoes, Hurricanes, Spitfires, Lancasters and Halifaxes. Towards the end of the war, women pilots ferried new aircraft and urgent supplies to the front line and retrieved damaged aircraft for repair. Their work was every bit as dangerous as that of their male colleagues and seventeen women lost their lives – including Amy Johnson. The ATA was not part of the RAF and while its status was never clarified it was certainly a civil establishment, even if its members were not civil servants. One harassed Ministry of Labour official described them as 'licensed bandits'!

The fame of the ATA recruits had not succeeded in opening minds at the Ordnance Survey. There the wartime influx of women was seen as undesirable; in fact an internal memo states clearly that it would be desirable that the whole recruitment should not be from women. Similar minds were at work in the Treasury:

> The sort of work you expect from these women draughtsmen (who it seems to us scarcely merit the title in the full sense) appears to be on rather a lower scale than that of the Office of Works employees; in fact we are inclined to think that the suggested title (Mapping Assistant) should be changed to Learner Tracer(s) (below 18) and Tracer(s) (from age eighteen and after completion of the probationary period).

Despite such views, women further strengthened their position in the mainstream civil service, although not all those who joined found the experience pleasant. The stultifying effect of the civil service was noted by Phyllis Pearsall (famous for devising the A–Z maps) when she was recruited by MI5. To mark her eightieth birthday, Pearsall was interviewed by *Sunday Telegraph* reporter Anthea Hall. Pearsall recalled that her intelligence work had left her with a lifelong loathing of the civil service, which she described as 'so completely dead, even in war time'.

We once received a note saying that there had been a cloud burst in the Peak District; men were starving and freezing. 'Take no action,' it said, 'this concerns other departments'. A colleague and I (you couldn't act alone or they'd think you ambitious) had a plane taking up food and clothing within an hour. A memo came back: 'On your own head be it.'

It may have been her bad luck to join MI5. During the war Jenifer Hart (formerly Williams) was secretary to the committee hearing appeals against detention orders; according to her obituary writer, Hart was struck by the disorganisation and illiberalism of MI5.

Not all women found the civil service so dire. For some it provided an opportunity to move from the provinces to London, an experience which they relished irrespective of the nature of their work. Peggy Wood's father had started work as a coal miner aged thirteen and had become a pit deputy before he was thirty. He was injured in his forties when he helped to free a colleague trapped by a fallen boulder. The mine owners refused to pay the cost of his hospital treatment, so Wood successfully fought them for compensation. But when the mine owners handed over the cash they also handed Wood his notice; thereafter he worked in the Attercliffe steel works.

The family lived in a small village called Ridgeway, situated outside Sheffield. Mr Wood was keen that his children should have a good education. Peggy gained a free place at her local grammar school, and her father wanted her to stay on to take the Higher School Certificate and possibly try for university. But Peggy did not want to stay on at school past the age of sixteen. At the critical moment, though, the school introduced commercial subjects, and she opted to take these with a view to obtaining work in an office. By chance, a fellow pupil sent for leaflets about the civil service exams and Peggy thought she would give the exams a try.

In September 1938, Peggy Wood, who had never been away from home on her own – or even into a café by herself – was packed off to stay with distant relatives in Manchester to sit three days of exams for a typing post. Although she scored 100 per cent in the arithmetic test, she did not do well enough overall to obtain one of the small number of jobs in Sheffield; she had the option of taking a post in London or waiting until one became vacant in Sheffield. She managed to persuade her parents to let her take a post in London, although they insisted that she applied for a transfer to Sheffield as soon as she arrived in the capital.

Peggy was posted to the Home Office in February 1939. She worked in a corner office from which she could see Big Ben and obtained wonderful views along Whitehall of state occasions; she saw the royal family several times and was particularly pleased to see the Queen and the Princesses Elizabeth and Margaret. Her work involved typing for the Home Office probation branch. She shared this work with two elderly women, one of whom was the daughter of a retired Indian Army major. This lady impressed Peggy with her silken summer frocks that she had worn in India. She took a motherly interest in Peggy, assiduously going through the in-tray to remove any documents that she considered too scandalous for an eighteen-year-old to see.

Peggy knew a girl called Anne Bishop, who had been in the year above her at school, and who had passed the clerical officer exam and now worked in London for the Post Office Savings Bank. Anne arranged lodgings for Peggy with a family called Dove who lived in Stamford Brook. Mrs Dove used to provide her lodgers with a packed lunch, which usually Peggy would eat in St James's Park. She would leave the Home Office by the side door into Downing Street and walk down the steps into the park (Downing Street was an open thoroughfare then), where on one occasion she saw George Bernard Shaw taking a walk. It was all such a contrast to life in Ridgeway, and Peggy enjoyed every minute of it. When her application for a transfer back to Sheffield was approved, she was not happy. She had become romantically involved with Graham Boorman, the son of a gardener who looked after the grounds of a grand house in Porchester Terrace. However, she felt obliged to fulfil her promise to her parents so she returned to Ridgeway a year after she had left for London. She worked in Sheffield's main Post Office; Graham joined the RAF. When the war ended in Europe, Graham travelled to Sheffield and he and Peggy were married in July 1945. He obtained a job as a village postman, which he thoroughly enjoyed, and Peggy remained at Post Office HQ in Sheffield until she left to have their first child in 1946. Graham rose to the rank of assistant inspector – in charge of all mail delivery drivers in Sheffield – and for good measure became captain of the Sheffield Post Office cricket team. Peggy and Graham celebrated their sixtieth wedding anniversary in 2004.

Given the valuable work so many women had carried out during the war, it might have been expected that the remaining inequalities in the treatment of female civil servants would have been removed by the Labour government which swept to power in 1945. It was not to be. The post-war Labour government took no action, and although the Conservative's manifesto for the 1950 election contained a promise of action, it was hedged with qualifications. 'We hope during the life of the next Parliament that the country's financial position will improve sufficiently to enable us to proceed at an early date with the application of the principle of equal pay for men and women for service of equal value.'

On 16 May 1952, Charles Pannell, the Labour MP for Leeds West, raised the issue in the House of Commons. Pannell pointed out that almost thirty-two years earlier the House had passed a resolution outlining 'that it is expedient that women have equal opportunity employment with men in all branches of the civil service within the UK … and should also receive equal pay'. He pressed the government to act, but Financial Secretary John Boyd-Carpenter would not commit himself. Boyd-Carpenter argued that such a move would cost £28 million a year. The most he would do was to state that the government was 'examining all these possibilities with a view to seeing if there is any step which they can take consistently with their responsibility for the nation's economic health'.

It would be almost three years before there was any progress. In January 1955, the Chancellor of the Exchequer, Rab Butler, announced a scheme under which women's pay scales would rise by seven equal annual increments – reaching the level of men's pay by 1 January 1961 (but only for non-industrial civil servants). Equal pay was one thing, but equality of opportunity was still far off (it still is). In 1954, Evelyn Sharp was appointed the first female Permanent Secretary. Just to keep the balance right, however, a Treasury mandarin briefed the head of the home civil service, Sir Edward Bridges, who was appearing before the Priestley Commission on civil service pay and superannuation. The mandarin noted that, in 1954, the Method I competition had produced 'a very high proportion of successful women candidates (11 out of 40)'. He suggested that it was 'likely a freak result', and forecast direful consequences if it were not.

Though the marriage bar had gone and equal pay had been achieved, there was still a battle to be fought against prejudice: it has still not been won. Although women are now in theory equal, the reality is that the attitudes of many male colleagues have not changed from those of the Post Office clerks of the 1880s, and women still find it difficult to break through the glass ceiling. In fact, women have probably fared better in the civil service than they have in the private sector, but that is small consolation for those remaining at the sharp end of discrimination. One of the most difficult forms of prejudice to deal with is how rules are interpreted; there is nearly always some latitude in interpretation, and proving that a hard-nosed interpretation is grounded in prejudice can be difficult. Where progress is made it is because some women fight against discrimination, just as their predecessors did in Victorian times.

We have come to expect that there should be opportunities for women (or men) to take career breaks to raise a family, but this is still a relatively recent development. In the late 1970s, a woman we will call Pat decided that she wanted to take just such a break and asked her department for three years' special leave without pay (SWOP). At the time you were only eligible for SWOP if you were studying for a degree, but Pat had heard that a man at the Department of Trade and Industry had been granted SWOP in order to train as a Buddhist monk, so she thought she might be in with a chance. Pat assumed the Buddhist monk case heralded a new approach by the civil service, but in fact it proved to be an aberration; Pat's application was rejected.

Her assistant secretary at that time insisted that the department's personnel section should refer Pat's application to the Treasury, but they too refused to budge and she was forced to resign. Shortly before doing so, she discovered that she had passed a promotion board to become a senior executive officer. Nine years later, after her second child had reached school age (and she had obtained a degree), Pat applied to be reinstated. She sought to work part-time, a request that was not greeted with great enthusiasm: 'I don't know what we'll do with you.' And though Pat was eventually reinstated, it was only as a higher executive officer; her earlier promotion was set aside.

Despite this treatment, Pat resumed work as if she had only been away on a summer holiday, effortlessly adapting to new processes and procedures in an area of work of considerable technical complexity. At the end of the year she received a glowing annual report, including a strong recommendation for promotion. But Pat was not promoted; she was not even selected for interview. Her manager, feeling that Pat had been unfairly treated, restructured her job and gave her a temporary promotion to the rank of senior executive officer. At the end of the following year she received another glowing report, with full credit for her work at the higher level and, once again, a recommendation for promotion. Once again, though, Pat was not promoted. It took another year before she was allowed to take up the promotion she had earned twelve years earlier.

The reason for the delay may have been due to Pat's desire to work part-time; many civil servants were still not prepared to accept part-time staff. I myself recall once hearing a colleague comment, 'Oh no, not another part-timer!' This was despite the fact that, in those places where part-time workers had been accepted and welcomed, they had proved their worth. In due course Pat demonstrated her ability to do higher-grade work, and when she left the civil service she had reached the rank of principal – and had also managed to keep working part-time.

It can be hard if prejudice comes from the very top. The establishment of the senior civil service in 1995 required that every post at assistant secretary level and above be evaluated. In one department, the official responsible for this exercise was called in to see the Permanent Secretary to discuss a particular post, which the Permanent Secretary thought had been graded too highly. The official launched into an explanation of all the factors involved in this particular assessment, but the Permanent Secretary interrupted him testily: 'Yes, yes. I know all about that – but she's a woman!'

While the discrimination is numerically obvious (only 40 per cent of senior civil servants are female, whereas in the whole civil service women slightly outnumber men), it is the result of a long-established mindset and is exceptionally difficult to overcome. Although women have made it to the top in increasing numbers, the picture of the senior civil service as viewed from the lower ranks across Whitehall is still predominantly one of a collection of grey-haired white males, most of whom have Oxbridge degrees. It is not a picture calculated to inspire junior female staff from ethnic backgrounds with much hope of significant promotion; it is hardly surprising that few put themselves forward for consideration.

Frank Scudamore noted back in the 1870s that for any given rate of pay, women workers would prove better than their male rivals. This was because so few civil service opportunities existed for women in the Victorian era that highly qualified women had to apply for jobs they were more than capable of doing, with only the most able among them recruited. Scudamore's view still holds some truth today. Women civil servants must outperform their male competitors in order to overcome the prejudices held against them and make it to the top (or anywhere near the top). That bias against women remains as strong as ever in the civil service demonstrates the robustness of the system Lowe and Lingen introduced back in the days of Queen Victoria.

# CHAPTER 8

# AND THE CONSEQUENCES WERE...

The civil service created by Robert Lowe, being based upon a false premise, was not destined to bring about the end he had in mind – as perceptive people in some departments had foreseen. The so-called lower classes, despite the handicap of Lowe's elementary education system and its legacy, managed to produce some of the best academic minds in the country, and plum jobs in the civil service were theirs for the taking. No doubt such developments would have pained Lowe, but the final twist was that clever people could now not only use the system to grasp the levers of power, but also to become aristocrats.

John Anderson, born in 1882, was a scholarship boy whose father was a fancy stationer in Edinburgh. Early in the new century, Anderson took the civil service exam, scoring the second-highest mark ever. By the age of forty, Anderson was a Permanent Secretary; at fifty he was Governor of Bengal. Six years later he succeeded Ramsay MacDonald as MP for the Scottish Universities, becoming Home Secretary only a year later, before being appointed Chancellor of the Exchequer during the war years. In 1951, Anderson entered the House of Lords as Lord Waverley. He chaired a committee that looked into the export of works of art; the rules that his committee drew up are still in force.

Other people came from even more challenging backgrounds. One of my earliest bosses was a Yorkshireman called Bill Twells. Twells had been a coal miner, fighting with his friends over who should get to work in the pits on any particular day. He retired from life as a miner after winning a scholarship to Ruskin College in Oxford. Following his graduation, he joined the civil service as a war-time temporary senior administrative assistant. Appropriately enough, Twells was posted to the Ministry of Fuel and Power's coal division; he was promoted to principal two years later. He allocated fuel to bomber stations and contributed to the work of William Beveridge in producing the report that ushered in the welfare state. Twells ended his career as an assistant secretary at the Ministry of Power, having acquired an OBE along the way. He had done well, but those lucky enough to have had an early start could achieve much more.

Douglas Henley's father was a gardener and caretaker, and in Robert Lowe's view of the world, he should therefore never have aspired to more than mechanical work. Henley passed the 11-plus and won both a state scholarship and a Leverhulme scholarship to the London School of Economics; he was well placed to breach the academic barricades Lowe had erected to keep the masses away from government. In 1946, after his war service, Henley joined the Treasury; ten years later he became the Treasury's representative in Tokyo. In 1964, he became an under-secretary, and, later, a deputy secretary at the Department of Economic Affairs. In 1970, he was appointed a Companion of the Order of the Bath, and two years later became a Knights Companion. In 1976, Henley became the fourteenth Comptroller and Auditor General.

Few might worry that the Victorian administrative reforms were flawed as a piece of social engineering, but they were also flawed when it came to creating the more effective administrative machine that Trevelyan had intended. They put power in the hands of academically gifted people, yet, as Trevelyan himself had noted in his comments to the select committee in 1848, academically gifted people did not always make the best managers – particularly of large organisations with complex operations. Lowe himself proved Trevelyan's point; Lowe was intellectually gifted but predisposed towards bigotry, reluctant to accept facts that were inconveniently at odds with his views, and distrustful of anyone not unquestioningly on his side.

Perhaps the key to understanding why the reforms failed is to go back to Jowett's original reason for his involvement. Jowett's aim had not been to secure better-quality administrators, but to provide careers for graduates unwilling to enter either the Church or the Bar; it was essentially a negative policy.

It is no chance happening that nearly all of Jowett's early protégés in the Education department lacked an interest in educating the poor – the main function of the department – and instead used their jobs to finance personal literary ambitions. It must be remembered, also, that Jowett did not consider there was anything more to administration that 'getting up a few technical details'. This statement might have held some truth in Jowett's day, but knowing a 'few technical details' was not enough to cope with the demands of administration in the late nineteenth century, much less in the twentieth century. Yet Jowett's interventions created a lasting legacy. When one high-ranking civil servant came to grief in the 1970s after failing to do his work effectively, he was eased out gently. A colleague lamented, 'What a shame. He only joined the civil service so that he could go on writing Latin poetry!'

During the industrialisation of Britain, the entrepreneurs who made it happen had to develop new management techniques in order to cope with problems posed by large flows of raw materials, finished products and a large workforce. These entrepreneurs succeeded because they were practical men, and knew how to solve practical problems. If they failed to solve their problems, they went bust.

The civil service created by Lowe deliberately cut itself off from practical men: civil servants were not to be recruited after proving themselves in the real world, nor could they rise from the ranks. Of course, there were practical men who also happened to be brilliant classicists, but the bias veered towards impracticality. Remarkably cultured and learned impracticality, it is true, but this was not really what was needed for the government of the country as it entered the twentieth century. Indeed, as Trevelyan's own incompetence in respect of Irish famine relief and the Crimean War demonstrated, it was not what was needed for the government of the country at any time. The need to recruit men of practical experience had been an important point to make in 1848, when Trevelyan first raised it to the House of Commons Select Committee; given the changing nature of civil service work, it became crucial.

The civil service of Lowe and Trevelyan vanished within a couple of decades. In 1893, the Board of Trade established a labour department and began to involve itself in settling trade disputes. In 1902, the Board of Education, finally breaking free from Lowe's legacy, established the grammar school system and launched a hundred years of increasing government involvement in education. In 1906, a Liberal government was elected that initiated the development of the welfare state.

From then on, augmented by the demands of two world wars, the government machine grew and grew. By 1983, the public sector accounted for 22 per cent of all UK employment, and while that figure has since fallen to some 13 per cent, it remains a huge number. Nor has the public sector grown only in size; the scope of its activities has dramatically diversified and touches our lives in many different ways. The national infrastructure (transport and utilities), social security, pensions, health and safety, the NHS, the security services and the emergency services are either run or supervised by the state; in some cases, such as health and pension provision, the state both provides and supervises private provision.

In mid-Victorian Britain, the overwhelming bulk of state activity was concerned with raising taxes to pay for the armed forces (as it had been since the late Middle Ages); now it involves the provision of welfare state services or the supervision of private sector alternatives. The work of those engaged in these activities is far removed from the operations of Trevelyan's clerks, and has been for many years. The work of managing the vast bureaucratic machinery of government is every bit as demanding as the formulation of policy, yet the distinction between the small corps of intellectual civil servants and the large number of mechanical workers remains embedded in the civil service mindset, and in various ways it has been reinforced over the past decade. This distinction has also tended to reinforce the culture of poor management engendered by the academic bias of the selection process.

Although Trevelyan held sensible views about recruiting practical men when he appeared before the select committee in 1848, his report proposed to exclude from the competition system mature people with practical experience of running other organisations. His reasoning was that graduates could be moulded into the right frame of mind more easily than mature, experienced people, and could be paid less than older people with business experience. Trevelyan recognised the risk (which is currently materialising) that good outsiders would not be won over by the salaries the civil service could afford, and that only private sector failures would be attracted. Graduate recruits were to be shielded from the outside world and bent to the mindset of their seniors. Having been so moulded, it then followed that the investment must be fully realised. So the remuneration package was geared to retaining staff via a good pension scheme.

It would have run counter to all Lowe's instincts to change this when he drew up the 1870 Order in Council. The press and some politicians today like to lambast the 'jobs-for-life culture' of the civil service, as though it had been invented by civil servants themselves. Actually, it was a carefully thought-through policy decision taken by Gladstone and Lowe for what they considered to be perfectly sound financial reasons.

Despite the vast changes that were taking place in the country, the role of the civil service and the scope of learning in the universities, the theory underlining open competitive examination remained unchallenged until 1912, when a royal commission (the McDonnell Commission) recommended that a committee should consider a new scheme for the examination. The McDonnell Commission thought that what it described as Macaulay's ideas were based upon conditions that no longer existed. Many new subjects were being studied at universities. The Macaulay system was condemned as giving too much weight to the classics and excessive preference to Oxbridge candidates.

The Civil Service Commission, in its evidence to the McDonnell Commission, pointed out that from 1906 to 1910 the successful candidates for the British and Indian civil services and the Eastern cadetships totalled 464, with 389 of these coming from Oxford and Cambridge. The Civil Service Commission also pointed out that of those 464 successful candidates, only seventy-three had not passed through the hands of a 'crammer'; Lord Ellenborough's prophecy of 1853 was still holding up.

The commission's recommendation was put on hold with the outbreak of war, but in the summer of 1915 the commission wrote to the Treasury and suggested that a committee be set up. The following year a committee under the chairmanship of the First Civil Service Commissioner, Sir Stanley Leathes, was appointed. In its report of 1917, the committee pointed out that the present exam system had 'grown up by the addition of subject after subject until thirty-eight subjects are on the list'.

The committee saw the existing system 'as designed to test the results of university in general, and not the results of a special education preparatory to public service'. Having identified this important point, committee members then duly ignored it, taking the view that 'the best qualification for a civil servant is a good natural capacity trained by a rational and consistent education from childhood to maturity'. They then addressed themselves to the issue of possible bias in favour of those with a classical

Oxbridge education. Most committee members were Oxbridge classicists, so perhaps unsurprisingly they saw no need for change: 'We are not inclined, nor do we think it to be our duty, to put any handicap on the widest, the most systematic and the most consistent humanistic education that at present exists in this country.' They paid tribute to that 'great band of scholars equipped by the tradition, the organised learning, and the experience of 400 years' who kept that humanistic system going. They did propose a new exam system, which they saw as relevant to contemporary university education and putting all universities on an equal footing; it looked very much like the old system.

The Civil Service Commission could not be accused of precipitate action in implementing the committee's suggestions, for it was not until 1936, as a result of discussions with the universities, that the regulations for entry into the administrative ranks were modified. From now on, entry would be determined by an exam consisting of three compulsory general papers accounting for 300 marks, a choice from among seventy optional papers carrying a maximum of 700 marks, and an interview accounting for a further 300 marks. The optional papers were framed in a way that would enable a candidate with a good degree in any of the major faculties to compete, and to take the exam immediately after finals without a need for cramming.

The changes came into effect in 1937, but despite all the universities theoretically being put on an equal footing, Oxbridge maintained its vice-like grip on the process: in 1939, 90 per cent of successful candidates came from Oxford and Cambridge.

The long run of Oxbridge male classicist supremacy in the competitions, combined with an absence of recruitment of mature people with experience outside the civil service, cemented in place the disadvantages of Lowe's system. A closed culture was established in which the predominant civil service virtue was 'being good on paper'; rigorous efforts to establish facts, or to subject assertion to appropriate statistical analysis, were subordinated to the need to present policy papers in elegant prose liberally scattered with appropriate Latin tags: 'In reply to your note about the transposed figures in the table, I can only cry *peccavi!*' It was the culture that Lord Monteagle had foreseen in 1854, when he compared Trevelyan's proposals with the Chinese civil service system.

The problem was probably exacerbated after the First World War by the reduction in the size of the civil service, which would have reduced recruitment and thus produced an ageing work force. It was certainly compounded by the decision in 1919 to revamp the Treasury, to give it greater centralised control of other departments, and to award the Permanent Secretary the title of head of the civil service, with a role of advising the Prime Minister on all senior civil service appointments.

The man chosen for this new post was the chairman of Inland Revenue, Sir Warren Fisher. Born into a family of independent means, Fisher had initially hoped to join the Indian civil service but failed the exam. He attended a crammer and in 1903 he came thirteenth in the home civil service exam. Fisher held a high opinion of himself and had little regard for most other people. He was a philanderer and separated from his wife in 1921; when he passed away he left his wife with nothing and she died in poverty.

At least one top mandarin thought Fisher 'rather mad'. He was forty when he became head of the civil service, and spent the next twenty years shaping it to reflect his view that what were needed at the top were not experts but generalists. In 1930, he wrote to a royal commission, warning members to guard themselves 'against the idea that the permanent head of a department should be an expert; he should not be anything of the kind'. The day of the gifted amateur had arrived.

Fisher took one further step that helped to reinforce his control of the civil service: he established the principle that the Treasury only recruited staff from other departments. The theory was that Treasury staff would all have experience of working in other departments; they would then acquire the practical experience that would enable them to become heads of those departments in due course. The reality, however, was that civil servants quickly realised you had to get into the Treasury, and once there you then needed to demonstrate you possessed those qualities that Fisher admired. Since most of the permanent secretaries in post in 1919 had retired by 1939, Fisher had ample opportunity to make his mark on Whitehall; his impact was visible in the 1960s and to some extent it still is.

The Second World War did bring into the civil service many hundreds of people from the outside world, and their impact was significant. In part they had an effect because they came from different backgrounds, but their main contribution to the war effort stemmed from the fact that so many were specialists – engineers, scientists, economists, statisticians, authors and artists – who had established reputations in their own fields, and who brought whole new areas of expertise. It also helped that these recruits were able to work unencumbered by the conventional wisdom of permanent civil servants. In no small measure it was the work of these new people that enabled the war to be won.

For some people, the war provided complete career changes. In September 1939, an economics lecturer at Leeds University was invited to a meeting with an unnamed person in Oxford. The lecturer found himself being interviewed by Professor Lindeman, who duly recruited him to head up a new economics unit in the Admiralty under Winston Churchill. The lecturer served Churchill throughout the war, and though he returned to academic life when the war ended, it involved work with the UN and the Organisation for Economic Co-operation and Development. When Churchill regained power in 1951, the lecturer returned to Whitehall and eventually became the government's chief economic advisor. When he retired from the civil service, he was invited to take up the position of economic advisor at the Confederation of British Industry, and after leaving the CBI he continued to provide unofficial advice to the government until shortly before his death in 2004. The lecturer's name was Donald MacDougall, and his autobiography, *Don and Mandarin: Memoirs of an Economist*, is a hugely entertaining read.

Although some wartime experts stayed in the civil service during the post-war reconstruction, many left to resume their interrupted careers, and by sheer weight of numbers the Treasury men gradually reasserted their grip. It is worth recording that Donald MacDougall was fond of Hilaire Belloc's *Cautionary Tales for Children*. He particularly liked the story of Godolphin Horne because it bore a close relationship to the workings of the civil service selection board.

During the Second World War, there had been two initiatives that could have had a significant effect on recruitment, but neither came to anything at the time. In 1941, the First Civil Service Commissioner put forward a paper which sought to broaden the basis of recruitment, giving greater importance to personality tests, providing a more rigorous probation period and including experience of administration outside the civil service as part of fast-stream training. All told, it was a sensible package, but it ran into significant opposition.

A meeting at the Treasury considered the paper on 17 September 1941. Sir James Grigg of the War Office set the tone, saying he disagreed with those who advocated personality tests as a reliable guide for choosing candidates. The man from customs and excise questioned the need for three compulsory English papers. But he was shot down by the First Civil Service Commissioner, who said the commission had found such papers 'a valuable test of the qualities of lucid and concise writing and the ability to summarise complicated arguments which was an important qualification for the home civil service'. Sir James Grigg agreed that home civil servants must be able to write clearly and succinctly, but rather bizarrely he offered the thought that 'for the Indian civil service this did not matter so much'. Grigg did not explain why members of the ICS could be rambling and diffuse in their writing.

Perhaps the most interesting comments were made by Sir

Thomas Gardiner from the Post Office, who complained that the Post Office was unpopular with new entrants so it tended to get only candidates from the bottom of the list. The quality of these people was extremely poor, Gardiner said, and they compared unfavourably in intellect and personality with men promoted from the engineering and other technical branches of the Post Office. Gardiner thought reform of the recruitment process was essential, and said it must include the use of selection interviews. He said these had worked well when appointing older men from outside the service to technical posts, as the selection board had 'valuable evidence in the shape of reports from previous employers'.

The Post Office could see that two key planks of the existing system (which could be traced back to Trevelyan) – a lack of mature external recruits and the failure to promote mechanical workers – deprived the civil service of some exceptionally talented people. There was opposition from others to the notion of personality tests. Ernest Bevin, the Minister of Labour, sought to limit the scope for even examining the possibility of introducing such tests, having, as one Treasury mandarin put it, 'a healthy distaste for all things psychiatric'.

Separately, and no doubt influenced by the impact of the wartime recruits into the civil service and his own military experience, Deputy Prime Minister Clement Attlee wrote a note in 1942 which was then circulated to the Cabinet's committee on the machinery of government. Attlee suggested creating a civil service staff college, where civil servants and private sector employees could rub shoulders and exchange ideas.

A Civil Servant, on being posted to an office, necessarily gets his training in the routine of a particular department which may or may not be up to date, and that unless he is transferred somewhere else he has little opportunity of taking a critical and informed view of the method of doing business. It is, I think, desirable to correct this.

Attlee foresaw the need to study organisations outside the civil service and other administrations. He saw 'great advantage in the joint consideration of problems by persons who come from different spheres of activity' and had 'noticed this particularly at the Imperial Defence College'. Unfortunately, nothing came of his idea, because when a committee was invited to examine the proposal it was comprehensively rubbished. In its report, the Assheton Committee on the training of civil servants proved dismissive:

> The idea of a central institution where training of all civil servants would be carried on has only to be mentioned to be seen as impracticable. The entrants each year are so numerous (running into many thousands), so scattered over the country and engaged on such diverse work, that no single institution would be capable of grappling with them all.

Attlee wanted staff to be able to break out of the closed thinking of individual departments, but the committee opined that civil service training needs were best met at the departmental level, particularly in the case of clerical and executive grades. Committee members were equally clear in dismissing the possibility of mixing administrators and people from the private sector in any training. The committee did concede that the administrative grade might benefit from some central training, but only for new entrants and definitely not at any staff college.

> From the evidence we think there is a danger that such an institution would end up by becoming a commercial college concerned with office methods, and that a real opportunity of assisting the Civil Service administrator to a rapid comprehension of the nature of his problems and the lines of thought and action he should follow would be lost if such training were merged in a generalised administrative course for both business and the Services.

The first significant opportunity in ninety years to undo the work of Jowett and Macaulay in closing Haileybury was thus ditched, and in such a style characteristic of the civil service that Jowett and Macaulay had created – bold assertion unsubstantiated by argument or debate.

As the Second World War drew to a close, the Civil Service Commission had begun to consider how to carry out selection procedures for those whose education had been interrupted by war. The commissioners, probably keeping in mind the paper written in 1941, concluded that they should emulate War Office Selection Board procedures and establish a civil service selection board to devise a series of tests and exercises spread over forty-eight hours. These tests would throw light upon the personality, character and ability of candidates not only as individuals but as members of a group.

It was thought the tests would work best in a residential setting, so the commission chose for the exercise the village of Stoke d'Abernon, and a country house that was in government ownership. Candidates first had to pass a written exam broadly comparable to the pre-war general papers, and were then brought to the house in groups of seven or eight. They were subjected to psychological tests, written and oral exercises and interviews on a one-to-one basis. Stories used to circulate about candidates being observed after the tests ended, to see, for example, how they coped with cherry stones in the dessert. Some 4,000 hopefuls took the written exam, and 3,050 then went to Stoke d'Abernon. A total of 488 successful candidates took up posts with the home civil service while 244 joined the foreign service; 67 per cent of the successful candidates had been Oxbridge students.

The election, in 1945, of the first Labour government with a majority, and full-blooded socialist programme to match, completely changed the nature of work in great swathes of Whitehall. But somehow the mandarins contrived to imagine their lives could go on unchanged. Others proved more perceptive. In an editorial on 7 October 1945, *The Observer* noted:

The Civil Service was built up as a defensive body, safeguarding the old way of life, not as a creative body laying down the pattern of a new way ... The Victorian State ... asked of its officials care, deliberation and thrift, and the whole Civil Service technique was fashioned to provide these.

The paper pointed out that what had suited Victorian laissez-faire economics had begun

to seem out of place with the growth of social reform. With the coming of Socialism it is potentially ruinous. If the Socialised industries are to be subject to all the current habits of Whitehall ... the community will suffer bitterly from the extension to peacetime commerce of the muddles and delays which have often driven us frantic in war time.

*The Observer* returned to the issue in March 1946, pointing out again that the task of administering socialism was a task for which the civil service had not been designed. On the whole, the paper was sympathetic to the civil service and tended to blame ministers for problems: 'The senior members [of the civil service] have been subjected to prolonged strain and are, in many cases, shockingly overworked. Yet whenever they go to the office they may find that their minister has lightly tossed them some new industry or profession to run.'

Backbench MPs also noted the nature of the problem. In February 1946, Wing Commander Geoffrey Cooper, the recently elected Labour MP for Middlesbrough West, wrote to Attlee seeking a select committee to examine how the problem of recruiting experienced people into the civil service might be addressed.

Sir Edward Bridges, the Cabinet Secretary and head of the civil service, took charge of the case. He thought a select committee would create too much work; instead he wrote to some of his Permanent Secretary colleagues, enclosing a copy of Cooper's letter, and suggested they meet one Saturday morning to discuss it. At least one of these colleagues had a sensible initial reaction. Sir Percival Robinson, at the Ministry of Works, noted in his reply that it was difficult to get the right people and suggested the government 'must ... recruit at various stages in the hierarchy appropriate people to deal with industrial [production] problems at the government end'.

At the meeting, which took place on 2 March, others made the same point, though there were also those like Sir John Woods at the Board of Trade who argued that 'it was possible to exaggerate the extent to which the civil service was "going into management"'. Perhaps the most revealing intervention was made by Oliver Franks, a civil servant in the Cabinet Office (who later wrote the report whitewashing the Thatcher government over the Falklands War):

> The old distinction between administration and execution no longer held good. The civil servant would have to acquire some of the qualities of the businessman. But the introduction of businessmen was not in itself a solution. Public administration was on a far larger scale than any business, and this was a fact seldom appreciated by people outside the fields of public administration.

There were two very good insights here: one concerning the blurring of the split between administration and execution, and the other about the scale of public administration. But neither Franks nor anyone else picked up on these points and their implications. If the division between administrative and executive work (Trevelyan's intellectual and mechanical work) no longer held good, then neither could the associated division between administrative and executive grades.

To the extent that the meeting considered executive grades, it was to opine that all potential recruits from them to the administrative grade had been promoted already; indeed a great many had been over-promoted because of the exigencies of war. No one addressed Franks's point about the large scale of public administration, yet the bizarre implication of his comment was that it was better to have large organisations run by people with no business ability, rather than people who did possess such skills albeit from smaller organisations.

Some within Whitehall did seem to realise that significant change was needed. In subsequent correspondence, Sir Henry Markham at the Admiralty reverted to the need for an administrative staff college, commenting that 'there is very little evidence of any effective thought being given to the general principles of administration ... If a substantial group of under-secretaries or assistant secretaries could meet ... to discuss such matters they should all benefit considerably and useful results of a general character might well emerge'. Markham's suggestion seems to have fallen on deaf ears; indeed, the whole thrust of the exercise was that it was characterised by little effective thought, and certainly by scant evidence of purposeful action.

As 1946 progressed, people were becoming increasingly angry with the government's failure to address urgent needs such as housing. In September, the Communist Party of Great Britain organised a mass squat of some 1,000 people in empty flats in Kensington, and several smaller squats in the suburbs. Commenting on these events, *The Observer* felt that ministers and officials were equally guilty: 'The root of the trouble is that Whitehall officials, and Whitehall ministers simply cannot visualise the dreadful plight of families in blitzed towns and other places where housing is more than usually scarce. This complacent remoteness is a vice to which all civil services and all governments are prone.'

The reality was, as some of the newspaper's earlier editorials had revealed, that the civil service at the end of the war was simply not structured or staffed in a way that enabled it to address the problems caused by six years of conflict, let alone the Labour government's requirement to turn the economy on its head.

Opportunities to change had been considered, but on the whole they had been rejected.

After the reconstruction exercise, normal service resumed in 1948, with a system under which 75 per cent of vacancies were filled by those taking Method 1 (broadly the pre-war written exams and interview) and 25 per cent by Method 2 (broadly the Stoke d'Abernon experience). Method 2 candidates had to possess at least a second-class degree. A further change was the introduction of a minimum mark. Because success in the pre-war scheme had depended simply on the total marks gained, candidates who performed lamentably at interview could still be successful.

The civil service commissioners had noted that the Stoke d'Abernon exercise might have deterred diffident people, but they questioned whether diffident people deserved to be administrators. The commissioners had no doubt that all that mattered was intellectual ability, drafting skills, and being able to get on with colleagues and outsiders. They did throw in the thought that administrators should be able to 'control subordinates', but this was the nearest they got to the concept of management. There was no mention of the collection and analysis of facts. Indeed, there was little between their view of what the job required and that of Trevelyan and Lowe, or Jowett. The mindset of those who chose potential mandarins, and of the mandarins themselves, was neatly summed up in the early 1970s, when a principal told a new assistant principal: 'You don't find the romance of the civil service in a benefits office.'

In the post-war period, Oxbridge slowly lost its absolute grip on the top jobs. But whether the clever graduates now came from Oxbridge or other red-brick universities, they were no more or less likely to prove competent administrators. The problem was that the Jowett/Trevelyan/Lowe legacy had created a career path for graduates, but had failed to create a profession in any meaningful sense of the word. There was no body of knowledge for graduates to master, and no facility for training them, other than 'sitting by Nellie'.

This was the inevitable consequence of believing that there was no more to administration than possessing a good mind and mixing with similarly gifted chaps at university. Such a view had not made any sense in the nineteenth century; it became unsustainable during the early part of the twentieth century and by 1945 was a huge hindrance. Despite individual ministers and civil servants showing an interest in training, it was not until 1963 that a Treasury Centre for Administrative Studies was established. All assistant principals now had to attend a three-week course after they had been in post for six months, and in their third year they returned for a twenty-week course. It was the start of a slow march back towards the point the East India Company had reached some 150 years earlier.

Although such high-powered training was confined to the fast-stream, less privileged civil servants were also beginning to get a look-in. By the late 1950s, individual departments had started to provide training for wide ranges of staff, and some interdepartmental training courses were organised. In July 1965, the Prime Minister's private secretary noted that Harold Wilson had shown interest in training, 'in particular the idea of a staff college to provide immediate post-entry training for the administrative staff'.

In late 1965, a sub-committee of the House of Commons' Estimates Committee, chaired by Dr Jeremy Bray, recommended that:

> a committee of officials, aided by members from outside the civil service … should be appointed to initiate research upon, to examine and report upon the structure, recruitment and management of the civil service, and the position should be reviewed by the government immediately upon receipt of the report; the government should report to Parliament the action they proposed to take; and if a further enquiry by a royal commission be then found to be necessary such a commission should be appointed forthwith.

On 1 November, Chancellor of the Exchequer James Callaghan wrote to the Prime Minister, telling Wilson he thought 'the case for a wide ranging inquiry has been made out'. Callaghan was not attracted to a two-stage approach, instead favouring a single committee. On 3 November, he and Wilson met and agreed on the way forward. The following February, Wilson announced the establishment of the Fulton Committee.

The Fulton Committee, and to some extent Wilson and Callaghan, foresaw the possibility of producing a report 'as important as that of Northcote and Trevelyan'. The committee members actually did a great deal better, not least because they sought evidence from a wide range of individuals and bodies, and then drew sensible conclusions from what they learned. 'The home civil service today is fundamentally the product of the nineteenth-century philosophy of the Northcote–Trevelyan Report. The tasks it faces are those of the second half of the twentieth century. That is what we have found; it is what we seek to remedy.'

Although there was one dissenting voice (Lord Simey), the other committee members were clear that Britain lacked a professional civil service. Committee members attracted considerable criticism from some top civil servants for giving currency to the jibe that top mandarins were gifted amateurs. In a note of 9 May 1968, just before the committee's report was published, Sir William Armstrong wrote:

> Where I think the committee have missed the point is in their assertion that the service is still essentially based on the philosophy of the amateur, the generalist and the 'all-rounder'. To my way of thinking this is only true in the most superficial sense, and it misunderstands one of the essentials of administration. This is surely that administration means taking into account and giving proper weight to what may be in a particular case a large number of differing specialist aspects and specialist advice.

It is not very convincing. The committee was not addressing the processes of administration but the abilities of the administrators;

whether they had the competence to 'take into account and give proper weight to' various issues. The committee had formed the view that those who needed to do the taking into account were not, in fact, well placed to give proper weight to 'specialist aspects and specialist advice'. On this point, the committee was pretty uncompromising. Of the administrative class, it said:

> Often they are required to give advice on subjects they do not sufficiently understand, or to take decisions whose significance they do not fully grasp. It can lead to bad policy-making; it prevents a fundamental evaluation of the policies being administered; it often leads to adoption of inefficient methods for implementing these policies.

Armstrong rather undermined his case (and strengthened that of the committee) in a different part of his note, where he complained about the slow speed at which the 'literary' approach to administration was giving way to a quantitative or scientific approach.

The committee also took a swipe at Trevelyan's split between intellectual and mechanical work; it found the system of classes had caused the civil service to become too rigid and made it difficult for staff to move between the various classes. The committee thought that the word 'class' in Britain had developed social connotations which could produce feelings of inferiority. Despite all this, the committee tended to frame its recommendations with a bias towards the administrators.

One committee member had already raised the issue of bias with Downing Street. In August 1966, Sir Philip Allen, Permanent Secretary at the Home Office, wrote to Harold Wilson's private secretary:

> There is a natural tendency on the part of these high-powered people to think primarily about the administrative class and top

professionals, and to pay much less attention to the big armies below. The committee rationalise this: 'If you get the top right, the rest will follow.' But that is doubtfully true, and the committee in any case do mischief if they produced a report which seemed to the armies to concern itself only with the general staff. We are doing our best to push attention downwards. But a hint from the Prime Minister not to forget the clerical officer would be helpful.

There is no indication on the file if such a hint was dropped, but although the conclusions of the committee were indeed heavily focused on senior and fast-stream staff, the proposal to abolish the class system did address handsomely Sir Philip Allen's point.

Despite all the criticisms, and the committee's own belief that its remit was too limited, the outcome was a sensible set of recommendations directly addressing the issues that had made the Victorian reforms so damaging. The opening up of opportunities at the top to specialists and to the executive class created the basis for a wider spread of talent and experience in the running of departments. The creation of a department to assume responsibility for the Civil Service Commission, and for pay and management of the civil service, significantly weakened the absolute Treasury control bequeathed by Lowe and Lingen, while the establishment of a new college went a long way towards undoing the consequences of Jowett and Macaulay's destruction of Haileybury, and began the slow process of turning amateurs into professionals (though the issue was never couched in those terms and is still far from complete). The recommendation for more exchanges of staff with outside organisations would, in time, lessen the stultifying effect of not recruiting mature people with experience outside the civil service.

The Victorians achieved one small victory: the committee recommended the establishment of policy units in each department. In an echo of James Wilson's dispute with Trevelyan over splitting policy from its implementation, Evelyn Sharp (former Permanent

Secretary to the Ministry of Housing and Local Government) wrote in the *Sunday Times*, 'Thinking about long-term policies, divorced from any responsibility for current ones, does not seem likely to be fruitful. Everyone knows that, in practice, ideas for the future are wrung from grappling with present problems.' Despite her censure, policy units sprang up all over Whitehall.

The reforms proposed by the committee attracted mainly favourable comment, and in a statement to the House of Commons Harold Wilson announced that 'the government have decided to accept the main recommendations of the report and to embark on the process of reform outlined by the committee.' He was particularly eloquent on the implications of the abolition of the class system: 'This will mean that for everyone in the civil service, whether from school, whether from a college of technology, or from a university ... for all of them there will be an open road to the top which, up to now, has been in the main through the administrative class.'

The committee's recommendations and Wilson's statement were circulated to all civil servants, together with an exhortatory message from the head of the civil service, Sir William Armstrong: 'This will be a process to which all can contribute ... our object being to create a service which, while offering all its members the fullest opportunity for the development of their talents, will serve our fellow citizens even better than before.'

The Civil Service department was set up in 1968, but it was abolished by Margaret Thatcher in 1981 and the Treasury regained control. The open grading system fared rather better; it was not until 1995 that the government announced the creation of the senior civil service, effectively reintroducing the split between intellectual and mechanical civil servants – a move that would have been fully endorsed by Robert Lowe for creating a small elite to which entry is particularly difficult for those possessing the 'wrong' credentials.

I do not believe the creation of the senior civil service was intended to produce such a result. I suspect there is little current knowledge in Whitehall of the thinking behind the Victorian reforms, but the intentions of the Fulton Committee on this issue have certainly been extensively undermined. One development that has modified the impact of the reversion to elitism has been the belated implementation of the committee's recommendation on greater exchanges with outside bodies. During the 1970s and 1980s there were inward and outward secondments – mostly involving the Ministry of Defence and the Department of Trade and Industry (in 1980 the MoD and DTI accounted for just over half of all secondments) – and some direct recruitment of people into middle-management grades (including ex-servicemen). On the whole, the secondments and direct recruitment schemes produced good results, though not enough care was always taken to ensure outward secondees received proper jobs. Where civil servants simply shadowed top management but had no specific function, the results were less satisfactory. That it should be considered appropriate to shadow top management is in itself revealing of a blinkered attitude; as the TV series *Back to the Floor* has shown, more can be learned from shadowing workers than the (mainly) men in the boardrooms.

A review of secondments undertaken by the Civil Service department in 1980 found that civil servants who had been seconded out improved their management and numeracy skills, as well as boosting their knowledge of management techniques. But the interest in secondments waned, although it never entirely died out. More recently, some significant effort has gone into direct recruitment at the most senior levels; again, the results seem beneficial and if the process continues it may help offset the risk of the senior civil service being staffed exclusively by Oxbridge graduates, just as the old administrative class was.

However, the extent to which successful mature recruits bring new attitudes and insights to departments may be less than might be expected; the most successful will tend to be those who adapt to 'the system', and the least successful those who are overwhelmed by the bureaucratic tide of paper and emails that most newcomers find so daunting. One reason for the success of ex-servicemen in the civil service was their familiarity with, and chiefly contempt for, bureaucratic processes; they knew how to work the system.

The permanent abolition of the divisive grading system would have been a major achievement, but although it was easier for mechanicals to become intellectuals, the process was highly secretive and the creation of the senior civil service has made switching between mechanical and intellectual even more difficult (but not as hard as in pre-Fulton days). In the circumstances, it is perhaps unsurprising that in 2017 women accounted for only 40 per cent of the senior civil service (but 54 per cent of all civil service staff), ethnic minorities 7 per cent (compared with 11 per cent) and disabled people 5 per cent (compared with 10 per cent).

Equally as important, Oxbridge's grip on the fast-stream process remains as strong as ever. In recent years, Oxbridge candidates have made up slightly more than 10 per cent of fast-stream candidates but have taken nearly 50 per cent of the places. Many good mechanical candidates are deterred from even applying; they perceive that their record of achievement will fail to carry the day against clever young Oxbridge men. There is some evidence, too, that women graduates are also put off; the number applying to join the fast stream in 2004 was the lowest for seven years.

I have suggested that the Victorian Whitehall offices resembled a gentlemen's club, and in some ways this is still not a bad analogy for the senior civil service; indeed, I have heard one Permanent Secretary remark that he did see his department as a club, with its own rules and traditions. Like the members of most clubs, the senior civil service feels most comfortable with new members who are moulded in its own image; consciously or not, the civil service possesses one of the most effective cloning processes the world has seen.

The civil service college's fortunes waxed and waned over the years, but at its best it offered a wide range of training for all grades and the quality of the training was usually high. A particular benefit was the mixing of officials from different departments. Despite its value, ministers still tried to close the college in 2010. Stalwart action by the civil service's top brass partially saved the day, and the college, though scaled down, became the National School of Government. But the new school was saddled with an unsustainable private finance initiative deal and eventually closed in 2012. Training was pushed back to departments, or done remotely by e-learning. As the Public and Commercial Services Union commented, 'The suspicion remains that this is purely a cost-cutting exercise to deliver training on the cheap, and this can only be a bad thing for the civil service and for the running of government.'

# CHAPTER 9

# WHAT DO ALL THESE PEOPLE DO?

This chapter heading stems from a question posed by a civil service secondee, who could not understand why so many people worked in his unit but seemed to produce nothing. The man's question was unfortunately not too wide of the mark. It wasn't that civil servants in his unit did nothing (though some did next to nothing), but that the work they did was to a large extent unnecessary.

A key factor was that the head of the unit was an assiduous ascender of the greasy pole, and since 'management' was the 'in thing', he needed to have a large empire to manage. It didn't matter that he knew nothing about management; what was important was that he could claim to manage a large workforce and show that he did all the right things: holding team meetings, setting up cross-disciplinary teams and anything else that happened to be in fashion.

At one point, the relevant minister decreed that no one had a managerial job unless at least four people reported to them. Four people did report to this unit head, but one was a part-timer. The unit head grew nervous. The part-timer was unceremoniously bundled out of the unit and replaced by a full-time member of staff, even though there was insufficient work. The tactic worked; the head of the unit moved to a more important and better-paid job.

The ability of any bureaucracy to remain in existence, irrespective of need, is legendary. Charles Dickens immortalised the process in *Little Dorrit*, with the character of Mr Tite Barnacle of the Circumlocution Office, who 'died at his post with his drawn salary in his hand, defending it nobly to the last extremity'. Tite Barnacle provides an enduring and, I fear, altogether convincing image of public service, but in real life overstaffing is not only confined to the public sector. All big organisations, unless well managed, possess their share of Tite Barnacles who conjure up empires out of thin air.

Imperial Chemical Industries' old headquarters, Millbank House, was known throughout the company as 'Millstone' House; and the inability of top management at Marks & Spencer to reduce staff numbers at its Baker Street bunker frustrated shareholders for years. An attempt was made at a Procrustean downsizing, by proposing a move to a smaller HQ which could not accommodate all the existing staff. But the M&S bunker-dwellers were equal to such a move, and the company eventually acquired other buildings to house those Tite Barnacles who would not fit into the new HQ.

And if governments have a problem, the issue is even worse for international bureaucracies. The European Commission is popularly supposed to acquire its functionaries first and think about their functions later – if at all. The story is told of a person who, in the early days of the commission's existence, decided it would be a good place to work. He walked into the commission's offices clutching some folders, walked around until he located an empty office – and then phoned the accommodation office to ask where his furniture was. After the furniture arrived he started turning up at meetings and, at the end of the month, phoned the pay section to complain that he had not been paid. In due course his money arrived, and from then on he was on the books and treated as though he had been properly recruited.

If all that seems far-fetched, it is only slightly so. Bizarrely, the day after I wrote about the phantom EC worker, the media reported the strange story of a man called Jonathan K. Idema. An American rejoicing in the nickname 'Mad Jack', he gulled NATO peacekeepers on three separate occasions into supporting him in 'military' operations against his own chosen targets – including the deputy director of the court of appeal in Afghanistan. Mad Jack pretended to be a US serviceman, and everyone believed him. It makes the EC story sound quite plausible.

In seeking to establish why there are so many civil servants, it is important to avoid simplistic assertions. The reality is that the Tite Barnacles of this world are only marginal contributors to the size of the civil service. What really swells civil service numbers is the fact that politicians insist on giving it tasks to perform: to dish out money or rake it in, and to provide a legal framework for everything, from driving vehicles to watering the garden. Most of these functions affect large numbers of the population, so it should come as no surprise that they require significant numbers of civil servants to administer them.

Until early Victorian times, the major functions of the civil service were to raise revenue then spend it on the army and navy. The mid-eighteenth-century civil service numbered some 17,000, and about 14,000 worked in revenue-raising departments. The boom in Britain's economy during the nineteenth century imposed new requirements, and brought reforms that changed the size of the civil service as well as the methods adopted for selecting staff.

The growth in the Victorian civil service was dominated by the Post Office, which had been a department of state since its inception in the Tudor period and would remain so until the mid-twentieth century. In 1805, the General Post Office employed 1,000 staff, making it the third largest department after Customs (7,200) and Excise (7,100). In contrast, the Admiralty and Navy had a total of 477 employees, while the War Office and Board of Ordnance had 660. Other departments such as the Foreign Office, Home Office and Board of Trade each employed only a couple of dozen staff.

By the time the war with Napoleon ended at Waterloo in 1815, numbers at the Admiralty and Navy departments had grown to 619, while War Office and Board of Ordnance staff totalled 1,094, just below the Post Office, which had reached 1,200. In the late 1820s, Parliament sought to pare back the civil service to its pre-war size, and total numbers were reduced by nearly 6,000. But the Post Office continued to expand – reaching just over 1,800 employees in 1832. This reflected a growth in population as well as in the levels of business activity. Two new and important factors also boosted Post Office numbers. One was a growing desire to spread education to the lower and working classes, an effort closely linked to the pressure for cheaper postage rates. The other factor was the growth in the number of newspapers. Sixty-one were published in the British Isles in 1782, but by 1833 that number had grown to 369. In evidence to Parliament, the inspector of letter carriers testified in the mid-1830s that it took 200 sorters in the London office, with additional help from letter carriers, to get some 45,000 newspapers onto outgoing coaches each evening.

The 1840 introduction of the Penny Post had a major impact on the volume of postal deliveries, which meant more people had to be hired by the Post Office. Ten years later, a determined effort was made to get letters delivered directly to rural households. Rural reorganisation was overseen by Anthony Trollope, who walked, or more usually rode, all the postmen's walks himself to make sure the Post Office squeezed the most out of the maximum sixteen miles a day a postman was required to walk (after walking to work in the first place!).

There is some difficulty in establishing a baseline for postal deliveries before the introduction of the Penny Post, as the Post Office had no real idea of the volume of letters carried each year. But a parliamentary committee took the view that an estimate of about 78 million items each year was probably reasonably accurate. By 1855, the number of letters carried had increased to 450 million, and by 1875 it had reached 1,000 million. The Victorians were rather proud of the Post Office. As *The Times* put it in 1868, commenting on the Post Office's annual report:

> Possibly there is no government department which so clearly shows the increasing vitality of this Empire as that of the General Post Office. The correspondence of a country is at once a test of its commercial activity, its social intercourse and its educational status. The history of the Post Office is, in short, the history of the progress of the nation.

It was indeed nothing if not vital, and by the turn of the century Post Office staff numbers had grown to just under 77,000. The rest of the civil service totalled 30,000. The next biggest department after the Post Office was the Admiralty at 9,000, followed by Inland Revenue with 5,000 staff, and Customs and Excise with 4,000.

But governmental changes were starting to impact on numbers. A Board of Education had been established in 1899. The board's work grew with the expansion of education and the development of the school medical service, and by 1902 its staff totalled 1,125. The Board of Trade had also seen a considerable increase in its remit. Originally consultative in function, it was later entrusted with an increasing number of executive duties, including the supervision of weights and measures, the compilation of agricultural statistics, the supervision of the School of Design, the registration of designs and of joint stock companies and the administration of Acts relating to railways and navigation. Unsurprisingly, this extra work was reflected in increased staffing levels. In the 1840s, the board appointed its first librarian. When the Select Committee on Expenditure of 1848 asked about the librarian's duties, J. G. Lefevre, an assistant secretary at the board, explained:

> The duties of the librarian are principally connected with the library; to take care of it, to keep up the catalogue, to purchase such

books as are necessary, to ascertain what books are necessary, and also to take care of papers after they are done with; to bind them up and arrange them. The librarian has nothing to do with the current business of the office at all, except that in as much as he is a very intelligent person his assistance is occasionally asked for on particular subjects.

In 1863, the board appointed its first translator. Sheaves of dispatches concerning tariffs and trade, and written in various languages, would arrive in the morning and had to be translated by the afternoon. The expansion of the board's work continued; by 1902, staff numbers had risen to just over 1,000, and by 1911 to 1,500. The Labour Exchange Act of 1909 and the National Insurance Act of 1911, which sought to address problems associated with unemployment, entailed vast amounts of work in a new field and necessitated the recruitment of a large workforce. By 1914, the Board of Trade's workforce had grown to 2,500, but the Post Office continued to be the civil service's main employer. In 1914, the Post Office employed 209,000 people, compared to a total civil service workforce of 278,000.

The First World War witnessed a major expansion of some departments and the creation of new ones. The War Office grew from 1,600 to 18,000; the Admiralty from 4,400 to 20,400, and the Ministry of Munitions from 1,200 to 65,000. By the end of the war, the Air Ministry had come into existence, employing 4,600 people. Other departments grew because of the consequences of the war for employment and production. The Ministry of Labour doubled its staff numbers to 8,500, while the Board of Trade grew from 2,500 to 7,000. The Ministry of Food was created and employed 9,000 people by the war's end. A new Ministry of Pensions began its spectacular growth, reaching 8,500 employees by Armistice Day. Through it all, the Post Office's workforce remained at around 200,000.

After 1918, contrary to what some critics of the civil service would have you believe, the size of the 'war departments' fell quite quickly; by 1920, they were about one-third of the size they had been in 1918. But in the same period the Ministry of Pensions grew to 25,000 and the Ministry of Labour to 17,000, with both increases reflecting the legacy of the war. By 1930, the total number of civil servants had fallen to just over 300,000, with the Post Office accounting for 194,000, the Inland Revenue 21,000, the Ministry of Labour 17,000 and Customs and Excise 12,000. The Ministry of Pensions had shrunk to just 6,000, despite the fact that in 1928 it organised the commencement of an old-age pension payable at local post offices to some half a million people aged between sixty-five and seventy. The preliminary work, noted *The Times*, had been done well and there was little confusion or delay. (Perhaps those folk making such a hash of Universal Credit could nip down to the Public Record Office and see how it was done.)

As the impact of the First World War dwindled, the inevitability of the outbreak of a war against Hitler began to make its mark. The first developments came at the Air Ministry. During 1934, exercises conducted by the RAF had demonstrated the vulnerability of London to air attack. An Air Ministry official, Albert 'Jimmy' Rowe, analysed some fifty files on air defence in the ministry's archive; his gloomy conclusion was that without new scientific developments any war fought by Britain in the next ten years would be lost.

Rowe's work led to the establishment of a committee for the scientific survey of air defence under Henry Tizard, and the start of research that resulted in the development of radar and the adoption of operational research as a practical tool of war. By April 1935, a research station had been set up at Orford Ness on the Suffolk coast, and within twelve months it was joined by a new station at Bawdsey. As the likelihood of war grew, the rest of Whitehall began to ponder the consequences for their own spheres of activity. In late 1938, a research and experiments branch was set up at the Home Office to take over the work on air raid precautions. In April 1939, a meeting was convened at the Board of Trade to discuss the consequences of setting up an export licensing department in the event of war, a draft handbook having previously been circulated. If the department were to be set up, 'the work would be strenuous and would doubtless involve the abandonment of regular hours'. 'The officers would have to take a good deal of responsibility in dealing with individual applications.' The latter comment was particularly perceptive, and was still relevant fifty years later as the Scott Inquiry into defence sales to Iraq demonstrated.

As the prospect of war loomed ever closer, it brought changes to how civil servants worked. Towards the end of March 1939, the Home Office made arrangements for duty staff to sleep in the office overnight; my father-in-law noted in his diary entry for 10 April that he had spent the night in the office for the first time. He heard '1, 2, 3, & 4 o'clock strike on Big Ben though I was not awake continuously all that time'. The charlady 'called with tea and hot-water about 7.35', after which he popped down to Whitehall on a bus and breakfasted at Strand Corner House; it was, he opined 'quite good'.

The outbreak of war triggered an immediate increase in civil service numbers. This expansion had been meticulously planned from early 1939, and in his book *Whitehall*, Peter Hennessy gives a detailed account of how it was managed. When the war started, yet more new staffing needs were identified and more people recruited to meet those needs. After the war the numbers employed in war departments fell quite rapidly, from 157,000 in 1945 to 91,000 by 1949. The Post Office was still far and away the largest department and it continued to grow until, by 1969, the year it ceased to be a government department, it totalled 415,000. Although no other department has ever come near such a size, the impact of increasing wealth and more inventive ways of avoiding tax drove up numbers at the Inland Revenue, which peaked at

85,000 in 1978. The increasing range and complexity of benefit payments pushed up DSS numbers to 125,000 by 2004. The MoD peaked at 250,000 in 1978.

Total civil service numbers reached their post-war high in 1969, when 885,000 were employed, and though reclassifying the Post Office as a public corporation nearly halved this figure, expansion of other departments quickly pushed numbers to a new peak of 736,000 in 1978. Mrs Thatcher's arrival in Downing Street heralded an era of cuts, and within six years numbers had fallen by over 100,000. The fall continued, fuelled by a mixture of cuts, privatisation and contracting out. Where services were privatised, as in the case of air traffic control, there were no real cuts, just a rebadging of the service that left the same people doing the same tasks. The same held true for contracted-out services such as those provided by the National Physical Laboratory.

When Labour won the 1997 election, civil service numbers stood at just under 480,000. All departments but one had suffered losses; owing to the popularity of putting people in prison, the Home Office had increased its staffing levels by 50 per cent, though not all of this increase was accounted for by the Prison Service. The Ministry of Defence, Foreign and Commonwealth Office and Department of Trade and Industry all shed about 50 per cent of their staff, while numbers at the Ministry of Agriculture, Fisheries and Food, Education, Employment and the Inland Revenue fell by some 30 per cent. Social Security lost only 8 per cent.

The total number of civil service staff continued to fall, reaching a low of 460,000 in 1999, before increasing rapidly, with over 510,000 staff by 2003. While some of this increase might reflect Labour's propensity for job creation in the public sector, a significant part of it was due to the roll-out across Whitehall of resource accounting and budgeting. This switch from traditional cost accounting was one of Kenneth Clarke's last acts as Chancellor of the Exchequer and was intended to make the real costs of government much clearer. But while there is no reason why Whitehall should not run its accounts like the rest of the country, the change has proved hugely labour intensive (it is estimated that the manpower needed to complete financial paperwork has more or less doubled) and in reality the cost of government remains as obscure as ever. The whole exercise has been described as the biggest ever scandal in Whitehall. Oddly, though, it has attracted only minor criticism of departments which were tardy in getting their accounts into the new form.

Similar consequences have stemmed from the decision to abandon central pay negotiations. In the recent past, some twenty civil servants conducted pay negotiations for the entire civil service, but now each department must conduct its own negotiations – meaning some 2,000 civil servants are engaged in a totally unnecessary task.

There is a certain irony about all this. The Victorian-era parliaments got exercised over the fact that civil servants in different departments were paid different rates for doing more or less the same work. Eventually uniform pay was achieved, but only for the generalists, and over the years a whole raft of departmental grades came into existence, each with their own pay rates. During the 1970s, this system was gradually dismantled, but hardly had the last departmental grade vanished than the government reverted to the Victorian model of a free for all, meaning that staff in different departments who perform broadly similar tasks receive considerably different salaries.

While politicians often criticise the civil service for being too big, and Chancellors of the Exchequer relish announcing job cuts, the fact remains that it is politicians who create the jobs in the first place and who pay insufficient attention to cutting out unnecessary tasks. At various times, Parliament has taken an interest in such matters. Between the two world wars there were regular returns of established civil servants employed by departments, and brief explanations had to be given for any growth. In 1938, for example, increases at the Home Office were attributed to expansion of air raid precaution services; at Health to extra work flowing from the Widows', Orphans' and Old Age Contributory Pensions (Voluntary Contributions) Act of 1937; at the Unemployment Assistance Board to additional work transferred from local authorities; and at the Board of Trade to work relating to the 1937 Coal (Registration of Ownership) Act, the Patents and Designs Act of 1932 and the Trade Marks Act in 1938. Overwhelmingly it is legislation that creates jobs, and it is Parliament that passes such legislation.

Even legislation that is more or less dead makes demands, albeit small ones, on the time of civil servants. The Easter Act 1928 provided for Easter to become a fixed Sunday in the United Kingdom, the Channel Islands and the Isle of Man, but the Act requires that before a draft order is laid before Parliament, 'regard shall be had to any opinion officially expressed by any Church or other Christian body'. So far none of the churches have sought to fix the date, probably having better things to occupy them, and perhaps mindful of the ructions at the Synod of Whitby in 664, when the present method of calculating the date of Easter was established. Nonetheless, someone in the bureaucratic machine has to be able to answer queries on the issue (a parliamentary question about the subject was tabled by Lord Norton of Louth in 2005), so some poor mutt has that responsibility (as well as others). And though people might think such recondite issues would never cause real problems, they have a nasty habit of doing precisely that, and their impact can be surprisingly important. In the run-up to the 1966 general election, the relevant person at the Home Office failed to note the impact on the Bank Holiday (Ireland) Act of 1903, and it was only at a very late stage that appropriate action was taken to keep the election legal.

It is not merely specific pieces of legislation that must be kept in mind, but also procedures and precedents for implementing them. During and after the Second World War, an official called the Custodian of Enemy Property had responsibility for looking after property that belonged to enemy nationals. For many years it was a significant task, but as the years went by the volume of business fell away. Eventually the post was allowed to lapse, but within a few years a decision was taken to return to their heirs the property of German Jews who died in concentration camps; all the old files had to be speedily retrieved and examined to ensure correct procedures were followed. The work occupied a number of staff for three or four years. In a similar vein, when economic sanctions were imposed against Iraq after the invasion of Kuwait, the Bank of England had to recall a retired member of staff, because there was no one left who had experience of running exchange control procedures.

From time to time, the courts can add to the bureaucracy. In 2005, the Secretary of State for Defence, John Reid, was ordered by a High Court judge to reconsider his decision not to designate merchant ships sunk during the war as war graves. The Secretary of State had argued that doing so would be a huge bureaucratic exercise, but the judge pointed out that there was nothing in the relevant Act that allowed the government to define which vessels might be designated as war graves on the grounds of avoiding administrative effort. It is difficult to think of a more emotive subject than that of war graves, and most people would sympathise with the idea of protecting them, but it is undoubtedly true that doing so (over 5,000 merchant ships were lost in the two world wars) requires bureaucratic effort. In 2006, the Secretary of State appealed against the High Court's ruling, but the appeal was dismissed by the Court of Appeal.

In the 2004 spending review, Chancellor Gordon Brown announced cuts of 84,000 civil service posts. Mark Serwotka, general secretary of the Public and Commercial Services Union, denounced these cuts as 'politically driven' and claimed they were designed to 'pacify a public whipped up by politicians and sections of the tabloid press to believe any deficiencies in service are the result of waste and bureaucracy'. While it is true that cutting the civil service always appeals to politicians, it is equally true that in any big organisation there will be waste and bureaucracy. What is required is to have systems that identify waste and inefficiency, and managers willing to use these systems.

Of course it can be done, and has been done, but it requires managers to realise that it needs doing, to find ways of doing it and to be supported by their senior managers while they achieve it. In one of the few publicly documented cases, two members of staff of the DTI, Liz Santry (a senior executive officer) and Peter Lawrence (a grade 7), explained in an article for the journal of the now defunct Royal Institute of Public Administration how they improved things at a Department of Trade and Industry licensing unit. They increased productivity from nine cases per week to fifty-one, and reduced average turnaround time from nine weeks to two-and-a-half weeks. They tackled the procedures, developed performance targets and, perhaps most importantly, changed their management styles. Because they were seen to be taking an interest, staff responded well. One employee commented that 'no one ever used to worry about backlogs'. But as Santry and Lawrence pointed out, 'We had worried about the backlogs, but we had not before found a suitable means of getting this message across to the people who counted.'

Increases in productivity of this order are clearly immensely valuable, and the figures actually understate the benefits. As a result of a faster turnaround, the huge wasted effort of dealing with complaints about delays, expediting urgent cases and the general confusion and muddle associated with overflowing in-trays are avoided. The effort simply goes into getting work done, so that it can be carried out in a more accurate and more efficient manner. Lack of muddle also gives the Tite Barnacles no cover for their incompetence, and they tend to find the pace of life too demanding; they find more congenial postings, leaving the work to the well-motivated and efficient.

Santry and Lawrence did, however, end with a cautionary note that goes some way to explaining the reality behind the Tite Barnacles, as 'left to themselves, case officers appear to have an inexorable tendency to find over time more complicated ways of doing simple tasks'. This problem is a long-standing one. In the 1780s, the commissioners of public accounts reported that:

> The Imprest Roll is all written in an abridgement of the Latin language. The sums are both expressed in characters that are, in general, corruptions of the old text ... the sums so expressed cannot be cast up. Most of the accounts in the Exchequer are made up twice; first in common figures, that they may be added together; and then turned into Latin and the same entered into Exchequer figures.

It was some years before the Treasury reluctantly gave up this archaic practice.

The point noted by Santry and Lawrence has been commented on by others. Lord (Derek) Rayner made the point specifically about the benefits system, after Mrs Thatcher appointed him to run the Efficiency Unit. The system had become so complicated, he said, that many staff did not understand it. This remains true today, as anyone who grapples with the system can testify. It is partly the result of an inadequately rigorous analysis of proposed changes, and partly the result of trying to bolt innumerable stable doors.

It would change people's perceptions of civil servants if they realised how many of them seem to resent paying out money which the government and Parliament say should be paid. In the early 1980s, for example, a Rayner scrutiny of regional development grant payments found that way too much effort was expended in 'saving' small amounts of money, and that far from any savings to the public purse there was a considerable cost – in the order of several hundred pounds spent for every pound 'saved'. In close consultation with the National Audit Office, the rules were changed; all the effort now went into the relatively few big cases where savings were much greater than the cost of achieving them. Staff were reluctant to allow small firms to 'get away with it', and it was only after the department's own audit teams insisted on the new rules being followed that the change became effective and real savings were made.

The propensity towards over-complication is complemented by a tendency for office functions to grow by the accretion of extra work; this is usually something that happens slowly. A new manager arrives who likes things done differently – financial reporting, procurement procedures, quality control – or who believes in the importance of ISO quality control or Investors in People accreditation. He may have authority to recruit staff to carry out this new task, or he may need to seek authority from above (or want to let his bosses know what he is doing to buttress his case for a bonus). The case will be made that his proposal is sensible and defensible, and only requires a small increase in resources which will be more than repaid by efficiency gains. More senior managers, who probably selected the new manager in the first place, congratulate themselves on their choice, noting that the new recruit is already making an impact, and readily accept the proposal. Over the years other managers come and go, and the process is repeated until someone starts jibbing at the corporate overheads, or profits nosedive.

What usually compounds the problem is that the new manager seldom bothers to halt any existing activity, either because the thought never arises, or if it does the threatened functionary deploys defensive (or aggressive) ploys. All but the most determined managers find it easier to concentrate on achieving what they want rather than scrapping what they don't want.

On a slightly grander scale, the process stems from the top. For example, a minister comes up with a shiny new initiative which will require X number of staff. That number is usually found from within the department's existing staff, most often for reasons of speed, but all these workers have to vacate their existing posts which must then be filled. The vacancy-filling process works its way through the system until it manifests itself as a recruitment need. Because of the nature of filling vacancies in government departments, those who are recruited might prove to be different types of people compared to those who filled the posts originally.

Let us suppose a Secretary of State has a (fictional) new initiative to encourage more effective supply chain management in the watercress industry (they've done worse!), and that this new unit will be based in London (where very little watercress is grown!) and headed up by an assistant secretary. Ostensibly the post has been pitched at this level to ensure industry sits up and takes notice, but industry generally has only the haziest notion of what such arcane nomenclature means, and the real reason is probably to do with empire-building further up the line. The new post is filled by transferring an assistant secretary from another part of the department, and a principal from the same unit is then promoted to fill the vacancy created by the assistant secretary's departure. That person is in turn replaced by a principal technical specialist from a government laboratory, who wants wider administrative experience, and his job is taken by a technical senior executive officer in Birmingham, where he has occupied an administrative post (to gain more experience), and who is seeking a transfer to London so he can look after his elderly parents. After five or six further iterations, the final vacancy in the chain is filled by recruiting a new messenger from Bootle, who has been unemployed for a year, and is happier than all the rest put together. The extra staff all get lost in the noise, and with 500,000 civil servants there is plenty of noise!

There is a further complication. While most workers do a decent day's work even if such work is not really needed, a significant minority do not (irrespective of whether their work is necessary), and unless they are properly managed they will be content to draw a salary and do nothing or very little. These are the characters who so annoyed Charles Trevelyan, and are also perhaps the people

Irish poet Louis MacNeice had in mind when he wrote the line 'Sit on your arse for fifty years and hang your hat on a pension'. They are the people who refuse to answer phones for absent colleagues; who leave faxes in the machine; who fail to reply to letters promptly (or at all); and who never return phone calls. They take sick leave for minor ailments, arrive late and leave early, take long lunches, and spend time gossiping and making lengthy personal phone calls.

Everyone in a large organisation in the private or public sector could take you immediately to an office with such occupants. They impose on colleagues and give their employers a bad name, and of course they cost money while adding no value. Such characters are to be found at many levels in different organisations, and come in varying shades of incompetence. I have been struck during the writing of this book by the number of people in different parts of the public sector who have complained to me about the proliferation of such people in their organisation, and the inability or unwillingness of management to address the issue – usually for the same reasons as those identified by Trevelyan in the 1850s.

There is one big difference between the private and the public sector. If I am unhappy with my builder or banker, I can find another, but I have no choice about my tax collector or social worker, or any of a host of public servants who can have such a large impact on my life. In his report of 1854, Trevelyan fulminated against a civil service that provided careers 'for the unambitious and the indolent or incapable'. Trevelyan grossly exaggerated the extent of the problem, but Lord Laming's report of 2003 made it clear that such staff had been well represented in the various offices when eight-year-old Victoria Climbié was murdered by her guardians three years earlier.

It is a justifiable criticism of the public sector that unsuitable people are recruited for work which can have a serious impact on the public; that they are not properly trained or managed; and that they are not dismissed when they fail to change their ways.

What Laming found in 2003 differed little from what an internal Home Office inquiry discovered in 1856: that equal rewards were 'given to the idle and inefficient, as to the diligent and useful, officer'. It doesn't have to be like that. What is needed is the sort of robust approach that the secretary to the Commissioners of Excise adopted in a letter to the supervisor of Pontefract in 1774:

> The Commissioners on perusal of your diary observe that you make use of many affected phrases and incongruous words, such as 'illegal procedure', 'harmony' etc., all of which you use in a sense that the words do not bear. I am ordered to acquaint you that if you hereafter continue in that affected schoolboy way of writing, and to murder the language in such a manner, you will be discharged for a fool.

More recently, robust management brought the UK Passport Agency from the brink of collapse to a high level of efficiency. A colleague who runs another agency was attending a hideously expensive away day, run to fatten the wallets of a firm of consultants, when he was asked what got him out of bed in the morning (they probe deeply, these management consultants!). His reply was 'anger'. This reference to raw emotion was unexpected and he was asked to explain himself. He pointed out that he had never forgiven Mrs Thatcher for her constant carping at the inefficiency of the public sector, and he was determined to demonstrate his agency was run efficiently; having visited most of that agency's offices, I think he was succeeding.

Poor service is a function of poor management, and for the reasons that I have set out the public sector is prone to have poor managers. In the early 1980s, the Treasury and Civil Service Committee reported that:

> There is no clear orientation towards the achievement of effectiveness and efficiency at the higher levels of the Civil Service or in government generally.

While the broad intentions of policy are often clear enough, there are too few attempts to set operational objectives and realistic targets against which to measure outturn. Measures of output are inadequate. Consequently there are no systematic means of guiding and correcting the use of resources.

Although there has been progress since then, it has tended to be in operational areas such as the executive agencies and not in policy areas. This means that while the agencies are increasingly efficient, the policy areas (and support services too) remain immune, producing perverse results in spending reviews, with agencies that have growing workloads being denied extra resources while resources are wasted in their parent departments. Ministers seek to modernise the management of the public sector, but none of them seems to have a clue as to how this might be done. This sense of frustration, coupled with the continuing widespread inability of top civil servants to understand even basic management techniques, means that, in an effort to be seen to be doing something to improve management, vast avalanches of new initiatives are unloaded onto the staff below. These initiatives are usually half-baked and serve only to hinder staff in getting their work done. Such a state of affairs is nothing new. The point was well made by Emperor Nero's courtier, Gaius Petronius Arbiter, way back in 210 BC: 'We meet any new situation by reorganising, and a wonderful method it can be for creating the illusion of progress while producing confusion, inefficiency and demoralisation'. We have had over 2,000 years to absorb that truth, but so far neither ministers nor civil service top management have got the point! Indeed, John Reid's reorganisation of the Home Office seems to be a potent example of such illusory progress.

According to a report from the National Audit Office published in 2010, reorganisations of Whitehall departments and quangos in the five years following the May 2005 general election cost some £1 billion and achieved precious little. When the report was published, the chairman of the House of Commons Public Accounts Committee, Sir Edward Leigh, remarked that designers of logos and makers of nameplates had much reason to be grateful for central government's passion for constantly reorganising and renaming departments.

It is worth comparing this management by confusion with the style of someone who ran a large organisation effectively. Arnold Weinstock built up the General Electric Company (GEC) through good management, and his technique was clarity of management style (his own preferred term). In November 1968, when General Electric and English Electric merged, Weinstock sent a note to all his managers, which included crystal-clear statements of responsibility:

> The real success of our company depends on the individual managing directors of our many production units. Our help (or lack of it) from HQ does not relieve you in the least of the responsibility for that part of the business which is in your charge. You will, of course, see that your sub-managers are given well defined, specific tasks and objectives and then discharge their duties effectively.
>
> Our philosophy of personal responsibility makes it completely unnecessary for you to spend time at meetings of subsidiary boards or standing committees. Therefore all standing committees are by this direction disbanded ... If you wish to confer with colleagues, by all means do so ... But remember that you will be held personally accountable for any decision taken affecting your operating unit.

Some twenty years later I got to know one of GEC's managers well. He told me that he met Weinstock twice a year: once to set a target for his contribution to profits, and once to assess the outcome. The meetings were tough (Weinstock was said to be quick to chide and slow to praise), but for the rest of the time my friend was left alone to achieve the agreed contribution to profits in whatever way he saw fit; it was a style my friend relished. He left GEC in the early 1990s when its hands-off approach became a finger-in-every-pie approach.

The Weinstock style is fully adaptable to the circumstances of the public sector, both in respect of service delivery and policy-making, and the whole machine would work much better if it were so applied. But ministers have a strong tendency to confuse activity with achievement, and since the former is easy to do, and easy to demonstrate, the top managers of the civil service have honed their skills as prestidigitators and created a system that tends to promote the creators of impressions rather than the achievers of results. It is such creators of impressions who fail to understand how to manage poor performance, and probably never notice it in the first place.

The civil service did have a useful mechanism for limiting the waste of manpower; it was called staff inspection. The process had been foreshadowed by Sir Charles Trevelyan in his inquiries into departments of state during the run-up to his major report. Departments were not always content that their work had been understood, but, irrespective of their value in other respects, the inquiries certainly found skeletons in some cupboards. At the office of the chief secretary in Dublin, the Treasury had approved the appointment of a chief clerk who was to be 'thoroughly acquainted with the whole of the detailed arrangements of the office business'. This post was needed to substitute for the under-secretary, because of the frequent absences in London of the chief secretary which required the under-secretary to stand in for him. The post of chief clerk commanded a salary of £800 a year, and Trevelyan discovered that in 1847 a Mr Theobald M'Kenna had been appointed to the post. Two years later, without Treasury approval, the job title was changed to assistant under-secretary and the salary increased to £1,000. The inquiry's report continues:

> It appears, however, upon inquiry, that the Assistant Under Secretary does not perform those important duties, nor does he take the active part in the business and discipline of the office which

was evidently contemplated by the minute of his appointment. At present there is scarcely any portion of the business disposed of by the Under Secretary which passes at all under the review of the Assistant Under Secretary; and it is evident to the Committee, that under present circumstances most important directions may be and are given of which the latter officer is perfectly ignorant.

Perhaps in an effort to shore up his position, Mr M'Kenna later added the roles of clerk of the council and deputy keeper of the privy seal to that of assistant under-secretary, but he vanishes from the record in 1857. He was a QC and he perhaps found the salary useful while building up his practice.

The financial control over other departments that the Treasury established during the nineteenth century meant no post could be created or abolished in the civil service without Treasury approval. In 1874, a proposal from the Home Office to employ a third char-woman was approved by the Financial Secretary. That same year the Treasury was asked to approve the suppression of a clerical post and the retirement of the office keeper (aged eighty) and housekeeper (aged seventy) at the Companies Registration Office in order to fund a 15 per cent pay rise for the registrar, assistant registrar and senior clerk. Even though officials ultimately took over the donkey work, the Lords Commissioners of the Treasury remained formally in control. As a committee of officials gleefully reported in 1947:

> Up to 1939 the nineteenth century management of complement control retained most of its pristine simplicity. Not one additional clerk or cleaner was to be engaged without Their Lordships' author-ity. Each post was authorised for a certain part of each office and was in no circumstances to be moved without Their Lordships' authority.

In 1933, the Post Office was allowed to vary its complement with-out prior Treasury authority, but only for grades with a maximum salary of £600 a year (later raised to £1,000). This was an appallingly inefficient system, but it was not until 1949 that other departments received delegated authority to create and abolish posts (again up to certain salary levels), provided that regular work surveys or staff inspections were introduced. Departments had been asked to set up such systems in 1947 where they did not already exist. The idea was that all units in a department would be reviewed on a rolling programme. Work would be examined to ensure it was necessary and that enough staff (but no more) were available. Eventually all posts below assistant secretary were delegated to departments, and staff inspectors examined the work to ensure it needed to be done and was properly loaded and graded.

Operated properly, this system proved very effective, and helped to drive out useless staff who found a properly loaded and graded post a bit of a trial. The great strength of the system was that it worked from the bottom up (junior staff seem surprisingly willing to tell people from outside their unit things they would never tell their bosses) and was carried out by those who understood the culture and mode of operation of their department, and thus where the bodies were likely to be buried.

The system had two major problems, though. Firstly it was not always staffed by good operators, as management was not seen as a way to get on, and secondly weak top management would not force issues with poor local managers. But one advantage this system did have over similar exercises conducted by external consultants was the fact that, having carried out an inspection, there was always a chance the inspectors might at a later date be transferred to that unit; it happened often enough to make good staff inspectors think carefully about their recommendations.

In recent times, there has been a tendency to think that changes in budgetary control have made staff inspections superfluous, but in fact the need is as great as ever. If project management requires special reporting tools and gateway reviews, why should it be assumed that ongoing business does not? Can incompetent project managers be capable managers of an ongoing business? Are they competent policy managers? The logic of the current civil service suggests that the top management believe they are, and this might go a long way to explaining some policy delivery failures.

One of the most positive aspects of staff inspection was that it enabled underused or misused staff to be redeployed where they were genuinely needed. It was possible to find units where staff in one office would be working overtime, while in an adjacent office they would be twiddling their thumbs, yet no one made the small leap of imagination required to reconcile those imbalances. Preparatory work for a staff inspection of a regional operation in 1983 revealed that staffing levels in the offices bore no relationship to workloads. Offices with a high caseload had low staff numbers and vice versa. There were offices where workload and staffing levels were appropriate, but these were a minority. The central management unit had not realised there was such an imbalance; to be blunt, it had not sought to find out what the position was.

It was because staff inspections revealed such a poverty of management skills that they were so detested by senior management. While only a small thing in itself, the case of the assistant secretary who allowed his personal secretary to slit open incoming envelopes, but not to remove the contents, goes a long way to illustrate the nature of the problem. Trade unions were usually quite worked up about staff inspections, but often were far more in tune with reality than managers, and frequently a lot more sensible in negotiating the final outcomes of any inspection.

The staff inspection process was centrally supervised by the Treasury, which also provided training. In theory, the system should have delivered more effective operations across the civil service, but the failure of top civil servants to understand the nature of management fatally undermined its effectiveness. The situation was neatly summed up by a principal establishments officer, who responded to the proposal to abolish a senior post which was so lightly loaded as to be non-existent by saying, 'I must have somewhere to put my hospital cases!'

Staff that were useless or had no real work to do were usually pensioned off, often on fairly handsome terms (rather like useless directors in the private sector today). In the case of the Board of Trade in 1866, a proposal was made following an inspection that there should no longer be two Permanent Secretaries. In his reply to the Treasury, one of the two secretaries, Northcote's brother-in-law Thomas Farrer, wrote, 'As regards the Joint Secretaryship, I am to acquaint you that Sir J. Emerson Tennent, the senior Joint Secretary, has expressed his readiness to enter into an arrangement for giving immediate effect to this proposal and to accept compensation for the abolition of his office.'

Farrer added that in view of James Emerson Tennent's record – fifteen years as Joint Secretary of the Board of Trade, Secretary of the India Board, Colonial Secretary to the Governor of Ceylon and Secretary to the Poor Law Board – 'my Lords are of the opinion that he has a claim to a special allowance of the most liberal order'. They proposed that Sir James should retain his salary; I am sure the beneficiaries of the Poor Law Board would have concurred! The Lords Commissioners of the Treasury did.

The Treasury finally delegated pay and staffing issues to departments in the first flush of the 1990s financial management initiative, and the requirement to hold regular staff inspections lapsed. There is no longer any regular system of challenging the work of civil servants to determine whether it is still needed. Inspection processes are a common feature of bureaucracies. Inspectors of prisons have done much to reveal the appalling state of the prison service and the Commission for Social Care Inspections launched a major consultation exercise in 2004 to improve the quality of information about children's homes and those for elderly people.

Interestingly, the commission had the wit to ask the children how they thought inspections could be improved. The children suggested inspectors should visit at weekends and in the evenings when the children were in. They also suggested that inspections should be unannounced, and that when testing showers the inspectors should not just turn on one shower but all of them at the same time, to check there was enough hot water to go round. With real imagination, the commission is piloting a scheme where youngsters from one home go with inspectors to another home so that the inspectors can get a child's-eye view. These children sound pretty sharp, and reading between the lines one can't help feeling that there are still some rivals to Dotheboys Hall in existence.

In 1835, three commissioners were appointed by Parliament to examine the workings of the Post Office. When the commissioners turned their attention to the packet boat services, their findings triggered a thoroughgoing condemnation of the operations. The use of Holyhead as a general repair station for packet boats was strongly criticised: it seemed foolish to take a Weymouth packet, for example, to Holyhead for repair. The official in charge of packet boat services was George H. Freeling, the assistant secretary of the Post Office, who just happened to be the son of the Post Office's secretary. Freeling admitted that he had never visited Holyhead, nor did anyone else inspect the place. He also revealed that no one at the Post Office possessed a practical knowledge of how to manage a dockyard. Parliament dealt with such issues robustly in those days: the commissioners' recommendation that the packets be turned over to the Admiralty was effected by an Act of Parliament in 1837.

Just over 100 years later, in 1948, the Post Office began to license the use of mobile radios by taxi companies. Over the years the use of this sort of radio grew and the administration of it became increasingly complex. (At one point it seemed to slip back into a pre-Trevelyan mode – assignments of radio frequencies to users were made from the pub opposite the office of the Postmaster General!) By the 1980s, the administration of the scheme involved a computer system, which contained a topographical map of the UK, as well as details of the locations of all the base stations and the frequencies on which they operated.

Despite all this sophistication, and the hard work of radio engineers, it became more and more difficult to find frequencies for an ever-growing number of users; those who had frequencies were always complaining about interference from other users. Eventually, it was decided to make a physical inspection of every mobile radio system in the country. It was, I believe, the first inspection since 1948. This revealed that more than a tenth of licensees were no longer using radio, though they still paid an annual licence fee. No one had told the accounts department, so they went on paying. In a slightly smaller number of cases, the base station had been moved (illegally), and in a similar number of cases the equipment had drifted off frequency. All told, some 30 per cent of data in the computer system was duff. The whole administrative process had been rendered worthless because no one took the trouble to find out what was happening on the ground.

A similar failure to take even the most elementary precautions in the way of cross-checking allowed a Devon farmer, John Bowden, to claim grants under two separate schemes in respect of the same farmland. No one sought to cross-check his applications. Eventually, an official who had been transferred from the administration of one scheme to the other recognised Bowden's name. The fraud was discovered and Bowden was jailed.

When the Public Accounts Committee exposed the case, its members made great play of the fact that in submitting his claims Bowden had used bogus Ordnance Survey grid references to identify the land. One reference put the land in Greenland, another in the North Sea and the third in a patch of water between Ireland and Scotland. Rather plaintively, officials explained that they only used the last three grid numbers provided by applicants as a reference. But the fact was that Bowden had helpfully provided the Ministry of Agriculture, Fisheries and Food with evidence of his fraud, which the ministry had then failed to notice.

In 1979, Lord Rayner, chairman of Marks & Spencer, was brought in by Prime Minister Margaret Thatcher to tackle some of the major problems of the civil service. What Rayner created was, in essence, a beefed-up system of staff inspection carried out by civil service high-flyers, sometimes with the help of secondees from the private sector. These 'scrutineers' focused on specific activities rather than work units, and produced some effective reports. The 'scrutinies' undoubtedly benefited from the attention of the high-flyers, as well as from the fresh perspectives of outside secondees.

A key to the success of scrutinies was that each report was copied to the Efficiency Unit in the Cabinet Office, and that every review had to end with an action plan. Scrutinies were conducted to very tight deadlines, which sometimes meant that while they probably hit every available coconut, they did not always get everything right. This was where a follow-up team often added value, because in working up and carrying through an action plan, the right weightings and priorities tended to fall into place. Follow-up could prove particularly effective if one of the original scrutineers was involved. As with staff inspections, scrutineers might be posted to an area they themselves had reviewed, which tended to make recommendations carefully thought through. The impact of scrutinies was that much greater because, although they were carried out mainly by departments, any follow-up action had to be reported to the Cabinet Office's Efficiency Unit. The work continued after Lord Rayner returned to the private sector, but gradually ran out of steam. The technique is still used but not on a coordinated Whitehall-wide basis.

An attempt to apply the principles of external review to significant policy issues was attempted by Prime Minister Edward Heath in 1971 when he established the Central Policy Review Staff (CPRS), commonly known as the 'Think Tank'. Like other review bodies, the CPRS tended to pick up on points that, despite being made by troops at the front, were ignored by top management – then put conclusions together briefly and forcefully in a way that was easily digested by ministers. The CPRS passed a crucial test of effectiveness: everyone thought it did a brilliant job except when it trampled over their own departments. With Lord Rothschild at the helm and prime ministerial backing, it made some headway. But powerful departments such as the FCO saw it off (just as had happened to Robert Lowe 100 years earlier).

When Harold Wilson's Labour Party won the 1974 election, he decided to retain the CPRS, with Lord Rothschild as its head. Rothschild explained to the new Prime Minister that the work of the CPRS fell into three main categories: the preparation of presentations to Cabinet ministers on overall government strategy; undertaking studies in depth on long-term prospects, and policies in specific fields; and the presentation of collective briefs for meetings of ministerial committees, where the CPRS could offer distinctive contributions.

The CPRS had a chequered and brief career, finally succumbing to the Thatcher knife in 1983. The decision to kill it off was, perhaps, symptomatic of Thatcher's distrust of the civil service; her preference for seeking external advice from those lacking practical experience of matters on which they advised her, and her propensity to get policy decisions hopelessly wrong through a powerful combination of 'dogma and haste'.

The theory is that financial management regimes in departments act as a brake upon staff numbers, but if the financial discipline of the private sector does not prevent companies such as Marks & Spencer or Boots from developing bloated head offices, it is highly unlikely that the much weaker forces at work in the public sector will have any great impact. The absence of any effective manpower audit system for the civil service is an example of an institutional aversion to quantitative or scientific thinking. This is part of the inheritance of the Victorian reforms, and lies at the root of much that goes wrong in Whitehall today.

# CHAPTER 10

# FACTS AND FIGURES

That much does go wrong in Whitehall is beyond question. The failures embrace systems – such as the long list of failed government computerisation projects and the inability of the prison service to deport foreign prisoners at the end of their sentences – and major policy initiatives such as the Child Support Agency, the Criminal Records Bureau and Universal Credit. What makes failures particularly deplorable is that all too often the reasons are repeated in programme after programme; examples of similar failures can be found running back over many years.

While things go wrong for many reasons, two significant underlying causes of failure stem from the legacy of the Victorian reforms of the civil service; they are closely interrelated. The first is the wedge that Trevelyan and Lowe drove between policy development and policy implementation; if the two are separated, feedback is difficult and policy can easily become divorced from reality, but this is not widely understood. It was because Trevelyan failed to understand the potential problem that James Wilson opposed his attempts to reorganise the Treasury in 1854. A similar perception prompted Dame Evelyn Sharp's letter to the press in 1972, criticising the establishment of policy units following the recommendation of the Fulton Committee. A small example neatly illustrates the point. A senior civil servant who was prepared to get involved in the practical application of policy-making accompanied her staff on a raid of a pirate radio station. After the raid, a police officer told the civil servant about an enforcement difficulty that had been created by the way the relevant regulation was drafted. The civil servant considered the matter and then said, 'You're right. I'll go and see the minister next week and we'll get it amended.' The police officer gazed at her with incredulity. 'I wish we could reach the Home Secretary as easily,' he said.

The second cause of many failures is the legacy of a bias towards a 'literary' approach to administration, compounded by the failure of administrators to seek advice from professionals such as economists and statisticians. This was recognised by the head of the civil service, Sir William Armstrong, in 1968. In a paper on the likely recommendations of the Fulton Committee, he wrote, 'The usefulness of university studies up to first degree level is in fact small compared with the needs of the Service for a trained mind, and particularly one that is trained in quantitative skills and has been given a scientific attitude'.

Armstrong also noted 'the relative slowness with which the "literary" approach to administration is giving place to the quantitative and scientific approach'. He believed that 'in too many cases "the quantitative approach" is still being neglected'. He criticised the partial failure in some branches of the service of the administrator in seeing and ensuring that the specialist advice in all the necessary aspects of problems is both available and given full weight.

Armstrong clearly hoped that matters would improve, but they have failed to do so to any great extent. In 2000, a report by the Cabinet Office's Policy and Innovation Unit pointed out that few administrators (and even fewer ministers) had any idea what range of problems professional specialists could help to resolve. As the report tactfully put it, 'demand for good analysis is not fully integrated in the culture of central government'. The report provided a clear analysis of the problem, and an equally clear prescription for improving matters, but it seems to have gathered dust in the 'not understood and not wanted here' pile.

This view is supported by a National Audit Office report on the e-borders project in 2015, which says the Home Office has a 'culture that does not demand and use high-quality data'. It would require a vast culture change among bureaucrats and an even more fundamental shift in ministerial behaviour. It would also require more professionals to work in government departments, and more recruits from outside the system who have proved their ability to get the best out of such professionals.

The poverty of government statistical analysis is a long-standing problem. In the nineteenth century, the weakness was highlighted by the parliamentary committee examining the case for the Penny Post. In considering the proposal, the Parliamentary Commissioners appointed in 1835 to look into the workings of the Post Office, very sensibly, sought an estimate from the Post Office of the existing volumes of post, since this was crucial to price-setting calculations. In one year the Postmaster General quoted three wildly differing figures: 170 million, 42 million and 67 million. The Secretary of the Post Office topped off proceedings by producing two figures which were different again – 58 million and then 70 million. The parliamentary committee, after pointing out that the Post Office had no accurate records, concluded that Rowland Hill, the advocate of the Penny Post scheme, was probably nearer the truth with his independent estimates of between 78 and 88 million. The committee thus calculated possible reductions in the rates based on his figures, rather than those of the Post Office.

The traditional attitude of administrators to specialists scarcely changed during the next 100 years. It was illustrated beautifully in a 1954 note prepared by a Treasury official as part of the briefing for the head of the civil service, who was appearing before a select committee and who hoped to head off any moves towards specialists getting the same pay as administrators. The administrator, it was claimed in the briefing note, must take a wider viewpoint, while 'the specialist's contribution to policy (if any) is confined to specialist considerations'. The administrator also took 'the main impact of ministerial, parliamentary and PAC requirements', and 'cushions and carries the can for the specialist'. In a damming throwaway final sentence, it was argued that 'recruitment is much more selective: the average assistant principal entrant is a superior article to the average scientific officer'.

In 1966, then Housing minister Richard Crossman complained that the Ministry of Housing and Local Government had only three statistician posts when he arrived and that only one of those was occupied – by someone who had been in post just six months. A few years later, the number of statisticians employed in the entire civil service totalled 302 – rather less than the number of laboratory assistants working in government departments! While things have improved slightly, there are still fewer than 2,000 such specialists in the civil service. The work of these professionals remains an area of considerable ignorance, and hence great fear, but the one thing above all others that characterises government is size (the NHS is the biggest employer in Europe) and it is in dealing with large-scale activity that these disciplines really come into their own.

A common response from administrators to any proposal for better analysis of policy is that 'you can't measure it'; this might in some cases be true, and it could even be true in areas of more routine work, but it doesn't rule out help from the statisticians. In the Second World War, Coastal Command was anxious to achieve greater success in depth charge attacks against German U-boats. Operational researchers interviewed the crews of the flying boats that were depth charging the U-boats and established that their estimates of the depth of the U-boats when they attacked was greater than the standard depth charge setting; the setting was duly changed and the results were so striking that the Germans believed a new type of depth charge had been introduced.

The key point of this story is that significant results were obtained on the basis of estimates made by bomb aimers during fast attacks, often under fire, not on the basis of precise measurements taken in a time and motion study. If these good results could be obtained in such difficult circumstances it is unlikely that the tranquil corridors of power would prove too steep a challenge. But many administrators, while prepared to agree that routine activities can be addressed in this way, simply do not see intractable policy problems in terms of professional analysis. Yet virtually all policy issues involve the assessment of quantifiable information and the creation of hierarchies of importance, and these are issues that statisticians and operational and social researchers could help to resolve, particularly issues relating to risk.

Peter Hennessy makes a revealing comment in his book *Whitehall* in which he discusses Lord Rothschild's tenure as head of the Think Tank during Heath's government. He says of Rothschild, 'He had a brilliant way with statistics, applying them to the most surprising phenomena.' Tantalisingly, Hennessy gives no examples of Lord Rothschild's brilliance (except that Lord Rothschild could calculate how many miles of cigarettes he had smoked!), but the chances are that though the author was surprised, few statisticians would have been. Despite the skills being available, and a proven record of success, statistical analysis remains a major weakness of government. A study conducted in 2003 by the Institute for Public Policy and Research concluded that there was 'little statistically robust evaluation work carried out' by the government when taking decisions about financial assistance to companies. It may be that administrators fear the use of statistical analysis will reduce their policy-making mystique to a commonplace mechanical task, but statistics will not remove hard choices, just make decisions more informed and easier to defend. For politicians, the fears are often that their cherished policy will be shown to be based on flimsy foundations. All too often such fears prove well founded, but it is better if mistakes are discovered before the event, rather than see banner newspaper headlines announcing yet another government failure.

The deep-seated lack of understanding about statistics within government is responsible for the widespread adoption of inappropriate and over-burdensome targets. The Royal Statistical Society has pointed out (via its working party on performance monitoring in the public services) that 'performance monitoring when done badly can be very costly, not merely ineffective but harmful and indeed destructive'.

The Statistics Commission was set up in 2000 by the Blair government to restore confidence in government statistics, after the Office for National Statistics had endured a rather difficult couple of years having to constantly revise published figures by considerable amounts. In 2005, the Statistics Commission published a consultation document on the targets associated with departmental spending plans. The document demonstrates clearly why people are concerned about the whole process of target-setting by government, and strongly reinforces the point already made about the poor understanding of the use of statistics in Whitehall.

Examples of poor practice found by the commission include setting precise quantitative targets for improving services in the absence of any baseline data; setting a target without any means of measuring progress towards it; setting 'zero' targets (no patients to wait longer than seventeen weeks for treatment) where one failure means the entire target is missed, even though thousands of cases are handled within the target time; and setting targets where the data for measuring success will not become available until some years after the target year in question.

All told, the consultation document suggests that Sir William Armstrong's concern about the relatively slow pace at which the 'literary' approach to administration was giving way to the quantitative or scientific approach remains valid thirty-five years later. Given the propensity for waste and misallocation of resources in both the private and public sectors, we need much more relevant measurement, not less. The argument about what is relevant in the way of information-gathering strays into the area of tension between those seeking results and those charged with oversight, with the latter usually craving daily updates, weekly returns and monthly progress reports. The definitive position of those on the front line was most effectively set out in a dispatch widely (if doubtfully) ascribed to the Duke of Wellington in August 1812:

*Gentlemen:*

*Whilst marching from Portugal to a position which commands the approach to Madrid and the French forces, my officers have been diligently complying with your requests, which have been sent by HM ship from London to Lisbon and thence by dispatch rider to our headquarters.*

*We have enumerated our saddles, bridles, tents and tent poles, and all manner of sundry items for which His Majesty's government hold me accountable. I have dispatched reports on the character, wit and spleen of every officer. Each item and every farthing has been accounted for, with two regrettable exceptions for which I beg your indulgence.*

*Unfortunately the sum of one shilling and nine pence remains unaccounted for in one infantry battalion's petty cash and there has been a hideous confusion as to the number of jars of raspberry jam issued to one cavalry regiment during a sand storm in Western Spain. This reprehensible carelessness may be related to the pressure of circumstances, since we are at war with France, a fact which may come as a bit of a surprise to you gentlemen in Whitehall.*

*This brings me to my present purpose, which is to request elucidation of my instructions from His Majesty's government, so that I may better understand why I am dragging an army over these barren plains. I construe that perforce it must be one of two alternative duties, as given below. I shall pursue either one with my best ability, but I cannot do both.*

*To train an army of uniformed British clerks in Spain for the benefit of the accountants and copy-boys in London, or, perchance*

*To see to it that the forces of Napoleon are driven out of Spain.*

*Your most obedient servant*
*WELLINGTON*

I have not seen any equally vigorous case put for the other side, but the truth is that if the civil service were better equipped to carry out accurate, relevant and timely statistical analysis, a great deal of public money (our taxes) would be saved; real progress could thus be made in improving the quality of services provided to the public.

Factual information, and in particular statistical information, can be distorted as well as misapplied. Those charged with collecting it and those who interpret it need integrity and open minds. In 1821, in what may well be the first example of cost-benefit analysis – and one which sets the tone for all subsequent examples – the journalist and MP William Cobbett devoted a dozen pages of his book *Cottage Economy* to an explanation of how brewing home beer was cheaper than making tea. Cobbett launched a tirade against the immorality of tea drinking, which he saw 'as no bad preparatory school for the brothel'! He branded tea 'a destroyer of health, an enfeebler of the frame, an engenderer of effeminacy and laziness, a debaucher of youth and a maker of misery for old age'. Cobbett's exercise is amusing (though he was in earnest), but it illustrates how cost-benefit analysis can be (and routinely is) bent to support a desired end, and how those with a dubious end in mind will usually dredge up dubious statistics to support their case.

The grotesque statistical parodies produced by the Soviet Union to illustrate the success of each five-year plan were in a class of their own, but all countries and governments can cook the books when they put politics before principle. The famous dictum attributed to Disraeli about lies, dammed lies and statistics is so well known as to need no reinforcement, and yet every time a government minister produces some fairy-tale statistic to try to convince the public that trains are more reliable, or grannies less liable to die on hospital trolleys, they reinforce disbelief. In late 2005, the Chancellor of the Exchequer, Gordon Brown, announced that the Office for National Statistics would become independent of government, to try to reverse its lack of credibility.

While the collection of facts, whether historical or contemporary, will not of itself make anyone a good administrator (or even a good person!), an awareness of their importance, as well as an ability to assess their relevance and take decisions in their context, can make the task of administration much easier and greatly increase the chance of policies or procedures delivering the goods. Where good-quality analysis can make a huge difference is in recognising, quantifying and managing risk, and ignorance of this fact perhaps goes to the heart of at least some major administrative (and political) blunders.

All of us take risks every day. Mostly we never think about it, either because we don't recognise the risk or because we discount it – 'it won't happen to me'. Most of us don't regard our houses as being intrinsically unsafe, yet records show many deaths and injuries arise from accidents in the home. But most people never see such statistics, so we leave trip hazards on the stairs and electric cables trailing across the floor, and climb on rickety chairs to reach the top cupboard in the kitchen. People do this time and again, until one day someone takes one risk too many and becomes another grim statistic.

The practice is not confined to the home. Despite the fact that much research has been done to illustrate the pitfalls, real estate speculators have an ability to forget about previous booms that went bust and then charge hell for leather into the next one, funded up to the hilt by bankers with equally defective memories. This propensity has been termed disaster myopia; the longer it is since the last disaster the less chance there is that anyone will believe it could happen again. The global financial crisis of 2007–08 demonstrated how dangerous disaster myopia can be.

Although there is extensive literature on disaster myopia as it affects banking and property development, I have not come across any similar analysis related to politics. In the field of property speculation in London, the time from one bust to the next is in the order of eight to ten years; in politics it is probably as many months! Civil servants are generally highly risk-averse people – when they perceive the risk! This makes it all the more surprising that they have so little regard for risk analysis. The reason for their risk aversion is that over many years the civil service has engendered a 'blame' culture which stultifies many people who might otherwise achieve much. In part, this culture is a consequence of Gladstone's legacy of the House of Commons' Public Accounts Committee and the National Audit Office. The impact of these two institutions was summed up in 1946 by Sir Frank Tribe, Permanent Secretary of the Ministry of Agriculture, Fisheries and Food, in a way that would still be considered valid by today's civil servants: 'The outlook of the civil servant was inevitably influenced by the Public Accounts Committee, and by the fact that what he did today would be the subject of an inquiry in two years' time.'

The National Audit Office, which investigates the work of government departments and reports back to the Public Accounts Committee, has over the past decade or so made major changes to how it works. In great measure this is a result of the work of Sir Douglas Henley, who became Comptroller and Auditor General in 1976 and who moved staff away from the traditional activity of finding fault wherever they could, shifting them towards a constructive search for overall value for money. The same movement has not been equally noticeable among members of the Public Accounts Committee, who for all their good work find it difficult to resist bullying and harassing civil service victims in a way that probably does more to limit their effectiveness than they would care to admit.

In any case, it takes time to offset the impact of 150 years of the sort of ferocious nitpicking that Sir Frank Tribe had in mind. It is probably also true that most civil servants are inherently conservative; they are good at doing things we all value in our dealings with public servants, such as being honest, reliable and fair. These virtues are encouraged in the public sector and the work is often of a sort that appeals to such people. A workforce with a strong bias in this direction, reinforced by the Gladstone legacy of retribution, is likely to come up a bit short in the risk-taking department. While ministers and top officials periodically exhort a more entrepreneurial spirit, civil servants look at what happens to those who take risks that backfire (such as Dr David Kelly, who briefed a BBC reporter on Iraq's weapons of mass destruction and was driven to suicide), and then, sensibly, keep their heads down.

In 1946, Sir Frank Tribe offered a further thought in the context of the work of the National Audit Office, arguing that 'the qualities required for business management could not possibly develop under such conditions'. It is ironic that at a time when the new approach by the NAO might be hoped to be having a liberating effect on how bureaucrats work, increased litigation, the government's growing recourse to public inquiries and a rise in investigative journalism are all potent forces working in the opposite direction.

At least the National Audit Office and Parliamentary Accounts Committee have a reasonably good understanding of how departments really tick, as well as of the nature of the relationship between ministers and officials, and between departments and Parliament. This is not necessarily so with those charged with conducting public inquiries. Sir Richard Scott, the judge who headed the inquiry into defence exports to Iraq in 1990, seemed unwilling to accept that parliamentary questions involve a mixture of the finer elements of *Yes Minister* and *University Challenge*, and an all-in wrestling match.

Parliamentary questions can be sharp; they can also be crass. MPs may be fishing for information, or simply seeking an opportunity to get a minister on his feet in order to then trip him up and earn a pat on the back from the opposition whips. Questions can also be income earners for MPs. Sometimes the questions make so little sense that an attempt has to be made to find out what on earth the questioner had in mind. Ministers may favour short or long replies; they may differentiate between questioners on their side and the opposition; they can be cavalier or diligent in how they reply.

The way civil servants draft replies to parliamentary questions has remained consistent over a long period. In 1677, Sir William Coventry advised Samuel Pepys 'to be as short' as he could be 'and obscure, saving in things fully plain', adding that the 'greatest wisdom in dealing with Parliament in the world is to say little, and let them get out what they can by force.' In June 1847, Lord Clarendon, president of the Board of Trade, had to answer a parliamentary question from Lord Wharcliffe relating to sugar imports. Clarendon told his friend James Wilson he had 'no desire to give him more information than is to be obtained from official sources'. This is a line taken often by ministers. In the 1960s, when a new recruit was given a parliamentary question as an exercise, he was told, 'Remember BTU'. This was explained as being brief, truthful and uninformative and formed the basis of drafting in the insurance division of the Board of Trade.

In this context the civil servant drafting an answer has considerable latitude as to interpreting the meaning of the question, and of deciding how to approach the draft answer to submit to the minister. The more that civil servants come to expect their drafting to be crawled over, and subjected to minute textual criticism several years after the event, the more bland their drafting will become, which is not a good thing. It is certainly not what Sir Richard Scott would want, since he took the line that parliamentary questions were one of the ways ministers and officials could be held accountable by Parliament. In fact, Parliament is quite capable of playing by Queensbury rules when it is so minded, but most of the time it does not and the report of Sir Richard Scott's inquiry is a formidable testimony to the fact that truth is rarely discovered by ignoring the facts of life!

More recently Lord Hutton, who conducted an inquiry into Iraq's weapons of mass destruction and the events surrounding

Dr David Kelly's death, seemed to have some rather unusual ideas on what constitutes good personnel management. Civil servants pondering his report will probably consider themselves marginally more at risk of being dumped on by ministers and mandarins if things go wrong, and will be less likely to listen to exhortations to be less risk averse.

While the impact of the judiciary on administration is usually seen at its most spectacular in public inquiries, the increase in the scope of administrative law during the second half of the past century is having an increasing effect, probably slowing down administrative processes as people seek to insure their work against judicial review. Most people recognise that if they break the law they risk consequences, but, for example, detailed understanding of health and safety is thin and many people fail to realise that what they considered a sensible short-cut through cumbersome rules might be viewed differently by a court exercising the benefit of hindsight. When this point is grasped it tends to have quite an impact. The action of railway managers in imposing drastic speed restrictions during the heatwave in 2003 was a predictable reaction to their perceptions of an increased risk of prosecution under health and safety legislation.

Those who fail to understand how ministerial powers can be circumscribed by the law can receive a rude awakening – whether they are civil servants or ministers. In February 2000, a band of Afghan men hijacked an aircraft in order to escape the Taliban regime. In due course the men were tried, but the jury failed to reach a verdict. A retrial was ordered and the men were now found guilty, but on appeal their convictions were quashed because the jury had been misdirected. The men, who steadfastly claimed to have hijacked the plane because they were facing an immediate threat of death or injury, then applied for asylum. Their applications were rejected, but they appealed and in 2004 a panel of immigration adjudicators allowed the appeal on humanitarian grounds (while dismissing it on asylum grounds). So far the system had worked properly: the Home Office had taken a decision, but the machinery put in place by the government to deal with appeals had produced a different result.

What happened next was an appalling case of maladministration. The Home Office did nothing to implement the adjudicators' decision for seventeen months. Efforts by the men's solicitors to get an explanation for the delay were met with a wall of silence. Eventually, in late 2005, the Home Office decided that it was not appropriate to implement the adjudicators' decision. The hijackers sought a judicial review, and in 2006 Mr Justice Sullivan allowed the application and quashed the Home Office decision. In commenting on the conduct of the Home Secretary, Charles Clarke, which he labelled 'inexcusable', Mr Justice Sullivan made the point that as a public authority the Home Secretary has a duty to cooperate and to make candid disclosure, but that duty had not been observed. The judge said the 'entirety of the secretary of state's conduct ... deserved the strongest mark of the court's disapproval'. The important point was not whether it was a good thing to hijack aircraft, or whether the Afghans should stay in this country, but whether the Home Office had acted in accordance with its duty as a public office.

Government ministers greeted the decision with vociferous and ignorant criticism and took the case to the Court of Appeal. Unsurprisingly the court rejected the government's case, pointing out that ministers could not use Acts of Parliament for purposes which Parliament had not sanctioned. Perhaps because of the ferocity of the criticism that he had been subjected to, the court went out of its way to praise Mr Justice Sullivan's 'impeccable judgement'.

More and more cases involving public bodies are being made the subject of judicial review, and the courts have been robust in dealing with bureaucratic incompetence. There is an excellent booklet produced by the Treasury Solicitor's Department that covers the process of judicial review ('The Judge Over Your

Shoulder') but knowledge of its existence seems patchy. Administrators can, of course, make their work less at risk of judicial review by taking legal advice, but there is often a marked reluctance to consult lawyers at an early stage, since the perception is that they will be unhelpful. The nature of this lawyerly unhelpfulness often amounts to no more than pointing out that a proposed course of action is illegal, or would be open to legal challenge; lawyers, like the collectors of unpalatable information, are often criticised for giving advice that does not fit the political needs of the moment.

Getting sound legal advice is just one way of dealing with risk. Often, what looks like taking a risk to others involves very little hazard at all to someone fully conversant with all the relevant detail; as with every other aspect of administration, successful risk-taking requires the risk-taker to possess a detailed understanding of what the risks involve. On one occasion, I was involved in a row with another department over the cost of a government building; the issues were complex and the sum of money not great. I offered to split the costs 50:50, but the other department was adamant they would pay nothing. In an ill-tempered phone call, its chief accounting officer threatened to raise the issue to ministerial level – hoping to bully me into giving way. I said he was welcome to do so, and he then slammed down the phone. I appreciated, as he did not, that ministers dislike getting drawn into pettifogging squabbles between officials, and that with an offer of a 50:50 split on the table no minister would push the matter hard, and so it proved. A letter was sent to my minister, but his polite suggestion that 50:50 was a reasonable solution was accepted. That proved to be a simple issue, but often the issues are of great significance.

There are few ministers or top civil servants who would take a trip in a plane unless they were reasonably confident all pre-flight checks had been carried out, and that air traffic control systems for reporting near-misses and taking remedial action were fully operational. Yet those same ministers and civil servants will embark upon new policy initiatives – such as rail privatisation or Care in the Community – without giving systematic thought to the risks involved.

Major risks are run with other peoples' lives on the back of dogma and haste, and when no adequate risk analysis is carried out there are often no contingency plans in place to deal with problems that arise. This is why ministers and their departments often seem at a loss when something goes wrong. Even when contingency plans are developed they do not always prove robust enough. Contingency plans existed for dealing with outbreaks of foot-and-mouth disease, but the planning scenarios were all based on outbreaks occurring in only a few places. Departmental thinking had not kept up with developments in the livestock trade, so when the disease was identified at eighteen different locations in the first weeks of 2002 the government's plans proved inadequate.

The principles of risk management are applied to project management, being incorporated in the standard planning tools. They are also applied to health and safety matters and to business continuity planning. To be effective, all relevant risks must be identified, and the number of high-profile programmes that do go wrong (Jubilee Line Extension, Millennium Dome, National Botanic Garden of Wales) suggest there is room for improvement. A huge number of projects, both big and small, succeed, but inevitably these never make news. Compare the publicity attracted by the passport agency, when people were queuing in the rain to collect passports, and the almost total lack of press interest in the smooth transfer of the agency's operations to a new building a few years later.

There are many reasons why some projects succeed, and one of these is usually the existence of a robust contingency plan; possibly because the sorts of people who run successful projects do their planning thoroughly. The auction of the radio spectrum for third-generation mobile phone networks was a classic example of such robust planning. No such operation had ever been attempted;

the process relied heavily on state-of-the-art technology, and it was conducted for reasons of market force dogma. In short, it possessed all the ingredients necessary for a first-class cock-up. But the processes were meticulously planned and rehearsed; back-up arrangements were made and tested and the whole process went like a dream, with all the media's attention focused on the daft money companies were paying for licences, and virtually none on the fact that a bunch of civil servants had pulled off a brilliant piece of work.

There is much evidence that thorough planning processes are not applied to policy-making in the way they are (sometimes) to planning policy implementation, and yet the level of policy failure is such that the need is great. Care in the Community, which involved closing mental hospitals and treating patients in the community, could have proved a success story; many ill people do not need to stay in institutions and would be better off in the community. But because the policy was not thought through thoroughly and because, in particular, no adequate risk analysis was undertaken, it proved to be flawed in ways that resulted in the deaths of several people.

The public sector has no monopoly on failed projects. In 2004, Penguin Books committed the two most heinous crimes in project management when they moved to a computerised warehousing system; Penguin had no period of parallel running and no back-up when the new system failed. In the same year, Sainsbury's had to write off its computerised warehousing system, and when Morrisons took over Safeway, it discovered that the chain had introduced a new accounting system before testing it thoroughly, and had not provided adequate training for people operating the new system.

All these failures were expensive and some cost people their jobs, but in the public sector similar failures can have catastrophic effects – including people losing their lives. If a proper analysis of the results of babies' heart operations had been carried out at the

Bristol Royal Infirmary during the 1990s, the poor quality of the surgery there and consequent high death rate would have been revealed much earlier, and many babies' lives would have been saved.

The need for proper risk management in projects is well recognised if not always well applied. The need for greater use of risk-management techniques in policy-making is not well recognised, and even where it is it is not taken seriously enough (as the Cabinet Office report 'Adding It Up' admits), which may not be unconnected with the fact that most politicians are chancers. For many politicians their progress towards selection for parliamentary seats, and the outcome at the polls if they are duly selected, is uncertain. If they become an MP, they take a chance on whether their party will win the general election. They then take a chance on whether they become a minister if their party emerges victorious, and they also take a chance that they won't blow it at the first test.

In many cases, as if all these risks were not enough, politicians take absurd risks with their private lives. Irish nationalist leader Charles Parnell destroyed his political career (and set back the cause of Irish independence in the 1890s) by becoming romantically involved with a married woman, Katharine (Kitty) O'Shea. In 1963, the Secretary of State for War, John Profumo, was forced to resign after he had a liaison with a prostitute then lied to Parliament. Profumo made handsome amends with his subsequent social work in London's East End. In 1983, Cecil Parkinson quit as Secretary of State for Trade and Industry after revelations about his love child. The day of Parkinson's resignation was also the day his department published its weekly journal. By an unfortunate coincidence, the cover picture featured storks carrying bundles under the headline 'The Facts of Life'. In fact, the bundles contained not babies, but boxes labelled trade statistics; the picture was an advertisement for the department's business statistics office.

More recently, shortly after becoming Secretary of State for Trade and Industry in 1998, Peter Mandelson told his staff he wanted 'to live dangerously'; within the month he had resigned for reasons of financial impropriety, delivering on his promise more quickly than perhaps any politician in history! Having been forced to quit, Mandelson was then brought back in 1999, as Secretary of State for Northern Ireland. But he had to resign from this position early in 2001, when stories surfaced about him using his influence to secure British passports for rich Indians. Mandelson was later exonerated, but the damage had been done.

Mandelson was in a class of his own until he was joined by David Blunkett, whose extraordinary behaviour as Home Secretary in speeding up the visa application of his former mistress's nanny forced him to resign from a post he clearly relished. It might have been expected that the former Marxist (who had earned considerable respect by fighting his way from poverty to the top) would have learned a hard lesson and kept out of trouble while awaiting a possible recall to office. Instead, Blunkett bought shares in a company which had benefited from Home Office work, took jobs without clearing them with the relevant advisory committee, and managed to give a woman the opportunity to tell tales about him to the press. This was all exposed after he returned to office in 2005 as Secretary of State for Work and Pensions; eleven months after his first resignation, Blunkett had to resign again.

These are but a few examples; the newspapers of the past 100 years are littered with reports of politicians committing one form or another of lurid political suicide. The behaviour range of politicians may be little different from that of the rest of us, but to the extent that most of them have only a transient hold on office, the quite bizarre risks they take with their private lives suggests that they have developed an altogether new approach to the precautionary principle. It may or may not be a comforting thought that the destinies of nations rest in such hands!

# CHAPTER 11

# FADS AND FANCIES

I t may well be that it is the approach to risk management taken by politicians that leads them to hazard so much on glib phrases as a basis of policy-making. Examples are all too plentiful – 'watch my lips'; 'the pound in your pocket'; 'you've never had it so good'; 'peace with honour'; 'a land fit for heroes to live in'. While those quotations all hail from the past century, the preference is as old as politics itself. Shakespeare clearly believed his audience would have no difficulty with King Lear's injunction to Gloucester: 'Get thee glass eyes,/And like a scurvy politician seem/To see the things thou dost not.'

It is a failure which politicians themselves have noted. Richard Cobden, vigorous opponent of the Corn Laws and general proponent of free trade, fulminated against this weakness: 'What nonsense is uttered even by the cleverest men when they get upon this least of all understood, and yet most important of all topics, the Trade of this country.' Cobden also commented (in the context of Lord Palmerston's gunboat diplomacy) 'with how little knowledge we enter upon the task of regulating the concerns of other people'. Both remarks might usefully be taken on board by those engaged in the Brexit debate.

More recently, Peter Lilley, while Secretary of State for Social Security, felt disadvantaged by a lack of historical information.

At the launch of a history and policy website in 2007, Lilley responded to a question about the role of Permanent Secretaries as 'historical memories of their department' by describing his own experiences.

> My Permanent Secretary [Sir Michael Partridge] had provided me with a several-page history of social security since Tudor times which was valuable. Also, he claimed to have been personally involved in drafting all of the dozen different pensions' policies over the preceding three decades and so acted as the historical memory on that. However, I would almost certainly have benefited from a departmental historical adviser to keep reminding me of previous attempts to tackle whatever problem I was addressing. I had been very conscious of the reluctance of civil servants to find out what happened abroad in social security policy. Any historical adviser would need to have knowledge of historical precedents overseas and not a narrow focus on one country.

It is a problem which is pervasive throughout the civil service and is relevant to just about any government activity, for it is the collection, analysis, marshalling and taking of action on the basis of relevant factual information that distinguishes the achiever of results from the creator of political effects.

Lord Rayner identified two other powerful reasons for the failure of politicians to achieve results when he suggested that some of Mrs Thatcher's more calamitous decisions were due to 'haste and dogma'. He was right, but the problem predates the Thatcher government and continues to the present day. Increasingly, in recent years, governments have seemed to believe that fundamental changes can be made to our systems – legal, educational and health, for example – and deliver promised 'benefits' within the span of a single parliament. In commenting on Mrs Thatcher's government, Lord Rayner makes the point that major changes were undertaken with hopelessly inadequate lead times and without appropriate resources; there was no proper experimentation and evaluation.

Interestingly, Lord Rayner specifically mentions that it took five years to make the changes he sought at Marks & Spencer; with governments usually lasting not much more than four years it is clear that such timescales would not appeal – despite the fact they might be necessary. Services that should sensibly be rolled out across the country in a phased programme are rushed out nationally. Civil servants then get stick when systems fail to deliver or, even worse, collapse in a heap as happened at the Child Support Agency and Criminal Records Bureau.

The problem has become more obvious in recent years because systems have grown so complex and huge. Ministers (and silly timescales are mainly their fault) seem unable to distinguish between changes that can be made reasonably quickly, such as an increase in fuel tax, and those requiring a long gestation period such as setting up a totally new tax or benefit, like the working tax credit. Part of the difficulty is that, never having run anything themselves, most ministers seldom have even the slightest idea about the complexity of running major departments of state; civil servants who point out difficulties are regarded as either negative, opposed to change or just plain difficult. When he decided that he had had enough of politics, Archie Norman, the former chairman of Asda, criticised the way MPs with no management training were put in charge of vast departments like Health. It was a state of affairs that Norman described as 'dangerous'.

There certainly are civil servants at all levels who will find out the facts then spell them out clearly, and there are also ministers who wish to listen, but there is a growing Whitehall culture of reluctance to tell ministers and more senior bureaucrats what they would rather not hear; it varies from department to department and minister to minister, but it impacts at all levels. It is clear, for example, from the published Treasury post-mortem on the exit of sterling from the European Exchange Rate Mechanism in 1992, that civil servants did not give advice to Treasury ministers that they thought would not be acceptable.

This culture has been reinforced in the UK by the growth of the use of special advisors whose advice ministers – especially in the present administration – much prefer and trust to that of that of their civil servants. The growth in the number and power of special advisors in the post-1997 Labour governments caused much comment, but the assertion that they have made a material difference to political interference in the civil service is difficult to justify. Ministers have always interfered in their departments' work and always will. The current preoccupation with special advisors 'giving orders' to civil servants seems largely contrived; if a minister wants something done it matters not whether the message is delivered by the minister, another civil servant, a special advisor or the Archangel Gabriel.

The important thing, as any civil servant should know, is to ensure that if there is any doubt about the origin or validity of a 'ministerial' request, a note (nowadays probably an email) should be written and circulated to those who matter, recording who said what to whom. It was a failure under time pressure to do this that resulted in the resignations of Cabinet ministers during the Westland Helicopters' affair of 1985–86. Colette Bowe, chief press officer at the DTI, and Bernard Ingham, the Prime Minister's press secretary, had a phone conversation about a suggestion that the Solicitor General's advice to ministers and the Prime Minister be leaked to Chris Moncrieff, chief political correspondent at Reuters' news agency. Depending on which source you go to, you get a different version of events. But it is clear that both Bowe and Ingham knew that whatever else civil servants do they never admit to the existence of advice from the law officers, let alone leak specific elements of it.

Both sides, it is claimed, did not think the advice should be leaked, so it is surprising that it was. Had the matter been put in writing there could now be no argument; whoever opposed the leak should have written a note of the conversation and circulated it to the other, as well as to the relevant ministers and lawyers (probably just threatening to do so would have done the trick). But it is easy to be cool and detached from the comfort of a writer's desk; in the thick of a political crisis with key players absent from the office it was assuredly less easy. This point was proved in 2001, when the World Trade Center towers were destroyed in New York. Jo Moore, special advisor to Transport Secretary Stephen Byers, was sunk after sending an email that suggested it was 'now a very good day to get out anything we want to bury. Councillors' expenses'? A few years later at the Home Office, an email proved crucial in establishing that Home Secretary David Blunkett had abused his position by fast-tracking his mistress's nanny's visa application.

A much more important and damaging effect of the use of special advisors, which outsiders tend to overlook, is that the relationship between ministers and special advisors may reinforce the propensity of civil servants not to offer good advice if they think it will be unwelcome. One senior official told one of his juniors not to make waves over a particularly silly initiative from a special advisor, commenting that if the junior official annoyed the Secretary of State over the issue, 'all our advice will lose credibility'.

As Prime Minister, Mrs Thatcher spent much energy denigrating and disparaging the civil service. She at least had had ministerial experience, whereas Tony Blair, who became Prime Minister in 1997, had never run anything. Nevertheless Blair followed suit, deciding that problems created by successive governments could all be blamed on public services in need of reform.

There is nothing new about civil servants running risks in delivering unwanted messages or being treated as scapegoats for failed policies. King Henry VIII dumped Cardinal Wolsey, and later Thomas Cromwell, because the two men failed to obtain the results he wanted. The head of the Roman civil service in 525 AD, Boethius, had time to write a book (appropriately titled *The*

*Consolation of Philosophy*) while in prison for having offended his political masters. He was eventually executed. Some of Mrs Thatcher's victims would have sympathised.

After more than twenty years of derision, the civil service has lost its confidence, and the risk of the current growth in the use of special advisors is that the civil service will become completely cowed. A cowed civil service is not something any minister should want. In the extreme it is the sort of pitiable object seen in North Korea, Stalin's Russia or Hitler's Germany. It is hardly surprising that a survey of public opinion undertaken by the Committee on Standards in Public Life in 2004 found that senior civil servants had a net trust rating of minus 16 per cent, putting them only marginally ahead of politicians. The chairman of the committee made it clear that civil servants needed to be more open about conflicting pressures, and should admit failures and then learn from them. I could not agree more.

There is an important distinction to be made between special advisors who have specific and significant expertise, backed up by rigorous analysis which they can bring to an issue, and those who are simply political aspirants in need of a meal ticket and have an agenda of half-baked political ideas. Perhaps the most famous expert special advisor was Florence Nightingale. Although widely known for her role in establishing a hospital for wounded soldiers during the Crimean War and for establishing nursing as a respected profession, Nightingale spent most of her life urging politicians to force through reforms of army administration in the teeth of ignorance. She once recommended that the War Office should be awarded the Victoria Cross for 'cool intrepidity in the face of facts'.

Nightingale took the trouble to learn the facts, and was able to assess the validity of what she was told on the basis of her practical experience in the Crimean War. She was opposed by those who were not interested in the truth, who chose instead to hold fast to baseless opinions. Anything that hinders the process of full and unbiased analysis of policy is worrying, because without such analysis it is often difficult to overcome political dogma that is usually based more on ignorance than knowledge. Failure to overcome dogma can cause major problems, and in some cases – public health, for example – the consequences can prove disastrous. Florence Nightingale campaigned to introduce proper sanitation into army barracks because the British Army lost more troops there than it ever did in battle. But military chiefs seemed oblivious and uninterested. Such reactions were not confined to the army.

At about the same time that Nightingale was campaigning for better hygiene and sanitation, Ignaz Semmelweis in Vienna, Alexander Gordon in Aberdeen, and Oliver Wendell Holmes Sr in Boston were each establishing that puerperal fever, which killed thousands of mothers and babies each year, was spread by lack of hygiene among doctors. Their views were greeted with scepticism and even hostility by the medical profession. The carnage in maternity hospitals continued until the end of the nineteenth century.

The task of those battling to improve public health was made more difficult because those opposing them on the basis of ignorance and bigotry were supported by people who believed that government action to prevent death from famine or pestilence was an unwarrantable interference in individuals' liberty. Such belief was widespread among the few people who had the vote and the even smaller number who held power in Victorian times. In 1859, Lord Palmerston's government withdrew proposals to enforce compulsory vaccination in the face of parliamentary opposition. Government health inspectors collected statistics enabling them to demonstrate the number of children whose lives had been saved by vaccination (average yearly deaths had fallen from 12,000 to 2,200). In 1861, a chastened Parliament passed a Bill to permit enforcement, though not before a rearguard action had been fought by the libertarians. One MP, the Radical Thomas

Slingsby Duncombe, claimed, 'There existed a feeling among the people of the country generally that the authorities had no right, in order to carry out a particular theory, to take polluted matter from one person's arm and place it on that of another.' He asserted that 'there were medical men who maintained that the matter produced in some instances scrofula, consumption and venereal disease'. It was not clear whether he thought people got all three together.

Such precedents make the task of dealing with an issue like the combined measles, mumps and rubella vaccination very difficult. The only way for administrators to extricate themselves from such difficulties is to conduct rigorous analysis. That was the basis of Florence Nightingale's success and, more recently, of the campaign against foot-and-mouth disease; it would seem also to have resolved the MMR issue. But as the Cabinet Office report 'Adding It Up' notes, few administrators are properly trained in the use of statistics as a tool of government.

More pertinently, some politicians – Mrs Thatcher was certainly one of them – seem to believe they have been given a perception denied to others, and that this perception enables them to leapfrog the painstaking and time-consuming business of establishing a case for any particular policy. The present problems of the National Health Service cannot all be laid at Margaret Thatcher's door, but a fair number can be. In her ruthless application of inappropriate 'solutions' she was in the same league as the nineteenth-century doctors in denial about the benefits of hygiene. Mrs Thatcher has her emulators still. Successive Education ministers have sought to impose a one-size-fits-all approach to the teaching of reading, despite clear evidence in schools throughout the land that not all children learn to read in the same way.

It is a commonplace that some people are good at initiating change, but lack the interest or ability to deal with the detailed follow-through. For them, having what Prime Minister James Callaghan described as a 'wait a minute man' is essential. Someone who will make sure bright ideas really are bright ideas before they are set in concrete, and that the right people are involved to ensure that ideas are brought successfully to fruition. This is precisely the role for which civil servants are (or should be) suited. Unfortunately, some ministers distrust their civil servants and would much prefer to listen to outside advisors.

On the basis of his experiences in the Thatcher government, Lord Rayner counselled politicians 'against embarking on major changes on the basis of theoretical advice from academics, or from consultants who are much better at running up fees than running things'. It is sound advice for politicians of all views.

The New Labour government elected in 1997 was supposed to be committed to 'evidence-based' policy-making, but it soon succumbed to the more conventional bogeyman-based policy-making. In the Education department, the bogeymen were teachers who sought to tailor teaching methods to the differing needs of pupils. But it would be wrong to suggest that bogeyman-based policy-making was new. Over the years there have been an amazing variety of bogeymen: tech giants and asylum seekers are currently top of the list, but it wasn't long ago that dogs were seen as the enemy. Sixty years ago in America it was suspected Communists, while 200 years ago in Britain it was Dissenters and 300 years ago it was Catholics. Four centuries ago women were denounced as witches.

The common factor in all these cases is that politicians (and church leaders and media moguls) for their own purposes whip up public hysteria, or leap on the back of a non-political movement, without any credible basis in fact and relying entirely upon prejudice and worse. Then momentum develops, which all too often involves innocent people suffering either as victims of the mob or of the state. Sometimes those who provoke hysteria get their due desserts, but not often. For his part in the Popish Plot of 1678, Titus Oates was put in the pillory, whipped from Newgate to Tyburn and sentenced to prison for life. But on the accession of William and Mary in 1689, Oates was pardoned and given a pension of £3 a week. Richard 'Tricky Dicky' Nixon made his name on the House Un-American Activities Committee, investigating alleged Communists 'with one eye on today's evidence and the other on tomorrow's headlines'. It was only after Nixon had become President two decades later that he was finally brought low.

The predilection of politicians for bogeymen probably reflects their nature as takers of bizarre risks. They are always looking for the winning ticket, and if they think they have found one, as the young Richard Nixon did in hounding alleged Communists, they will play it for all it is worth. The theory is that cautious civil servants exercise a moderating influence on impetuous politicians, but as already noted, in the interplay of personalities that characterises the real world, those roles may not be realised.

Bogeyman-based policy-making has its exact opposite: pampered-pet policy-making. As with bogeymen, pampered pets come and go, but one of them – the manufacturing industry – has a long lineage. An early classic example of the dangers of such policy-making is provided by the silk industry. In 1606, King James I decided to launch a major initiative to bypass foreign silk growers and English silk importers by introducing the culture of the silkworm into Britain. It must rank as one of the government's earliest forays into industrial policy-making, constituting what economists would now term vertical integration of the industry.

Like many subsequent escapades of this sort, it was done on a large scale. Two gentlemen were granted a monopoly to import thousands of mulberry trees. To ensure success, James I sent a letter to every lord lieutenant in the country, effectively ordering them to twist the arms of the gentry to buy 10,000 mulberry plants per county. Needless to say, the scheme did not go down well with the importers of silk, who made vigorous representations. However, the trees were imported and planted. Not content to be seen as a mere armchair industrialist, James I even organised large-scale planting himself, paying some £900 for the planting of four acres of land near the Palace of Westminster.

After the trees had been imported, a snag developed. The monopolists had imported the black mulberry, whereas the white mulberry is the species on which silkworms flourish. In addition, neither silkworms nor mulberry trees care greatly for cold weather, so some more northerly counties must have had little success in growing the trees at all. Although the royal family persevered with their black mulberry trees and produced enough silk to make a dress for the Queen, all told the initiative was a failure.

As has happened so many times, a failure to get the facts right scuppered a major government project. Although the scheme for vertical integration failed, the King's support for the industry did attract immigrants from the Netherlands, and for another 100 years or so there was a thriving silk industry in the Spitalfields area of London, though it did rely on imported silk. Even after the industry finally collapsed, at least in some places the trees remained (the last plantation in Charlton Park was not cut down until the nineteenth century). The plantation paid for by King James did not prove a total loss either; after the English Civil War, James's mulberry garden became a place of recreation, visited by Samuel Pepys. He found it 'a very silly place, worse than Spring-garden, and but little company, and those a rascally, whoring, roguing sort of people'. Later the site became better known as Buckingham Palace. Perhaps the shades of those 'rascally, whoring, roguing sort of people' found it not much of a change from time to time!

Three hundred and forty years later, the post-war Labour government managed to eclipse James I on a heroic scale, and with infinitely less excuse. An expected shortage of fats, and the success of east African smallholders in growing limited quantities of peanuts for their own consumption, led to the infamous Tanganyika groundnut scheme which cost British taxpayers some £23 million. At least King James I made just one mistake. In east Africa, there was a catalogue of basic errors, all the more unforgivable given that, in the period since James's little difficulty, the British had become pioneers of plantsmanship, and could draw upon the experience of the development of tea plantations in Asia and Africa, and of rubber plantations in Malaysia.

Perhaps the problem lay with the fact that the idea, which was certainly worth investigation, unfortunately captured the imagination of the new Minister of Food, John Strachey. It therefore began to assume the guise of a ministerial imperative, in the face of which no cold and discouraging facts should be allowed to stand. A special mission was dispatched to east Africa, but instead of a competent team of agricultural engineers and soil scientists, a 'visionary' was sent who returned with an inspiring image of a transformed east Africa, but not the slightest idea of how this vision might be turned into a reality.

Some 100,000 men volunteered to work in the scheme. However, upon arriving in east Africa, they found that there was no adequate equipment for clearing the dense scrub. When some highly inadequate kit finally arrived at the coast, workers discovered there was no sensible means of transporting this equipment to inland locations. In addition, the trees that needed to be cleared were occupied by vicious bees whose sting left victims requiring hospital treatment. As work on clearing the ground eventually got underway, it suddenly occurred to someone that testing the soil to see if groundnuts would actually grow might be a good idea. These tests proved positive, but those carrying out the work failed to pay attention to the soil's high clay content. (They said afterwards that no one had asked them!) The nuts would grow all right, but as soon as the rains stopped the earth baked hard and it became impossible to harvest them.

Back in London, officials were in denial about the scheme for months, proudly forecasting a great success; at last even the most foolishly optimistic had to admit defeat. Some 4,000 tons of groundnuts had been purchased for seed in 1947. But by the end of the second season's harvest, after two years of effort and the expenditure of £23 million of taxpayers' money, only 2,000 tons had been harvested.

A desperate attempt was made to salvage the project by planting sunflowers. For sunflowers the land did not have to be cleared and levelled, and harvesting would be easy. With all the grim inevita-bility of a Greek tragedy, the rains failed, and the sunflower crop with it. One of the last acts of the outgoing Labour government was to end the scheme. For a country that had just conclusively demonstrated the value of rigorous scientific analysis in seeing off a determined and highly efficient enemy, the failure to tackle the Tanganyika scheme in any way remotely resembling half-decent analysis and management beggars belief. It is a classic example of how a politically correct opinion, if proclaimed long enough and loudly enough, will sweep away any semblance of rational behaviour in the corridors of power.

The fad for pampering industrial pets was widespread. For something like forty years its most admired practitioners were the Japanese, whose industrial sponsorship policy was lauded by experts as the most successful among industrial nations, with programmes sponsored by Japan's Ministry of International Trade and Industry (MITI) held up as examples for others to follow. British industry (showing a rare degree of unanimity between company directors and trade union officials) was loud in its clam-our for similar programmes. By 1994, however, when researchers began to take a hard-nosed look at the facts, they began suggesting that MITI had picked losers not winners; that the conventional wisdom of MITI's ability, almost alone among the world's bu-reaucracies, to pick only winners and shun potential losers was no better than the average urban myth.

Researchers demonstrated that for each sector that received industrial support there was a negative correlation with growth. Far from assisting the 'Japanese miracle', MITI's policies ac-tually hindered it. By 2002, the Japanese Ministry of Finance's Policy Research Institute was advancing the same argument, commenting that 'the Japanese model was not the source of Japanese competitiveness but the cause of our failure'. The institute claimed that industries sponsored by MITI, such as textiles, aircraft manufacture and chemicals, became bloated and inefficient, while those industries exposed to global competition grew more market aware, efficient and profitable.

For many years the French government has followed equally protectionist policies; now these are coming under attack for the same reasons. In his 2003 book, *La France Qui Tombe*, Nicolas Baverez suggests that during the past twenty years or so the French have succumbed to special interest groups such as the farmers and otherwise declining industries, wasting vast amounts of taxpayers' money propping up concerns that should have been allowed to fail. It was the French who gave the world the concept of chauvinism, and it is they who have demonstrated its failure when applied to government industrial policy.

That the UK did not follow suit to any significant extent was not for lack of lobbying, but rather due to the stance of successive ministers, who when it came to dishing out money to industry, sought maximum political profile for minimum public expenditure. It was not so much that prudence dictated parsimony, as that an inability to screw more money out of the Treasury dictated the available cash be spread thinly and far and wide. British government policy was roundly castigated by economists (not all of them), and by trade unionists and captains of industry. Historians such as Correlli Barnett and Eric Hobsbawm (unlikely bedfellows) lambasted successive post-war governments for their failures to plan industrial policy; the saving grace of the British economy was that such policy-making was done in such a half-hearted way that the resultant damage was less than in other countries.

It was, of course, important to have a rationale for shovelling taxpayers' money into loss-making organisations, and so the concept of 'market failure' was born. This idea was based on the theory that very sensible decisions by hard-nosed business people with their own money at risk, and a detailed knowledge of their own market, could be second-guessed by government ministers and ministerial economic advisors. The policy, which was followed by governments of all political hues, rested on an implicit assumption that ministers really did understand, and could control, the economy; it was widely held, but was not without its critics, as the next chapter reveals.

The politically correct description of pampered-pet policy-making is protectionism. This is bad news for everyone and has no real justification, but once it has been obtained its beneficiaries hang on to it like grim death – no matter the consequences for the rest of us. According to Margot Asquith, the wife of Prime Minister Herbert Asquith, Lord Salisbury once asked her if she had ever known a man 'with a first-rate intellect in this country who was a protectionist?' Salisbury added that she need not be anxious, as 'free trade will always win against protection in this country'. How wrong he was. Free trade flourished for less than 100 years. It vanished in the 1920s and has only slowly and painfully been partly eased back in the period since the 1960s. But the tariff and quota battles in the World Trade Organization, between the EU and the USA and between the developed and developing countries shows how much further there is to go.

The grotesque consequences of protectionism were fully illustrated in 2005 when huge stocks of underwear imported from China stacked up in warehouses because of a deal negotiated by then EU Trade Commissioner, Peter Mandelson, to deprive the least well-off EU consumers of access to goods at world prices in order to protect wealthy clothing manufacturers running uneconomic operations in France, Italy and Belgium.

Compared with the horrors of the Soviet collectivisation of farms, and of China's Great Leap Forward, the industrial planning failures of Europe and Japan are small beer, and their consequences, though harmful, are not catastrophic. Industrial planning on a big scale was a child of the twentieth century, spawned to produce prodigious quantities of munitions for the Western Front in World War I, and given its most notorious manifestation in Lenin's New Economic Policy. In the UK it revived in the Second World War because of the needs of the military, and received its greatest and most damaging boost with the nationalisation of the 'commanding heights of the economy' after the Labour victory in 1945. From then on it was more or less downhill all the way. The final economic collapse of the Eastern Bloc, and China's switch to a market economy of sorts, were the death throes of industrial planning in developed countries.

There is a sound case to be made for industrial planning by governments in the special circumstances of a potentially overwhelming military or economic threat, though even in those circumstances such planning is likely to work only in the relatively short term because of distortions it introduces into the economy. The history of the twentieth century is an awful demonstration of how belief in a political dogma, whether of left or right, leads to a suspension of any attempt to act rationally, or to base policy on facts or to question that which is indisputably wrong. It is a supreme irony that perhaps the greatest waste of public money this country has ever seen should have produced one of the classic design icons of the twentieth century and, arguably, of all time, but, then again, perhaps it does illustrate the point that such policies are in the end all about image rather than reality.

A key factor in keeping the Concorde project going in the teeth of any rational consideration of the costs was that, as a joint Anglo-French operation, issues of national prestige were involved. Unsurprisingly, the same reason for failures can be found in wider foreign policy.

In her book *The March of Folly*, which provides an excellent introduction to the mindset of those involved in developing foreign policy, Barbara Tuchman illustrates how governments from the Trojan War up to the Vietnam War have followed policies that brought about the very ends that they were intended to prevent.

Tuchman's selection is good, but she was spoilt for choice! Her definition of folly is that to be so classified a policy must have been perceived as counter-productive at the time (not just with the benefit of hindsight); that feasible alternative policies must have been available; and that the policy should be that of a group or succession of people and not only a single individual. It is an interesting definition and one that can be applied to many areas other than foreign policy. It also hammers home the point that bad policies are the responsibility of people, not systems, and the people responsible for most ludicrous policies are ministers and their more senior advisors.

# CHAPTER 12

# PEOPLE AND POWER

Failures of central and local government are ultimately the re-sponsibility of elected politicians and it is by no means easy to get the right people into political office. It is often suggested that there was a golden era when politicians took their responsibilities seriously, behaved with probity and resigned when something went disastrously wrong; when a politician would undertake what Edmund Burke described as 'humble and persevering endeavours to do [his] duty'. On the whole, all of this is an illusion, but it is a long-standing illusion.

In the mid-fourteenth century, poet John Gower wrote that in olden days 'law and justice were secure ... and all the barony respected in their high estate'. Gower contrasted that with his contemporary world, where 'those who are the nations' guides have not good counsel from all sides', and uttered a heartfelt cry of 'God only knows what's to be done!' Two hundred years later, Erasmus was sufficiently exercised by what he saw to write that 'the sense of honour is extinct in public affairs'. In 1840, Disraeli declared, 'All confidence in public men is lost.' The reality is that not much changes. Julius Caesar's tactics of bypassing the Senate, intimidating opponents by force and terrorising Rome with hired thugs so that he had an excuse to 'restore order', would have been a credit to Adolf Hitler or Robert Mugabe. Fortunately, every age also produces its quota of principled politicians.

It has recently seemed to become exceptionally difficult to prise politicians' fingers away from the seals of office, even after they are caught doing inappropriate things with the public purse or someone's private parts. But this probably just seems to be a modern-day phenomenon because in the past such goings-on never appeared on newspapers' front pages.

Prime Minister Herbert Asquith, for example, would have needed no lessons from twentieth-century politicians on how to seduce young ladies, or on squeezing money from friends to finance his housing needs. He received little adverse comment in the press; when he turned up worse for wear to King Edward VIII's laying in state, journalists simply noted that Asquith had 'dined well'. The charge of 'sexing up' official papers, which caused a major political row for Tony Blair's government in 2004, was a charge levelled against Robert Lowe in 1864 when he was at the Education department. Lowe forced schools inspectors to change their reports to suit his political requirements under the threat of dismissal; it caused a furore and he was criticised sharply. Presciently, the writer of a critical article in the *Saturday Review* noted that Lowe's 'despotic disregard for the feelings of others is likely to make him miscarry in the administration of an English office'. Within ten years, precisely that trait would cost Lowe his job as Chancellor of the Exchequer.

Clinging to office in the face of scandal is nothing new. In 1912, the Marconi scandal involved the Chancellor of the Exchequer, the Attorney General and the former Liberal Chief Whip. They had all purchased shares in Marconi's US subsidiary while the government was negotiating a major deal with the UK parent company. Asquith supported the men, and they all survived but were eventually forced to apologise to the House. Like their successors who were exposed in the 'cash for questions' scandal during the 1990s, being caught out didn't seem to harm any of the three men's subsequent careers. But the Marconi shares slumped in value, so not only did the men lose their money, they had to also suffer the ignominy of being caught out.

Trying to prove black is white (particularly in the face of personal criticism) is no novelty either. Robert Lowe's biographer, Robert Winter, put it well: 'He admitted that his path had been full of twists, but adamantly denied he was a twister ... he was a politician with extraordinary powers of rationalisation.' Aren't they all.

The moral ambivalence of so many at the top raises a question: is there something about the personality of a leader that makes so many of them unpleasant people? Leaders tend to have unusual personalities and while these will be tempered by environment – spending your formative years in Grantham is bound to be different than growing up in Tikrit – and the nature of the power they exercise, there may not be too much difference between bullying office managers and party leaders who bulldoze through the next great policy failure in the teeth of sensible advice.

The problem is that while a forceful personality is good for cutting through bureaucracy and red tape, and for ascending the greasy pole, it is just as good for forcing through acts of stupidity – such as the Dardanelles campaign or the poll tax. It is also the case that large egos don't take kindly to competition, so a tendency exists for the great to surround themselves with yes men, or to terrorise staff into becoming acquiescent. While the impact of massive egos is sometimes made manifest in huge blunders, the effects they can have on the day-to-day business of government is usually less obvious. But this can be corrosive; the regular imposition of irrational decisions to do or not do relatively small things erodes the willingness, indeed even the ability, of subordinates to resist being bullied on great issues.

Bullying in the workplace is now recognised as an evil, but if it is blatantly exhibited at the top of many organisations – including government departments – is it any wonder that it persists at lower levels? The attitude of many ministers towards their staff, the public and the public purse gives ample support to Lord Acton's famous dictum that 'Power tends to corrupt, and absolute power corrupts absolutely.' It is interesting to speculate whether it really is the access to power which corrupts, or if the fault lies with those who will use power corruptly, who crave it and have the ability to achieve it. Such a thought lies behind Lady Macbeth's criticism of her husband: 'To catch the nearest way: thou/wouldst be great,/Art not without ambition, but without/The illness should attend it'. Certainly people do not achieve power in most countries without shedding a fair amount of blood (metaphorical or literal depending on the circumstances). John Major, as he lost his grip on power, referred to Cabinet colleagues as bastards. But is it possible to go from being a local politician in Bermondsey to standing outside the steps of No. 10 just by being nice? On the day she won her first general election, Mrs Thatcher invoked St Francis of Assisi: 'Where there is discord, may we bring harmony. Where there is error, may we bring truth. Where there is doubt, may we bring faith. And where there is despair, may we bring hope.'

But the Iron Lady seems not to have modelled herself on the saint much during the long march from Grantham to the doorstep of No. 10, or during her subsequent eleven-year reign as Prime Minister. Given all the circumstances, it is hardly surprising that many politicians eventually succumb to illusions of adequacy and, like Mrs Thatcher, are genuinely taken aback when they are overturned in a coup. Sir Basil Zaharoff, who spent many years in the nineteenth and twentieth centuries making a fortune for the British arms company Vickers by stroking the egos of the powerful across the world, noted that sooner or later nearly all politicians suffer from an exaggerated idea of their own importance.

The trend to self-importance is probably affected by the fact that politicians have a number of different functions, each generating its own opportunities for patronage, favours and pelf. A minister is a member of the government, but he is also a member of a parliamentary party, a member of a national party and a constituency MP. He may also have some particular interest or range of interests unrelated to his constituency or departmental responsibilities. Underneath all these functions there lurks a human being with a private life (perhaps more than one), seeking advancement and the perks of office (or worse from time to time). In any of these roles he may have agendas he wishes to pursue and will meet people who can help or hinder his progress. Equally, those whom he meets will have their own issues on which they may seek his assistance.

How ministers negotiate their way through this moral maze depends on their personal morality, but also, to some extent, on their experience of office. It follows that ministers' abilities in this area are not helped by long spells with one party in power; regular changes of power ensure continuity of ministerial experience and reduce the risks of a party long excluded from power losing the instinct for government (and spending far too much time getting its nose in the trough in a big way once it does return to office). Shadow ministers only have to grab the headlines, they do not have to live with the consequences of their hypothetical policies; real ministers must remember that a shiny new policy initiative has to be lived with long after it has failed to deliver the goods and has become a rod for their own backs.

Lloyd George's promise that after the First World War Britain would become 'a land fit for heroes to live in' was turned against him as the reality proved different, and he was accused of creating 'a land only heroes could live in'. Neville Chamberlain promised 'peace in our time' as he led the country into the Second World War, and John Major's Back to Basics campaign was ridiculed as his government sank under the burden of sleaze. Tony Blair promised to be 'tough on crime, tough on the causes of crime' and to make his top three priorities 'education, education, education', but he presided over record levels of public concern about crime and falling standards of education.

Lack of appropriate knowledge can also leave ministers vulnerable to the pressures of office. Hugh Gaitskell, as a minister in Clement Attlee's post-war government, fulminated in his diary about the ignorance of Cabinet colleagues, noting that scarcely comprehending briefs from their departments did not seem to inhibit them from spouting rubbish.

The problems that lack of ability and relevant experience can cause were particularly manifest in 1997 when the Labour Party came to power after eighteen years in opposition. Most ministers had not the faintest idea of what their jobs entailed, and in particular had no understanding of how to start working with the civil servants for whose actions they were now responsible.

In 1976, Lord Rothschild, in the light of his experience of running the Think Tank, advocated that new ministers should spend their first three or four months reading themselves in and avoiding decisions. In the run-up to the 1997 election, the Fabian Society organised discussion sessions for Labour's shadow ministers and a number of the top mandarins in Whitehall.

While this was clearly a good move and provided useful insights for potential new ministers, it was perhaps overdoing it to suggest, as the Fabian Society did in a publication based on the discussions, that 'Labour is the best prepared opposition of all time'. The article is admirably clear and concise and would repay reading by any newly appointed minister of any party, but in its published form is too simplistic to address the enormity of the gulf between a pleasant life on the opposition front bench chucking squibs at the government, and being on the government bench trying to cope with continuing business, while also seeking to address new problems as they arise and pushing for the implementation of long-standing policy objectives. The publication hinted at the hankering of the mandarins for policy work; a feeling that there had been 'an over-emphasis on management at the expense of policy development'. Here were the ghosts of Trevelyan's intellectuals, ever hopeful that an incoming Labour government would let them 'stop mucking around with management and get on with their real jobs'.

It is arguable that the 1997 Labour government was, despite the attentions of the Fabian Society, the least prepared of any government in the twentieth century. Only very few ministers had any experience of holding office, and the general consensus is that Labour did indeed waste its first term. Most MPs who reach ministerial office move from being a backbencher, often with no management experience, to being in charge of a large part of a major organisation that spends huge sums of money; usually they know little if anything of the work of the office.

But at least when an individual obtains office and has ministerial colleagues to hand who do have some experience, they can get practical advice – or sit tight and learn by watching how these colleagues work. When an entire government enters office with virtually no practical experience, the scope for disaster is great. The problem is aggravated by the febrile nature of politics; politicians aren't really happy unless they are at the centre of attention (favourable of course), or in the middle of a political plot to oust their leader or capture a seat on a select committee. So they have little time for acquiring anything like a thorough understanding of more than a few issues, and if those issues don't pose problems when they finally achieve power (or are given a portfolio unrelated to their interests) they are thrown back on quickness of wit and the seat of their pants. Since ministers, whatever else they lack, usually possess a commodious supply of both these qualities, this need not be a problem if their civil servants know what they are about, and if the minister is prepared to accept their advice. But all too frequently neither proposition is fulfilled – or given enough time to be fulfilled.

Too often there is a deliberate wish to cut away from the past and make a new start, which is all very well as a political statement, but pretty useless if it means ignoring the reasons for past policy failures and simply dressing up old discredited policy in a newly spun suit of emperor's clothes. Even when there is no systematic attempt to disconnect, the short shelf life of most ministers in any one department means they can never hope to master the full range of their responsibilities, particularly in areas where a minister has no special background or interest.

It is not the case that ministers are very often dim; British governments during the period since the Victorian reforms have contained many clever and highly educated individuals. However, it may be true that those who reach the top tend to be 'big picture' people who simply can't deal with detail. If such qualities are mixed with a fair amount of dogmatism, a large dose of self-confidence, special advisors with inadequate experience, and a civil service unable to make good the deficiencies, then the way is prepared for the sort of poor government that has been much in evidence during the past fifty or so years, as governments became increasingly involved in attempts to run the economy.

Harold Lever saw at first-hand how such factors affected the ability of the Wilson government to achieve anything despite the undoubted talents of many of its members, but Lever's comments could just as easily apply to any government since 1945. 'These governments, like most other modern governments, overestimated their ability to shape and manage the complex drives of a modern economy. They assumed they understood all the reasons for its shortcomings and so, unsurprisingly, were all too ready to lay hands on superficial remedies for overcoming them.' Much the same point had been forcefully made by the Permanent Secretary of the Ministry of Fuel and Power in 1946:

> The idea that the economic activities of the nation can be planned, directed and controlled under a system of ministers selected for their political abilities and appointed with no expert knowledge of the subject for which they have to deal, to take full and sole charge of a particular department for a period of two or three years and sometimes even less, is fantastic.

The difficulties faced by ministers in resolving all potentially conflicting personal, political, departmental and constituency interests were captured neatly in 1972 by William Plowden, a member of the Central Policy Review Staff. An exercise in resource allocation produced a dazzling series of multicoloured bar charts with equally florid transparent overlays. But at an early stage of the exercise, Plowden had suggested taking a rather different approach. Quite possibly Plowden delivered his comments with a fair amount of tongue in cheek, but he was nonetheless right on the button.

> It seems to me that it would be helpful to think in terms of the several ends to which ministers may want to direct public expenditure. There are the purely economic ones (what would be the effect on the economy of spending £100 on X rather than on Y?) which are probably the easiest to assess ... There is the objective of benefiting particular groups in the community; the old, the very poor, coloured immigrants, farmers, the very rich, etc. There is the familiar objective of doing something for specific geographical areas: Wales, the North-East, any area with a significant number of marginal seats. There are also specific problems, which since they may largely define the terms in which the public discuss the issues may also become the natural targets of politicians: can't we do something about cancer, noise, violence, road accidents, house prices? Finally in this list, there is the question of the timescale over which the investment will pay off.

It was not just Labour ministers who thought they could manage the economy. In a Cabinet discussion in 1962 on modernising Britain, Harold Macmillan took the line that people, 'particularly the young', felt they 'are or ought to be on the move', and were looking to the government for a lead. 'Do we or do we not', Macmillan asked, 'set out to take control of the pattern of events, to direct development, to plan growth, to use the instruments of government to influence or determine private decisions?' He believed that this was inevitable and that the 'forces at work are now too complicated to leave to market forces and laissez-faire'. There is little reason to doubt that Macmillan and his Cabinet colleagues, just like Harold Wilson and his Cabinet members, really did believe they were competent to second-guess market forces: there is pretty conclusive evidence that they were not. Sir Alec Douglas-Home was much derided for his comments about using matchsticks to help him understand the economy; he probably had a better grip on it than most Prime Ministers.

Ministerial lack of adequate knowledge is not confined to economics. In his autobiography, Douglas Hurd makes the point that when he was moved as a junior minister to the Home Office in 1983 he had, at the age of fifty-three, no relevant experience, and, in common with all other British politicians, received no sensible handover or training. A year later, when he was promoted to be Secretary of State for Northern Ireland, Hurd 'knew little more of the province than any other conscientious follower of public events' (i.e. more or less nothing) and again, of course, there was no meaningful handover or training. Ministers are not always as open as Hurd about their unsuitability for the offices to which they are appointed. It is a state of affairs that goes back at least to Victorian times.

In 1848, Lord (John) Russell explained to James Wilson that the duty of a statesman was to serve the Queen whenever he might be called upon to do so and not to consider whether the office in question was the one he could best fill. It was becoming more difficult to do this as the scope of government increased in the second half of the nineteenth century and the demands of office grew more complex. Given the range of issues that now face incoming ministers, the problem has become a major, if unacknowledged, reason for government failure.

This has been compounded by the changing nature of the relationships between ministers and civil servants. When Gladstone, Trevelyan and Lowe were pondering reform of the civil service, the distinction between ministers and civil servants was fairly blurred. Ministers moved to administrative posts and civil servants became ministers. A civil servant in Britain might take a quasi-ministerial post in India and then return to a civil service post in London. Ministers and their top civil servants came pretty much from the same class and had more or less the same culture. They mainly enjoyed each other's company and shared common perspectives and attitudes. They also ran reasonably small organisations which bore all the hallmarks of a London Club – and which frequently dealt with issues not much more demanding.

This comfortable arrangement was not destined to last; a combination of the unintended consequences of the reform of the civil service and the growth of the scope of government activity gradually eroded the relationship. While there are still ministers who get on well with civil servants, the second half of the past century saw a marked change in emphasis, and in particular the development of a ministerial, and prime ministerial, paranoia about being undermined by the mandarins. An early straw in the wind was, perhaps, Rab Butler's comment that the civil service was 'a bit like a Rolls-Royce – you know it's the best machine in the world, but you're not quite sure what to do with it'. What on earth are you doing at the top of an organisation if you don't know what to do with good staff? Good staff exist to be harnessed and utilised, and if people don't know how to do so then they have no right to be in charge!

Ministerial paranoia probably reached its height in the Wilson government. Richard Crossman records in his diaries:

> All the civil servants I worked with were imbued with a prior loyalty to the Treasury and felt it necessary to spy on me and report all my doings to the Treasury, whether I wanted them kept private or not. There was nothing I could do, no order I could give, which wasn't at once known to the Treasury, because my staff were all trained to check with the Treasury and let it know in advance exactly what each of them was doing.

It was a view not only shared by Harold Wilson but, in a less neurotic way, by Harold Macmillan, who thought Treasury officials had 'narrow and jealous minds'.

There is a clear foretaste in Crossman's diaries of Mrs Thatcher's distrust of civil servants, and it may have had the same root cause. Denis Healey described Crossman as having 'a heavyweight intellect with a lightweight judgement' and of finding it 'difficult to listen to others'. If you don't listen to people it is easy to decide they are not saying anything you want to hear. Crossman was outclassed, however, by Michael Meacher, who wrote a whole page of conspiracy theory for *The Guardian* in June 1979.

> There are three main ways in which the civil service subverts the effect of the democratic vote. One is the manipulation of individual Ministers, an exercise in man-management which is skilfully orchestrated and on which a great deal of time and care is spent. Second is the isolation of Ministers and the resulting dependence on the Whitehall machine, for which a heavy price in policy terms is paid. Third is the exploitation of the interdepartmental framework, in order to circumvent Ministers who may be opposing the Whitehall consensus.

One of Labour's own special advisors, Roger Darlington, wrote to *The Guardian* to point out that while civil servants could and did use techniques 'against ministers', Labour tended to blame civil servants 'for what are really the inadequacies of Labour ministers'. Darlington commented on 'the naivety and ignorance of ministers on first taking office', citing Richard Crossman by name. He also thought that too often ministers lacked 'clear political policies of their own', and that the 'sad truth' was that views of left-wing ministers were 'blocked by their Cabinet colleagues without any need for subversion by the civil servants'. This was certainly true in respect of Michael Meacher's relationship with his own Secretary of State, Edmund Dell.

When Michael Meacher was back in government, I wrote to ask him whether his latest experience had altered his views about the civil service. Meacher replied that his views had 'not been modified, so you can quote from the *Guardian* 1979 article as it stands'. This must have been immensely comforting to his staff. The reality is that only at the most trivial level do civil servants seek to circumvent their own ministers. It was a point Harold Wilson addressed forcefully in an interview with Ian Trethowan (later to become director-general of the BBC) in 1967.

> But, this idea of course that ministers don't know what's going on, and that civil servants keep facts away from them, if I could be told of the name of any minister who is subject to that situation, I don't think he would be a minister for very long. It rests with the minister to control his department. I find that civil servants do what is required when they get a clear lead. I think you could get that situation if a minister failed to give a clear lead, but then he shouldn't be a minister.

There is undoubtedly some truth in the proposition that when ministers seek to block the policies of ministerial rivals, civil servants are involved, but this is not the same as civil servants frustrating ministers' wishes off their own bat. In late 1966, Michael Stewart, then Secretary of State for Economic Affairs, wrote a secret and personal note to Harold Wilson complaining about how the Chancellor of the Exchequer refused to allow his staff to pass economic information – such as daily sterling balances – to him and his Permanent Secretary, and that in interdepartmental discussions Treasury staff were instructed not to cooperate with the DEA.

From personal experience, I can cite a series of occasions when a Cabinet minister sought to overturn decisions taken by ministerial committees of which he was not a member. When he heard of a decision he disliked, he would write to all the ministers on that committee, arguing that it was about time the subject was looked at, and suggesting they do more or less the opposite of what had been agreed. In each department, this letter would come down to the relevant official for 'advice and a draft reply'. When a copy landed on my desk I would phone two colleagues in other departments, and we would agree that one of us would put a draft reply for our minister to send – saying the equivalent of 'sit down and shut up' – and advise him that the other two ministers would write in support. My two colleagues would put the appropriate supporting letters up to their ministers and, as soon as the first letter was sent, the other two would follow in short order. We did this a number of times on different issues. No doubt the victim considered it a conspiracy, but we saw it as preventing the frustration of government policy by a maverick, and so did our ministers. Whichever side you take is determined by how you think government ought to be run.

Internecine spats between ministers pose an interesting dilemma for civil servants since the Civil Service Code states that 'civil servants owe their loyalty to the duly constituted government'. When this formulation first appeared I asked my principal establishments officer how, when two ministers disagreed, I was to know which one represented the duly constituted government; he confessed himself unable to offer advice.

Mrs Thatcher, though more inclined to hubris than paranoia, tended to distrust any ministers or officials who might have a mind of their own. She saw civil servants as executors of her will, and her ministers took their cue from her. In a telling interview in the *Financial Times* with Geoffrey Owens in 1991, Lord Rayner, who was a great fan of Mrs Thatcher, wondered 'whether the civil servants have been ignored in favour of outside advisors, and politicians have paid the price'. Possibly! There was, he suggested, 'an understandable but unjustified distrust of civil servants, the fear that they would always drag their feet'. I suppose it is only natural that, finding yourself dragged pell-mell towards the nearest abyss, you drag your feet; but Mrs Thatcher, like some other politicians, never saw the abyss until she was well and truly in it, and seemed quite incapable of realising that others could see what she could not.

There are, of course, plenty of precedents. One that seems particularly relevant is that of the able seaman who, in 1707, worked out by dead reckoning that his admiral, Sir Cloudesley Shovell, was sailing too close to the Isles of Scilly. In the Royal Navy at that time it was a capital offence for sailors to try to work out the location of their ship, but this sailor was so concerned that he raised the issue – and for his pains he was hung. The next day his vessel, and three others in convoy with it, did indeed run aground on the Scillies. Some 2,000 men were drowned.

The resemblance to Mrs Thatcher's more extreme policy initiatives is strong. Some idea of the Iron Lady's attitude to leadership is revealed by her comment that Lord Young brought her solutions, whereas other ministers brought her problems. While there are obvious reasons for letting the boss know you've been clever (I once saw a senior civil servant phone his boss from an international conference to let him know he had foreseen a problem which would shortly arise – but that he had developed a solution), it should hardly need stating that solving problems which others have failed to address is a key function of a leader. If managers at any level lack the inclination or ability to take the really difficult decisions that get thrown up in their organisation, they soon lose touch with reality, and eventually come to grief.

When the Labour government came to power in 1966, top civil servants were regularly referred to as mandarins. They were viewed as masters of their craft and were certainly intimidating, if not positively arrogant. By the time of Mrs Thatcher's fall in 1990, these last two attributes were firmly in the grip of ministers. Tony Blair's government has seen both the ultimate flowering of this transfer of power and authority and, if that were possible, a further downturn in ministerial regard for civil servants (I have the scars on my back!). Unsurprisingly, this has resulted in top civil servants becoming increasingly isolated. They perceive they have lost their influence over ministers, and so do those below them. A gap has now opened up between top civil servants and their staff.

The system which is intended to deliver government is split into three camps. In one sit ministers and their special advisors; in the second the top management of departments (usually directors-general and the Permanent Secretary); while in the third camp is the rest of the department. Perched precariously in between are a number of under-secretaries and agency chief executives, who must try to keep in touch with the top of the house while maintaining street cred with those they manage. It is hardly a recipe for good government, particularly if the relevant under-secretaries and agency chief executives are not effective managers or leaders.

Because ministers stay in post for such short periods, there is seldom much chance for them to become effective managers of their departments. Nevertheless, they should still be able to perform some sort of leadership function. If they are unable to do this – and many are – then the way is open for the sort of situation which John Reid inherited at the Home Office when he took over from David Blunkett. According to his biographer Stephen Pollard, Blunkett thought that it was not deliberate obstruction by the civil servants in the Home Office that frustrated ministerial policy but incompetence, which is not far from Reid's more accurate diagnosis of poor management and leadership. There is, however, a fair amount of evidence to suggest that the minister himself was a major contributor to that poor leadership. One of Blunkett's criticisms appears to be that his staff didn't always agree with him. They may have had good cause.

I have myself witnessed an incident in which a minister with the warmest, most approachable public image threw a tantrum at a meeting in the Cabinet Office, and as a result wasted a great deal of taxpayers' money. Those who see only the public images of politicians might suppose they are excellent at dealing with people, but the reality is often quite different; kissing babies, shaking hands and even addressing large meetings does not necessarily imply an ability to deal with individuals effectively, or indeed at all. Some politicians with a fairly dire public image, men like Nicholas Ridley and Norman Tebbit, were actually exceptionally easy to work with, while others, such as Michael Heseltine, who could have a Tory conference on its feet baying for blood in minutes, were difficult to engage with on a one-on-one basis. Where ministers find difficulty in working with people, and in particular their civil servants, ample scope exists for things to go wrong.

For ministers, their special advisors and their civil servants, the key to a successful relationship should be an effective private office. To be effective, the private office needs to generate trust in both directions. Most civil servants in a department will have no contact with their ministers and will know little more about them than they can read in the newspapers. They will know even less about any special advisors. Equally, ministers and special advisors will get to know only a small number of civil servants, and when new issues become live the minister will have to get to grips with a new facet of the department's work and the people who are responsible for it. Both the subject and the people may be quite new to the minister, yet if a particular issue is hot enough the minister's political future may be at stake. In the space of a few hours the minister must be briefed on the issue and its implications, helped to develop a response and to prepare for follow-up action, including the possibility of having to answer oral parliamentary questions.

The private office has a crucial role to play in ensuring that civil servants prepare their briefing in a way that the minister finds most helpful, and which takes account of the minister's known views and attitudes. There is, for example, no point in producing reams of briefing for ministers who can't or won't read much more than a page. I once had to brief a minister on the outcome of a complex multilateral trade negotiation that had taken thirteen years to complete, but the minister had a low reading tolerance and my final brief consisted of just ten sentences, each one line long. It may not be entirely satisfactory to have the country's destiny in the hands of people who are unable to read long sentences, but it is certainly better to give a minister a briefing he or she can understand than something they will not bother looking at.

Private offices have many other functions, but for the good governance of the country it is the role they play in ensuring an effective interface between ministers and their special advisors and civil servants that is most vital. But the value of a private office can be severely diminished, or even destroyed, by ministers who do not recognise the value of their staff, or who fail to understand the crucial importance of having an effective relationship with their civil servants.

In seeking to maintain such a relationship, a private office may often have to deal with inter-personal issues which might otherwise get in the way of business. During the early 1960s, I heard of one under-secretary who was very knowledgeable on his subject, but whose clothing was so exceptionally unkempt that it could easily put people off. When he had to see a minister for the first time, the private office would be at pains to prepare the minister to discount appearances and concentrate on what was being said. On one occasion, after the meeting was over, the private secretary asked the minister if he had found the advice given helpful. 'Yes,' replied the minister, 'but please tell him to do his flies up next time he comes to see me!'

When ministers find that a civil servant is just too irritating to endure, it will be the role of the private office to ensure that meetings are scheduled when the offender is otherwise engaged, so that other more congenial staff can attend to brief the minister. This is more difficult than it sounds, as civil servants usually ditch other commitments for ministerial meetings, but with a little effort the trick can usually be managed, as I observed when one of my bosses became *persona non grata* with one minister.

One other important function of a private office is to try to limit the workload of ministers. It is sometimes suggested that ministers' staff want to see their minister fully occupied, and others have suggested that it is ministers themselves who create silly working hours due to their own working style. In most cases the major issue is simply the volume of work that comes a minister's way, coupled with Parliament's odd working hours.

Some ministers, however, are driven by an inner compulsion to work silly hours. Sir Stafford Cripps was a notorious workaholic, and his long hours in the office drove not only his private office but other ministerial colleagues to counsel caution. He ignored them and paid the price, dying aged sixty-two. Working long hours not only damages your health, it also leads to poor decision-making. While he was running the Think Tank, Lord Rothschild had plenty of opportunity to see how these pressures affected ministers' abilities to take sensible decisions. In October 1972, he wrote an interesting letter to a Dr Broadbent of the Medical Research Council:

> Ministers and senior Civil Servants work extraordinarily long hours, quite often interspersed with gin & tonics etc., perhaps to keep them going – at least that is my experience. They may take very important decisions at 10.00 a.m., 6.30 p.m. (a rather tricky moment in the light of what is said above) and at 2.00 a.m. Can one demonstrate in a not more than three minute test, that their powers of judgement and decision-taking are worse at 6.30 p.m. and 2.00 a.m. than at 10.00 a.m.?

In his reply, Dr Broadbent opined that such a test would not be successful because the minister might pass it even if he were tired – and would thus be encouraged to go on as normal, or if he failed might simply repudiate the test's validity. There the matter seems to have rested, but it is worth noting that by the following October Douglas Hurd, who was then a political advisor to Prime Minister Edward Heath, was noting the onset of fatigue in the ministerial team. They were, Hurd said, increasingly 'missing their stroke' and were beginning 'without realising it to move through a fog of tiredness'.

There is a considerable irony in the difficulties faced by the Heath government. Before winning the 1970 general election, Heath had noted that working twenty-four hours a day was silly because it left people tired and prone to taking wrong decisions. Like many others, though, once in office he succumbed to the pressure to work ridiculous hours and suffered the fate he had so clearly foreseen from the leisure of the opposition front bench.

The importance of ensuring that ministers work well with their civil servants lies in this simple truth: it is the large numbers of relatively junior civil servants who are responsible for day-to-day implementation of government policy, and if they get things wrong the minister's head is likely to roll. An extreme example was provided by the furore over the deportation of foreign prisoners which cost Charles Clarke his job as Home Secretary in 2006. A month after Clarke's resignation, Lin Homer, the director-general of the Immigration and Nationality Directorate, told the House of Commons Home Affairs Select Committee that the issue of non-deportation was understood by junior staff. But she argued that employees had been overwhelmed by the volume of cases referred to them by the prison service, and had simply filed them away and taken no action.

Junior civil servants, for all that they were deemed mechanical by Charles Trevelyan, are people with complicated personalities, and how well they work will be affected considerably by the way they are treated. They are not some homogenous lump of humanity to be vilified in public as stupid, too numerous or overpaid, nor are they to be heaped with abuse in private because the nanny of a minister's mistress can't get a visa extension. They are a bunch of individuals with their own aspirations, ambitions, apprehensions and concerns. How these factors balance in any particular case will vary depending on matters such as how well junior civil servants are led by their bosses, and how well they are treated by their ministers. In the case of the Home Office deportation row, the director-general told the select committee that the whole department was 'under-managed'; the record of most recent Home Secretaries does not suggest that they took many pains to win the hearts and minds of their staff.

It might be thought that this point was so obvious as to not need stating, but it does seem as though ministers and top civil servants fail to understand that how well their staff perform will depend on the messages in word and deed that they receive from those they work for, and on any discrepancy between what is said and what is done. If, for example, ministers purport to encourage debate and discussion, but slap their staff down every time anyone says something they disapprove of, it will not take long for staff to form the view that the minister is hypocritical and untrustworthy. This is a bad thing because it means ministers will be much less likely to get independent and impartial advice from their staff, who will only tell them what it is perceived they wish to hear (as is happening now in Whitehall).

Ministers can be particularly good at spending most of the year behaving in ways that hack off their staff, and then sending round a jolly Christmas message, gleefully reporting on what a wonderful year everyone has had and how it will get even better next year; by mid-January they are back with the hatchet. Of course they mean it when they say 'Happy Christmas', and somehow contrive to forget all the aggro they have been causing, and they expect the staff to forget too – just like they expect the electorate to forget all the broken promises of past decades and concentrate only on the latest shiny new election manifesto.

But it is not just a question of whether a minister wants to run a contented office. The issue of how a minister runs his or her department goes to the heart of the question of ministerial accountability. The convention that ministers take responsibility for anything that happens in their department dates from a time when ministers did indeed take all the decisions in their department. As the size and role of government expanded – particularly during the twentieth century – it became unrealistic to expect ministers to know everything that was happening in their department, but the convention remained unchanged. The convention was not designed by civil servants to protect their backsides; it is a parliamentary convention and it is for Parliament to decide whether or not the convention should be changed.

In reality, the issue gets inextricably caught up in party politics and the parliamentary standing of individual ministers. Commentators who make the point that ministers cannot possibly know what is going on in every corner of their department, and should not therefore take the rap when something goes wrong, often fail to understand how important the attitude of a minister can be in determining whether a warning of imminent danger is sent up the line or not. Ministers may also so burden their departments with new initiatives, policy switches and image changes that the system breaks down under the strain; ministers may not be directly responsible for everything that happens in their department, but they may be responsible if little or nothing can be done effectively.

It is perhaps not widely enough appreciated that people can only be managed with their own consent. Many people failed to understand this in 1776, and as a result the United States came into existence. As Lord Chatham put it, 'Tyranny, whether ambitioned by an individual part of the legislature, or the bodies who compose it, is equally intolerable to British subjects...' What was true then remains true today, and it applies to office staff just as much as it does to whole populations. It is always possible to direct or coerce, but directing people cuts you off from the free flow of feedback which is such a valuable part of effective management, and, much more importantly, you lose people's loyalty; if people feel badly treated they will find many ways of fighting back – most of which may damage their organisation. Although often thought to be the exclusive preserve of government departments, I have observed this process at work in industry, when companies carved policies in tablets of stone and staff were not allowed to challenge them. In one instance, senior managers from two major multinational companies came to me to ensure my department adopted an effective new idea they had conceived. They knew they could not take the idea to their top management, because to do so would be to admit they had been thinking in ways that were contrary to company policy. In the face of my incredulity, they told me that once head office had laid down a policy, it was unchallengeable no matter how unsuitable for local circumstances, and no matter what bright ideas might be dreamed up by local staff. They explained that if the government adopted the idea they would be able to persuade their managements that they had to accept this new government policy, and that is exactly what happened.

The propensity for top management to lose sight of the need for management altogether and instead develop a good line in bullying has interesting implications. The Whitehall II health study carried out by Professor Sir Michael Marmot at the Royal Free and UCL Medical School suggested a link between illness and the extent to which people felt they had no control over their working lives: it is quite possible that the high absence rate in the public sector due to sickness is a result of the high level of poor managers in that sector. The steps taken to deal with such a high absence rate are usually directed at those workers who fall ill rather than their managers, and thus arguably address – and aggravate – symptoms rather than causes.

In the run-up to Christmas 2004, ministers decided to tackle the problem of absences from sickness in the public sector. As ever, it was the symptoms they went for; there was no mention of improving working conditions for those in grotty offices, or providing better security for those who faced violence in the workplace (the prison service and Department of Work and Pensions were singled out for special mention as notorious offenders), or dealing with poor managers who don't delegate decent work, or dealing with those who feel unable to seek promotion because they see the majority of managerial jobs taken by elderly white males. No, the way forward was to make everyone phone in from their sickbeds – possibly to the very person whose actions were causing them to be off work in the first place. This tremendous initiative was by chance taken in the same week that the government announced it was considering ending final salary pensions in the public sector.

If public servants are abused in ministers' speeches and memoirs or biographies, and if their pay and rations are made political footballs, it is really no wonder that the least competent go sick. But, of course, while some people do play the system, many others have perfectly valid reasons for being absent from work. The same day that the Minister for Work and Pensions announced his initiative, the BBC showed a film about the work of the social services' department in Bristol. It included footage of a social worker who had been violently attacked during a home visit. She was off work for several months, and despite being supported by colleagues on her return, she eventually resigned because the trauma had been too great. Lumping skivers in with the genuine is a good way to drive a few more borderline cases over the edge into the skiving camp, and to really brass off the diligent.

Anecdotal evidence certainly suggests that people seem to derive the greatest benefits and enjoyment from working for bosses who allow them to get on with the job, and feel least happy with those who are highly prescriptive and always interfering – particularly in the really interesting bits of work. While there are many who do let their staff do their own thing, there are still far too many who do not. Secondees into the civil service often make this point, being startled at the low levels of responsibility afforded to able civil servants. As one wrote in their account of their secondment, 'One of the remarkable differences between the public and the private sector is that the former can take very clever people and put them in an environment where it is impossible to achieve anything.'

If it is good practice to give staff their heads, that can only happen if staff know in what direction and for what purpose they are heading. This requires managers to know what it is they are about so that staff can be informed. While this may sound pretty obvious, it is nonetheless my experience that, in many cases, managers do not know what they are about, and simply react to events ad hoc and without any sense of overall purpose. In this I suppose it could be said that they are only emulating their political leaders, but it does mean that many in the public sector find themselves in some sort of administrative limbo in which they carry out a set of tasks but have no real idea why they are doing so or to what overall end, and from there it is but a short step to doing things which no longer have any purpose at all.

In 1967, the Public Accounts Committee lambasted the MoD for employing a clerk and an executive officer on maintaining a list of chronograph wrist watches issued to naval airmen. The list had been established in 1954. When the Comptroller and Auditor General's staff carried out a check in 1966, they found that nearly 100 watches were listed as held by air stations that no longer existed, or by officers who could not be traced or were no longer entitled to have an official watch. A complete check by the navy not only failed to find any of these watches, it also revealed that another 700 were untraceable.

When grilled by the committee, the navy had to admit that the list had never been updated; that it may have been started with defective data; that it was useless, and that they had been unable to establish why it had ever been set up in the first place. Somewhere up the line in the MoD there existed a senior official who was responsible for the work of those keeping the useless list of watches; it is doubtful if he knew this until the Comptroller and Auditor General took an interest.

The huge gulf between the intellectuals and the mechanicals can be best illustrated by the fact that very large numbers of civil servants will never have seen top mandarins in the flesh. Some will seldom have seen much in the way of senior management either. One person wrote to her department's staff newspaper to say she didn't believe senior civil servants existed because none had ever appeared in her office – and she worked in a London headquarters building containing most of the department's top brass! For those in isolated offices, or in large clerical factories such as Longbenton in North Tyneside, even middle managers are a pretty rare sight. One woman I knew worked for several years at Longbenton as a clerk, in what was then the Department of Health and Social Security; the only people she ever saw were her fellow clerical workers and an executive officer perched on a dais at one end of the very large room in which she worked.

Even when mandarins do venture to offices in the regions, they tend to closet themselves with the most senior form of life; they seldom just get out into the main office and behave like a fully paid-up member of the human race. These days most staff in a department will have some idea of who the top people are because efforts are now made to publicise such matters in staff newspapers, or on departmental websites. But while this represents some progress, it can have unintended consequences of reinforcing the gap between intellectuals and mechanicals because it rams home the point that most of the top people are elderly white males, and that must send a powerful message to all the young black females who work predominantly in clerical jobs.

It will always be difficult for those at the top of a large organisation to ensure that they are not isolated from those at the bottom, but the people at the top are allegedly there because they are clever, and clever people ought to be able to sort out such difficulties. Of course that does raise the issue as to why government departments are so big; as noted earlier, that is mainly a function of the tasks which at one time or another have been thought necessary by governments, but some responsibility rests on those who bring pressure on governments for change, including the electorate.

# CHAPTER 13

# THE AGENDA BENDERS

Although the range of government activity has spread hugely during the past 100 years, it is surprising how many issues have been problems for governments over long periods of time. Often these issues are outside the direct control of government, and yet they can become very important indeed for governments and their ability to govern; they are the sorts of issues that Prime Minister Harold Macmillan had in mind when he coined the phrase 'events, dear boy, events' to explain his administration's difficulties.

Chaucer's merchant in *The Canterbury Tales* wanted the sea between Harwich and the Hook of Holland kept clear of pirates; in 1696, protecting merchant shipping from Barbary pirates was a key duty of the newly established Board of Trade and Plantations; in 1945, the Royal Navy had to carry out anti-piracy patrols after the Japanese surrender left far-eastern waters without effective control. Piracy is still an issue for shipowners, mainly in the waters between Indonesia and south-east Asia and off the coast of Somalia; over 400 vessels were attacked by pirates in 2003 and some 100 crew members killed or kidnapped.

Dislodging squatters was a problem in the Middle Ages (caused by returning Crusaders) then surfaced again after the Second World War when Blitz victims became fed up with waiting for the government to rehouse them; and it still remains a problem, as Lambeth Council discovered when the courts handed one of their properties, worth some £1 million, to squatters who had lived in the property rent free for thirty-one years. Dealing with beggars was a significant problem for Queen Elizabeth I and has remained one for just about every government since. The reluctance of people to pay taxes has been a problem ever since there were wars to be financed, though it took a British government to realise that Benjamin Franklin's gag about nothing in life being as certain as death and taxes could be turned into a taxation policy, with the introduction of death duties. Keeping road users safe from theft has been a very long-standing issue; during the reign of Edward I, legislation was introduced to guard against the depredations of robbers by requiring trees and bushes to be felled for a distance of 200 yards from the sides of all high roads between market towns: an early trunk roads policy!

Those affected by such issues seek to persuade governments to do things (or stop doing things) so as to bring about change. The methods of persuasion are varied, ranging from the solitary letter writer to the mass campaign; from informed lobbying to rioting; from enlightened disinterest to sectarian bigotry. Whatever its form, external pressure inevitably produces a result – though not by any means the one desired by those bringing the pressure to bear.

The nature of the problem posed by external pressures has been complicated by the evolution of political power in the period since reform of the civil service began towards the end of the eighteenth century. Much of the early pressure for reform and the reforms themselves stemmed from Parliament, and were forced upon a reluctant or at least passive administration. In 1782, after a two-year battle, Parliament voted the Board of Trade out of existence (the board and its offices were to be 'utterly suppressed and taken away'), though it bounced back in 1784. The Post Office was strongly opposed to the Penny Post, but a parliamentary committee rammed it down the throat of the Postmaster General, as well as passing other legislation to reform abuse and incompetence in the Post Office. After the end of the Napoleonic Wars, Parliament insisted on cutting back the civil service to its pre-conflict size, and required returns to show that this was done. The extension of voting rights gradually eroded the power of MPs by putting the electorate in charge of the fate of administrations, and by creating a demand for policies and politicians which appealed to the masses. As MPs' powers waned, those of the whips waxed, and the legislative initiative passed to government ministers. But while ministerial hands were ready to grasp power, it did not follow that they, or the systems over which they presided, were capable of supporting them in adequately discharging the responsibilities that came with the power.

If the universal franchise has affected the balance of power between the legislature and the executive, 'people power' has also had a more direct impact on policy-making and implementation. The National Health Service was nearly overwhelmed in its opening months by the vast numbers of women with prolapsed wombs who flocked to hospitals to have an operation they had hitherto been unable to afford. This suppressed demand had simply not been identified, and provides a classic example of why adequate risk analysis is a vital component of policy-making.

Even where there are not significant unidentified elephant traps waiting for policy-makers, they often contrive to manufacture such traps themselves by making naive assumptions about how the population will respond to policy. In 1381 and 1989, people rioting on the streets saw off the imposition of a poll tax. Even when not tearing up the flagstones in fully fledged riots, people have gone to considerable lengths to make their views known via big public demonstrations, and while the outcomes of these have proved varied, there have certainly been some conspicuous successes. The Campaign for Nuclear Disarmament generated a great deal of attention, but CND is not the force it once was and Britain still has nuclear weapons. Mass protests in America against the war in Vietnam certainly weakened the resolve of the US administration, though in the end US policy fell over rather than being pushed over. Recently in this country, protests (and the threat of their repetition) have effectively prevented long-planned increases in fuel tax.

An unusual example of the impact of people power on policy-making was provided by the response to the 2004 Boxing Day tsunami in the Indian Ocean. The initial British government reaction to the disaster was feeble in the extreme, but the huge public response, generating £76 million in the course of the first week and even forcing credit card companies to waive charges, shamed the government into making a sensible and proportionate contribution.

Less dramatically, people can also exercise considerable power by taking decisions individually, especially if they do so on a large enough scale, as they often do, for example, in avoiding (and evading) taxes. The evidence is overwhelming that people dislike paying taxes, yet Chancellors of the Exchequer continue to assume that the public will cough up, and become indignant when taxpayers and their accountants discover ever more ingenious methods of tax avoidance. Inevitably it is the well-off who are best placed to avoid taxation, whether by clever accountancy or frequent cross-Channel booze cruises; the poor can seldom afford to follow suit, yet the policies followed by Chancellors of the Exchequer over the past couple of decades have dragged more and more low-paid workers into the tax net.

The attempted enforcement of doomed policies often develops a demented logic of its own, as the Americans discovered in Vietnam. As each initiative fails, some armchair strategist dreams up yet another, which is seized upon by administrators (and politicians) desperate to avoid being seen as 'defeatist', and that too is followed until its failure is too manifest to deny. An exemplar of this sort of thinking must be Major General Edward Braddock, who in 1755 tried to fight the Indians in Canadian forest country, with his scarlet-uniformed troops drawn up in a block formation. As his unfortunate footsloggers were picked off by the Indians, lurking behind the trees, the general rode up and down hollering at the Indians to 'come out and fight like men'. At least Braddock recognised the folly of his actions, for as he too lay dying, he told George Washington (who had tried to introduce a little common sense into proceedings) that 'we shall better know how to deal with them another time'. Perhaps a public fund should be created to place pictures of the death of Major General Braddock in the Oval Office, and in 10 Downing Street?

Just occasionally, governments prove able to break out of the spiral of defeat by doing the counter-intuitive thing. An example is provided by the peace process in Northern Ireland, where a resolute policy of digging a bigger and bigger hole, because to do anything else would be to 'surrender', was turned on its head and replaced by a Panglossian policy of papering over not only cracks but yawning abysses. It has worked so far and one can only hope that it will continue to do so.

While people acting on their own are seldom the cause of major problems for governments, they can waste a lot of time. A particular problem they do pose is how to distinguish the sensible from the silly, or indeed the insane. A well-used route for such individuals is to write to their MP. When Richard Cobden became an MP to help further the cause of repeal of the Corn Laws, he was taken aback by the attention he received.

First, half the mad people in the country who are still at large, and they are legion, address their incoherent ravings to the most notorious man of the hour. Next, the kindred tribe who think themselves poets, who are more difficult than the mad people to deal with, send their doggerel and solicit subscriptions to their volumes, with occasional requests to be allowed to dedicate them. Then there are the Jeremy Diddlers who begin their epistles with high-flown compliments upon my services to the millions, and always wind up with a request that I will bestow a trifle upon the individual who ventures to lay his distressing case before me ... Then there are all the benevolent enthusiasts who have their pet reforms, who think that because a man has sacrificed himself in mind, body and estate in attempting to do one thing, he is the very person to do all the rest.

Douglas Hurd had similar experiences, and offered the opinion that one in eighteen of those who came to his surgeries were 'unhinged'. Needless to say, MPs are swift to pass their correspondence to government departments. Here it joins the cases that come direct to departments, for MPs have no monopoly of unsolicited correspondence. Queen Elizabeth I's ministers were bombarded by letters from those who believed they had some divine message to impart; one believed he had been instructed to sound the last trumpet, another that he was the son of the Queen and God the Father. A modern counterpart was the man who wrote to the government denouncing economic sanctions against Yugoslavia, as part of 'the Pope's extermination plan that is codenamed as Operation Ferdinand and Isabella' being perpetrated by 'Catholics disguised as UN/EC functionaries'.

The barking mad are perhaps not too difficult; it is those who might just be sane who cause the real difficulty. A man who turns up well dressed and supported by apparently sane bankers, declaring that he has so much money in the bank of a certain country that if he withdraws it the country's economy will fold, needs at least to be given time to demonstrate that he is really in the same league as the denouncer of UN sanctions. Such happenings can be amusing, but they can also waste lots of time and distract bureaucrats from more sensible activities. A lady once complained about aircraft noise in an area where there were no aircraft routes; by chance she mentioned that she had raised the subject with the local police and luckily they were prepared to share their experience with the luckless officials who had to deal with the complaint. The police sent a copy of the report written by the local bobby.

On — I proceeded to Rose Cottage having received a complaint about aircraft that were said to be circling overhead. On arriving I looked up, but could see no aircraft. I saw Mrs — in her garden and I engaged her in conversation. She complained about the noise the aircraft were making; I looked up but saw no aircraft, nor could I hear any aircraft. I decided that I ought to speak with her husband, Mr —, who was indoors. When I mentioned his wife's complaint about the noise the aircraft were making, he too said how bad the noise was; I could hear no aircraft, and stepping to the window I looked up at the sky. I could see no aircraft. At this point I decided I would return to the station and report to the station sergeant.

The woman's complaint was conveniently 'lost'.

Sometime later, another lady from the Lake District wrote to the same office complaining about aircraft noise. She did not live near any military low-flying route, nor was there an airfield situated near her house. However, she was asked to log the times when she heard the aircraft. This she did, and it immediately became apparent that for whatever reason (probably a combination of particularly keen hearing and a low ambient noise level), she could hear aircraft that were flying over her house at 25,000–30,000 feet, planes which would not normally be audible to most people. It would have been easy to write her off as another person with a personality disorder, but she had been proved right and would have had every cause for complaint if her letter had not been investigated. The woman seemed content once she learned the source of the noise – and possibly rather chuffed at the clear compliment paid to her hearing.

These examples are deliberately chosen because they are harmless, but in reality some of the individual cases which go off the rails, sometimes with very serious consequences, do so because it can prove genuinely difficult to distinguish between a person with a real issue and someone with a totally imagined one. I once spoke to a member of the public who said he was being driven mad by his inability to get anyone in government to take his invention seriously; within a week or two the man had committed suicide. Such difficulties are compounded by the knowledge that governments have failed to pick up on sound ideas. It was only after Charles Algernon Parsons's boat *Turbinia* left the Royal Navy's fastest vessels standing at the Spithead Review in 1897 that his invention of the steam turbine was taken seriously, and Frank Whittle encountered much difficulty with the Air Ministry over his jet engine.

Members of Parliament can, of course, cause problems in their own right. There are 650 MPs, most of whom seek some sort of political power. But real political power presently rests with only a handful of Cabinet ministers and a few well-placed junior ministers (not all of them by any means at any one time), and sometimes with the chairs of some select committees. For much of their careers, MPs can expect to languish in opposition or to seethe with frustrated (or extinguished) ambition on the government back benches. It is not surprising that they sometimes become hooked on issues and causes. It is also perhaps not surprising that MPs have taken cash directly for various purposes, including asking parliamentary questions.

One of the 'cash for questions' MPs once phoned a civil servant to ask if they were responsible for a certain policy. The MP said he was acting on behalf of a company in his constituency. The civil servant knew the company and also knew that they were fully aware of the answer to the question being posed by the MP. The only reason for the phone call was to let the civil servant know that he (the MP) was taking an interest; it was a gentle but potentially effective threat to make life bothersome for the civil servant in the hope that the constituent's case would be given a fairer wind than might otherwise be the case.

No one could cavil at the work of good constituency MPs like the late Jo Richardson, who, despite being crippled by arthritis, would arrive at her constituency office on a Friday afternoon after a week's work and leave only when the last constituent had been seen, often late at night. An equally positive view was provided by Emma Nicholson's concern for the Marsh Arabs during the Gulf War and its aftermath, and Frank Field's for the socially disadvantaged. Every party in every parliament has its share of conviction politicians, and whether one agrees with their convictions or not they certainly raise the moral standards of parliamentary debate. As John Morley wrote of Richard Cobden, 'In the country his speeches excited the deep interest of that great class, who are habitually repelled by the narrow passions and seeming insincerity of ordinary politics.' When sitting through debates in the Commons, I have been struck by the way MPs talk through some members' speeches and listen intently to others; their choices seem to reflect the same point that Morley was making.

From MPs with special interests (declared or otherwise), it is a small jump to the professional lobbyist. One reason for the success of lobbyists is the ability of people to think in terms of boxes. For example, it is often perceived that there are a bunch of people called taxpayers while there is another group – apparently on some other planet – called workers, and yet another group called consumers, who are doubtless someplace else; it is a way of thinking that ministers have often encouraged, but their skill is as nothing compared with that of the single-issue campaigners – particularly those who seek to prevent the development of a transport or energy infrastructure suitable for the twenty-first century. Such sloppy thinking may start off as a convenient shorthand for more complex and therefore more realistic issues, but it is surprising how quickly a particular form of language can become built into government thinking and eventually, by constant repetition in speeches and papers, become enshrined in departmental folklore: 'My minister could never agree to the taxpayers' interests being ignored in this way.' It is true that these groups are not totally overlapping, but for most groups the degree of overlap is extensive enough to make such distinctions silly, but despite this, box-based policy thinking is alive and well.

It must be stressed that special interest groups can have a good influence on government policy – particularly those organisations which have attempted over the years to establish the factual basis of their subject and to avoid the seduction of boxes and bogeymen, as well as a temptation to grab headlines by destroying crops or interfering with freedom of navigation. The Howard League for Penal Reform is one well respected body, and the Royal United Services Institute is another in a very different field. They seldom, if ever, hit the headlines, yet they exercise a responsible influence on government in their chosen areas. Their work is invaluable as a means of providing some of the evidence-based thinking that can be so helpful in the formulation of good policy.

A different side of the lobbying coin is illustrated by the vice-like grip that farmers in the developed world have established on government money. For many years the farmers of the EU have run an extremely successful operation whereby, under the EU's Common Agricultural Policy, they receive some £28 billion a year. In the UK, 224 rather well-heeled landowners owning barely 2 per cent of the country's arable land share about £47 million a year for growing cereals. Most beneficiaries seem to farm in East Anglia. By chance, the same area provides a living for twenty-seven wealthy sugar beet producers who each get about £190,000 a year for producing their crop (about three times its cost on the world market). Fortunately, this subsidy is being phased out, but that is just one small triumph for sanity.

Similar stories abound in the United States, where in one recent year ten cotton farmers received a total subsidy of some $17 million, with one of them scooping $6 million. These subsidies are paid to the very rich by all taxpayers, most of whom are not wealthy, and who then, to add insult to injury, must pay more for their food or their clothes than if there were no subsidies. Subsidies enable extremely rich farmers in the EU and the USA to compete against the very poor farmers of the developing world. There is a certain irony here regarding Labour MPs who would express outrage against fox hunting, in the belief they were striking a dramatic blow in the class war, yet solemnly lined up behind their government's refusal to halt subsidies to wealthy members of the nobility, who thus continued to produce wheat at prices that undercut poor developing world producers.

To put the figures in a relevant perspective, Save the Children receives some £53 million a year in grants from the UK and foreign governments and bodies such as the UN and the EU. Such power has a long history. The Corn Laws were passed in 1815 to keep grain prices pegged at the high levels they had reached during the Napoleonic Wars. They were maintained in the teeth of campaigning by people such as Cobden and Bright until the point came when Peel realised he could no longer defend the policy.

Unsurprisingly, special interest groups seldom operate in the open and it is only because of research by bodies such as Oxfam (itself, paradoxically, a special interest group) that the scandal of farming subsidies receives regular airing. While the farmers' success has been spectacular, they are not alone – though they are probably in a league of their own. Press coverage in 2006 revealed how the system of all-party groups in the UK's Parliament was in danger of becoming subverted because the groups were using secretarial services provided by the very industries they covered.

If folly marches through industrial as well as foreign policy, the two come together in government support for exports. I am not aware of any economic study that has demonstrated that government support for exports achieves any significant impact on trade balances, but ministers can see that shiny new power station or dam on which they are spending taxpayers' money; they cannot see the myriad of small export contracts that are lost because feckless (or worse) government ministers in developing countries (and some in the developed world too) squander overseas aid on un-needed prestige projects – some of which have had major adverse environmental impacts.

The Paris-based Organisation for Economic Co-operation and Development (OECD) has performed a great service to the cause of good government by coining the phrase 'fallacy of misplaced concreteness', which describes a state of affairs when ministers dish out taxpayers' money to prop up a highly visible inefficient factory or industry, and ensure that by squandering this money they are putting others out of work who are not so obviously visible (or indeed preventing some even less visible unemployed people gaining work).

Basing policy on fact as opposed to fiction is particularly important because the public may not have easy access to relevant and accurate facts, and may be guided easily by those with a special case to make for supporting muddled policies. If Joe Public does not understand that his (or her) 'Spanish practice' is costing someone else a job, or that a strike can cause serious long-term damage to his or her own job security, then it is no wonder he (or she) acts just like Mr Tite Barnacle.

The failure of administrators to look with a more critical eye at the activity of the special pleaders is another manifestation of their reluctance to seek information, particularly when special pleaders are so ready with their own one-sided view of the world. Those who do not have an adequate depth of knowledge about the subject for which they are responsible will gladly seize upon whatever information comes their way and will have no real basis for critical examination of it. There is no reason for such ignorance; it is a matter of choice. It is possible to read widely about more or less any subject under the sun, and for many reading can be supplemented by academic discussions, trade conferences and seminars. Visiting companies, farms, universities, local authorities (or whatever they deal with) enables bureaucrats to see for themselves what the issues are, and to be seen to be interested.

Failure to do any of these things gives rise to a mafia effect, in which interest groups of a small number of organisations or people acquire a dominant position as the 'voice' of that interest group. Because these organisations/people are professional networkers, they tend to pop out from under every stone. They have their uses – and some can be good value indeed, but only if their views are tested against the views of those who are not establishment figures. All too often, bureaucrats with short deadlines and inadequate information will take whatever they can find from whoever can offer it, and the lobbyist with a ready supply of data which supports a specific cause will then move in to fill the vacuum.

The activities of the special pleaders are just one of the many pressures which have such a large impact on policy-making. One that seems to cause quite a lot of difficulty is that policy formulation and development take place against a background of a wide range of continuing business, which is constantly responding to changing internal and external events, and may well develop in a way that has implications for whatever policy is currently under consideration. What the historian Professor Geoffrey Elton has said of history holds equally true for policy development (which is, after all, history in the making): 'The whole difficulty of historical reconstruction and writing lies in this fundamental truth about history: it contains a multiple situation forever on the move.'

Much though they might like to do so, administrators can never stop the world moving on while they develop a new policy. In the late 1950s, the British government had examined its overall energy policy and decided to let the UK gas industry wither away. It was a perfectly sensible decision, but as the finishing touches were being worked out word reached the government of the discovery of natural gas under the Dutch section of the North Sea continental shelf. This news caused a major reappraisal; if there was gas under one part of the shelf then why not under another? Preliminary work suggested there was at least a possibility of gas being found under the UK section, so there was a major policy switch which resulted in the discovery of gas and oil under the UK shelf and the development of the national gas grid.

Rather more dramatically, in July 1990, the government decided to relax its arms embargo against Iraq. Before the ministerial group which had been set up by the Prime Minister had time to report back, Iraqi President Saddam Hussein began threatening Kuwait; the Home Secretary reported that it would be wise to wait until Saddam simmered down before announcing any change in policy. Several days later, Kuwait was invaded and the policy change was dropped: it was a very close call indeed.

If I had been writing this book before about 1980, I would have included a significant section on the role of the trade unions, for up to that time they were a major influence on government policy. They still can be influential, but the decline in union membership has reduced them to much the same level of importance as special interest groups such as the National Trust or the Royal Society for the Preservation of Birds. More to the point is the fact that because of their great success over the past 150 years or so, trade unions have achieved most of their original aims in terms of safety at work, hours of work and pay and conditions of work.

It was the trade unions (together with some of the more enlightened employers) who pressed for and obtained the appointment of women factory inspectors, and who stood up to the more intransigent exploiters of labour. In achieving their aims, trade unions have always been at risk of appearing as bad as their opponents. This aspect of the relationship between the two sides was neatly characterised by Sir Herbert Samuel, who chaired the Royal Commission on the Coal Industry in 1925. 'Anyone', Samuel commented, 'who had not met the mine owners would think the coal workers the stupidest people on earth'! Although it must rile the unions, it is a tribute to their achievement that the conditions they fought for are now taken for granted as being part of the natural order; few special interest groups can make that claim.

Regulation of the working environment by British governments has, over the years, been more beneficial than not and has made this country a safer place to work (and play), a healthier place to live, and a more honest place to do business. But it is still important to scrutinise all regulatory activity in order to minimise the damage that can be done by poorly thought-through policy and poorly implemented regulations. It is here also that bodies such as the trade unions, the Confederation of British Industry and the Institute of Directors continue to play useful roles.

Much regulatory policy is developed internationally in well-respected specialist bodies such as the International Civil Aviation Organization or the World Health Organization, and while debates in these forums can become very heated, and national interests can play a disproportionate part in policy formulation, their main impact over the years has been positive. To some extent this beneficial impact has been greatly helped by the highly specialised nature of their work, which often attracts little ministerial or media attention, allowing the international bureaucrats and specialists to beaver away to their hearts' content honing rules on the height of letters on runway signs, the precise radius of visibility of navigation lights or the details of the protocols enabling international telecommunications.

These bodies are just as likely as national bureaucracies to be overstaffed – providing tax-free sinecures for some lucky international bureaucrats. Some have a strong predilection for meeting in interesting places. One body concerned with international telecommunications used to be referred to as the Committee for Investigating Seaside and Pleasure Resorts. But on the whole, we all benefit from the international frameworks these bodies agree, and the near invisibility of much of this international regulatory activity is in sharp contrast to the high profile of what goes on in Brussels.

Although those who work for highly specialised international organisations have the universal bureaucratic potential to be highly irritating, they usually know what they are about because they work in specialised fields; this is not always the case in Brussels. In some cases, for the subject in question there may not be any real expertise available to some member states, and even where it is in theory available it might not be deployed at Brussels, which is often seen as the exclusive preserve of either of the national representatives in Brussels or an official of the country's Ministry of Foreign Affairs (often one and the same thing). It is by no means uncommon to see delegates enter a meeting, which will result in the drafting of highly technical and directly applicable EC regulations, carrying no papers (and with no understanding of the detail involved). No matter how much ignorance exists, however, each country has a vote.

Of course, some member states have people at meetings who do understand what they are about, but it only requires a little political arm-twisting of the ignorant for a poor regulation to be adopted. Another important area where knowledge may be lacking is in the commission itself. In some areas the commission has its own expertise, but in many it does not and cannot. In such cases, the commission official who has drawn the short straw can only rely on such help and assistance as he can obtain from member states' experts, or seek to remedy the deficiency by employing consultants. But, as happens with consultants the world over, the results are highly variable (and the consultants often turn out to be retired 'experts' from member states).

Most regulations and directives from Brussels are usually no more or less important for the man in the street than those of any other bodies. The reason they achieve a lot of publicity is that some newspapers have made it their policy to lampoon the EU for political reasons. It has been argued that the media are not so much agenda benders as agenda setters; certainly there is considerable (though superficial) evidence that on issues such as asylum seekers and prison sentencing the media exercise a considerable influence. Newspaper owners are often said to have their own political agendas, and while this may be true, it is also true that they often work closely with politicians. Many politicians enjoy intrigue and most seek publicity. Politicians also face major difficulties dealing with the speed of modern communications. The collection of factual information is often labour-intensive, and when political solutions are needed urgently to address to-day's headlines, time simply may not permit anything much more subtle than a knee-jerk reaction, or a bit of bogeyman-based on-the-hoof policy-making. It is open to question as to whether this is sensible or leads in any way to good government, but it is indisputable that it happens. The position was well put by the Conservative Chancellor of the Exchequer Norman Lamont in his resignation speech in 1993:

> There is something wrong with the way in which we make our decisions. The government listen too much to the pollsters and the party managers. The trouble is that they are not even very good at politics, and they are entering too much into policy decisions. As a result, there is too much short-termism, too much reacting to events, and not enough shaping of events. We give the impression of being in office but not in power. Far too many important deci-sions are made for thirty-six hours' publicity. Yes, we are politicians as well as policy-makers; but we are also the trustees of the nation. I believe that in politics one should decide what is right and then decide the presentation, not the other way round. Unless this ap-proach is changed, the government will not survive, and will not deserve to survive.

The Conservative government did not survive much longer, but paradoxically the propensity for instant government received an enormous boost when Labour won the 1997 election and sought to introduce the sort of 24-hour instant-rebuttal mechanism that had worked so well for them in the election campaign. Labour failed to realise that while it was relatively easy to look up election pledges and speeches in Hansard, it was quite a different matter to get sensible answers across the entire range of government activity. The point has long been understood by civil servants. In 1864, Sir James Emerson Tennant, the joint secretary in charge of the general and commercial departments at the Board of Trade, told a select committee, 'The quantity of correspondence and the number of documents that must be read, to arrive at a result which is conveyed in a single sentence, either affirmative or negative, is such as would scarcely be credited, except by a person who would undergo the labour'.

The difficulty is illustrated by an event which occurred in the period between Iraq's invasion of Kuwait and the Gulf War. In 1991, the *Sunday Times*'s Insight Team ran a story that 8.6 tons of depleted uranium had been exported to Iraq. In fact, there had been no such shipment, but the figures in the overseas trade accounts, one of which gave rise to the story, are compiled using such a Byzantine process that it took days to establish the facts. The truth was that the figure related to medical isotopes and included errors made by exporters incorporating the weight of lead shielding packaging, the use of a minimum weight for consignments recorded by direct electronic means. The erroneous figures had been further confused by Customs and Excise's practice of aggregating entries to preserve exporters' confidentiality. The Insight Team had obtained a published figure, but had run their story without establishing the facts behind it.

The government became aware of the story one Friday evening. By the Saturday afternoon before publication, the government had enough information to know that the figure was misleading, but insufficient detail to give a full explanation, and since it is banner headlines that sell newspapers irrespective of their veracity, the story was published. It took several weeks of research before a detailed breakdown of the figure was available. The full facts were later published by the Trade and Industry Select Committee, but it is to be supposed that few who clucked and expostulated as they read the original story would have also read the annex to the committee's report where the facts were published.

It would save considerable resource if such hares were not chased, but unfortunately politicians simply cannot resist playing the journalists' game, and spend far too much time chasing their own tails, or, more likely, their harassed staffs' tails, seeking to disprove stories constructed on the most flimsy 'evidence'. It is a pity, because most of this effort is wasted; few people ever believe the government of the day, even though governments often do tell the truth and quite frequently many newspaper stories contain significant inaccuracies.

Early in 2004, the British media gave considerable coverage to the allegation of the radioactive contamination of farmed salmon in Scotland. On the Monday of the week after the story broke, one national newspaper ran a story under the headline: 'Salmon shunned despite price cuts and reassurances'. The article reported that over the weekend 'supermarket shelves remained stacked high with salmon steaks and smoked salmon strips as wary shoppers plumped for fresh tuna, mackerel, haddock or trout instead. Many stores slashed prices in a desperate bid to shift salmon stocks off their shelves.' In a leader on the same day, the newspaper inveighed against 'this tendency towards visceral public reaction'. Readers were lectured sternly for giving way to panic. The following day the paper's consumer editor reported, without a blush (or any further editorial comment), a diametrically opposed view which stated that over the weekend in question 'supermarket chains were pleasantly surprised to find it (salmon) leaping off the shelves ... and some Scottish producers found that orders had gone through the roof ... the supermarkets said that generally they had not cut prices to prop up fish sales'. A supposed crisis which had threatened a major Scottish industry had vanished overnight.

The nature of the problem posed by poor reporting is compounded by the fact that over the years there has also been a great deal of very good reporting, so reports must therefore be investigated thoroughly – which takes time and resources. One of the most illustrious of newspaper correspondents, William Howard Russell, earned justified fame with his reports from the Crimean War for *The Times*, but his career had started earlier with coverage of events in his native Ireland – the famine and the political career of Daniel O'Connell. Russell went on to report on the American Civil War and the Franco-Prussian War. He had a justified reputation for integrity, and his work was all the more valuable for this reason. His qualities were the same ones that James Wilson drummed into his staff on *The Economist*. They are qualities which can and do bring about change in the way we are governed.

While many factors and interest groups impact on the formulation of policy and its implementation, a major source of conflicting pressures is Whitehall itself. People seem to believe that Whitehall has (or at least should have) a single view on any given policy issue. The reality is that departments often have quite sensible and sound policies that are totally irreconcilable with those of other departments. This reflects the fact that government is an uncoordinated set of often conflicting policies, which to some extent reflects the reality outside Whitehall (and often the position of members of the Cabinet).

A neat illustration of the problem is provided by a meeting I attended in Washington. On the UK side were representatives from the Ministry of Defence, the Foreign and Commonwealth Office, and the Department of Trade and Industry. The US team included representatives from the equivalent US departments. There was a high level of agreement between the MoD and Department of Defense, between the State department and the FCO, and between the Commerce department and DTI; there was, however, no agreement among the members of the UK team or between the members of the US team.

What happened at that meeting happens regularly in capitals all over the world on just about any issue that comes up for discussion. It illustrates how the evolution of policy, which takes place against a wide range of different influences, is heavily affected by the culture of the department in question – a culture which for some departments has developed over several hundred years (or, in the case of the Treasury, since the Norman Conquest).

Departmental officials see themselves as responsible for subjecting any policy initiative from another department to an examination for its impact on whatever areas of government policy they cover. These sorts of pressures are endemic to government. The frictions they sometimes produce can best be handled when government departments cooperate fully with an agreed common purpose and a shared understanding of the policies and issues involved. Usually interdepartmental (or intradepartmental) wrangles are resolved by a decision taken on the basis of some form of collective agreement involving the lowest common denominator, often on the basis of the first text to be put on the table. It follows that where ministers have distinctive agendas, and civil servants stick closely to departmental cultures, there can be little hope of coherent and consistent policies emerging.

At times, pressures from departments on particular issues can become intense. Mrs Thatcher was right when she said that 'in politics I have learned that it is the half-hearted who lose. It is those with conviction who carry the day.' Those ministers and civil servants who heed her advice are likely to carry the day. But it would be foolish to believe that such determined people are necessarily sound thinkers, or that good arguments always win cases in Whitehall!

# CHAPTER 14

# SOME WHITEHALL FARCES

Evidence to support the assertion which concluded the last chapter is not difficult to find; what makes it worse is that the procedural mistakes and policy failures of the present often have a distinct resonance with those of the past. The current attempt by politicians to crush all inclination for learning out of children, by subjecting them to endless tests, repeats a folly of our Victorian forbears who introduced a system of payments by results into elementary schools.

This was done by Robert Lowe and his Permanent Secretary, Ralph Lingen, when Lowe was the minister in charge of the Education department. It was done in the teeth of opposition from teachers, and it was done not to further the cause of educating the working-class children who attended these schools (about whom neither Lowe nor Lingen cared in the least), but to keep education expenditure to the level of 1861; it succeeded in doing that for a decade, but at a cost of damaging the education of children.

The system was eventually dismantled in the 1890s, but the legacy of 'rigid, mechanistic, mindless habits' that it left behind took years to eradicate. Such a bitter feeling did it leave in the profession that in the 1950s I remember my primary school teacher fulminating against the system to her sympathetic East End charges. An example of the sort of rote learning of trivia that the system engendered is provided in a book called *Sententiae Chronologicae*, which contained a list of 500 dates to be learned by rote in the form of sentences from which the dates could be 'extracted' (the author's own word) by taking the first letter of each word beginning with a consonant and remembering which initial consonant represented which number. There is a certain irony in the fact that the first date to be remembered, using the snappy phrase 'read of Adam's sin and sore repentance', is that of the Creation in 4004 BC!

The effects of the testing system today are not greatly removed from those of payment by results, and while the current system has been established to raise standards of literacy and numeracy rather than to save money, it seems to be having no impact on raising standards, perhaps because it shares so many of the disadvantages of Lowe's scheme. A recent Ofsted survey of maths teaching in English schools and colleges found that, just like their Victorian counterparts, teachers were drilling pupils to learn by rote without any understanding of what they were learning. More worryingly, the survey found that the teachers could not act otherwise since they lacked any understanding of the concepts they were supposed to be teaching! A few years ago, Oftsed officials compared the UK's primary education system with those in Finland and Denmark, and found that in the relaxed, test-free environment of these two countries, children fared better than their English equivalents; the response of the UK government was to extend testing to even younger children.

If Lowe made a mess of elementary education, he did at least succeed in his stated policy of saving money. There was no such redeeming feature of Charles Trevelyan's failure to manage the supply of equipment to British troops in Crimea. In 1854, the commissariat (presided over by Trevelyan) failed to supply the army with adequate or appropriate equipment, and when the appalling conditions endured by soldiers were exposed in *The Times* by William Howard Russell, Trevelyan staunchly maintained that all was well and that the alleged failures were 'an immense crop of lies'. The failure to supply troops with adequate and appropriate equipment has been repeated regularly since then. In 1939, the British Expeditionary Force had insufficient ammunition; during the Falklands War, the MoD supplied boots that fell apart; in the Gulf War, troops were armed with rifles that did not work; during the 2003 invasion of Iraq, there were insufficient desert combat clothes and boots. The inability to admit the existence of the problem is also a state of affairs that is still with us. In 2003, the Secretary of State for Defence, Geoff Hoon, told the House of Commons Select Committee on Defence that 'all the requisite number of boots clothing and equipment were there [in Iraq]'; a year later, in April 2004, Hoon admitted that 'some of our personnel may have experienced shortages of equipment' and that the shortages 'were more serious than we believed to be the case at the time'.

In May 2004, the recently appointed Head of Defence Procurement, Sir Peter Spencer, told the same select committee that 'poor performance was endemic' in the organisation he had just taken over. He cited 'bureaucracy, lack of effective decision making and an inability to fully assess defence requirements'. Sir Peter pointed out that while his agency had devised a system called smart procurement, based on seven key principles, only one of these had been implemented. He said it would be his task to implement the other six. Faced with such a firm sense of purpose from the new broom, the committee's chairman commented that he had heard many times over the years that the MoD would put its house in order. He was right to sound a note of caution; a year later a parliamentary select committee reported that the MoD was still failing consistently to apply smart procurement rules.

Britain's railways provide an example of the failure to learn from the past, where the government's role has concerned supervision rather than direct operation. The great Victorian railway building spree was beset with problems of safety from the outset.

William Huskisson, a former president of the Board of Trade – a post which included responsibility for railway safety – was killed at the opening of the Liverpool to Manchester railway. That accident seems to have been caused by lack of understanding about the speed of locomotives, but many early railway accidents were due to inadequate equipment and poor regulatory supervision.

A few years after Huskisson's death, Robert Lowe, president of the Board of Trade, offered his Cabinet colleagues the view that the board should not take powers to prosecute companies which did not follow the safety rules strictly, but leave such matters to the courts – presumably after the event, when it was too late. Lowe was concerned that the government was being pressured to nationalise the railways; he believed that if this happened and a major accident occurred, the government would be in jeopardy. Lowe commented that 'a single fearful accident like that at Abergele would turn out a government'. On 20 August 1868, the Irish Mail crashed into some runaway goods wagons carrying paraffin; all thirty-two passengers in the front three coaches were killed in the fire that broke out. For Lowe, political convenience and utilitarian principles walked hand in hand.

Lowe's chief official responsible for railway safety was Captain Douglas Strutt Galton, an officer in the Royal Engineers. Appearing before the select committee on railway safety in 1858, Galton ducked and weaved as committee members pressed him on why the Board of Trade would not set better standards for safety. His line was that if the board set a standard for equipment such as brakes, and an improvement in brakes was then made, it would prove difficult to upgrade the standard in line with the new technology.

I think it would be very hard upon the railway companies, after having compelled them to incur an expenditure, perhaps, of £10 or £12 a carriage upon all their stock in order to adopt a particular system of breaks [sic], that you should, after the expiration of a few years, call upon them to revise that, and perhaps incur a further expenditure.

His questioner made the point that it would be 'very hard upon the people who travel by railways, if a better description of brake should be discovered, that their necks should be broken for the sake of putting so much money into the pockets of the companies.' Captain Galton agreed, but thought 'the question is so very complicated that I do not see how the thing is to be done'. Under continuing pressure, Galton fell back on Robert Lowe's utilitarian line: 'I do not see the point at which you can stop short of taking the whole management of the railways into the hands of the government if you interfere in these details.'

The debate about forcing companies to dig into profits to fund safety improvements is exactly the same one which was held after the Ladbroke Grove disaster of 5 October 1999. The technology had been available to improve safety by fitting trains with an automatic train protection system, which would prevent them from passing red danger signals. But Thames Trains had rejected such a move as too expensive some two years before the crash in which thirty-one people died. As a result of the inquiry into the Ladbroke Grove disaster, an interim system was fitted to trains, and in 2002 Railtrack announced that more than fifty trains which had passed red signals had been prevented from crashing.

But the interim system works only when trains are travelling at less than 75 mph; for complete protection the full system is needed. However, that will involve serious sums of money and the government remains unwilling for the improvement to be made. So passengers will continue to be put at risk, and the rail operating companies' pockets will be that much fuller. Similar cost considerations have dogged the issue of level crossing safety. According to the Rail Safety and Standards Board, level crossings are likely to account for nearly half the risk of future serious train crashes. Yet the rail industry – whether privately or state-run – has dragged its heels in applying the most obvious safety precautions, because of costs.

The 1988 inquiry into the Kings Cross Tube station fire of the previous year highlighted the need for an effective radio system for emergency services; eighteen years later, in the report on the 7 July 2005 terrorist attacks in London, the lack of such a system was still being cited as a major impediment for emergency services. Successive governments have tolerated this cavalier approach to the safety of passengers.

In the longer historical perspective, the failure to learn from the past can be seen most vividly in the sphere of military activity, and no finer introduction to government can be made than a close perusal of the history of military blunders. It's not just that governments have blundered at the strategic level – though they have – or that mad emperors, crazy dictators and elected politicians have committed armed forces to unwinnable wars; it is also the fact that in battles, and even during peacetime, individuals sometimes commit acts of folly which undermine the good work of their colleagues – and these individuals have exact counterparts in any modern civil organisation.

At the 1879 Battle of Isandlwana, during Britain's war against the Zulus, a quartermaster effectively ensured a British defeat in otherwise favourable circumstances by insisting that the proper paperwork was completed before releasing ammunition to his hard-pressed colleagues, and by opening only one box of ammunition at a time. Every modern organisation has his counterpart – often a number of them – and their effect on fellow workers can be just as dire as that of the quartermaster at Isandlwana. The role of this person is well understood by many in the organisation, but somehow he or she continues to exercise a baleful influence – just like someone from Dilbert (the strip cartoon character) – probably because senior managers are unaware of their existence. (Dilbert, despite its private sector context, exactly captures key elements of the bureaucratic mindset.) An important point about

Isandlwana is that it demonstrates that anyone at any level in an organisation can cause a crisis, if they are in the wrong place at the wrong time and doing the wrong thing.

The ability of some politicians and bureaucrats to keep their work free from the influence of previous relevant experience is equalled by their ability to carry forward programmes of work without reference to other contemporary activities. This goes some way to explain why governments, and even individual departments, can simultaneously espouse contradictory policies. Promoting arms exports while also participating in international peacekeeping and humanitarian relief activities is an example of very long standing. Another is to try by draconian means to prevent smuggling, while at the same time pursuing a tax regime that encourages it. This is a piece of folly that was denounced by the then president of the Board of Trade, William Huskisson, as long ago as 1825. The futility of such actions had already been exposed by William Pitt in 1786.

In the second half of the eighteenth century, tea smuggling into Britain had reached a stage where contraband supplies accounted for somewhere between a half and three-quarters of all consumption. Pitt reduced the duty on tea from 119 per cent to 12.5 per cent and killed off the smuggling overnight. He raised replacement revenue by increasing the window tax (which could be avoided to some extent by bricking up windows, but could not be evaded altogether); within a few years demand for tea had increased so much that the revenue from the lower rate of tax was above the level of 1786 and still rising.

Despite the availability of such compelling evidence, Chancellors of the Exchequer have continued to follow policies which encourage tax avoidance – particularly of alcohol and cigarettes. The advent of the single market and the cheap trips available through the Channel Tunnel, or on cross-Channel ferries, enabled people to buy alcohol cheaply and perfectly legally for their own use on a much larger scale than hitherto, and it might have been thought that the Exchequer would have sensibly thrown in the towel.

Chancellors have instead tried to implement draconian measures against those acting in perfect accord with the law. A particularly bad consequence of such policy failures is how easily they
can turn civil servants into oppressive instruments of the state. In
2001, customs officers turned a group of friends out of their car
as they were about to enter the Channel Tunnel. The officers then
seized the car and the legitimately purchased goods, and dumped
the friends at Folkestone to find their own way home to Gloucester. No doubt the customs officers justified their actions by something broadly equivalent to 'we are only obeying orders', but it is
wrong that civil servants are required to act like this in defence of
policies that were demonstrated to be counter-productive by Pitt
and derided as ineffective by William Huskisson.

As it happened, the car owner in question took Customs and
Excise to court and won, but many other people have been treated
in a similar fashion and not all of them had the ability to fight
back. It is exactly the situation faced by the Windrush generation,
who encountered hostile officials when seeking to establish that
they were in the country legally.

Similar thinking to that which motivated Pitt and Huskisson
caused the select committee on the Post Office of 1835 to inveigh
at length about the losses of postal revenue, which committee
members saw as a very strong argument against postage rates
pitched at a level that tempted evasion. Members of Parliament,
for example, were entitled to free postage and would frequently
allow their friends and relatives to send letters under cover of their
franks. They also no doubt from time to time would take money
for allowing others to do so.

Evasion was widely practised by inventive use of newspapers,
which attracted a lower rate of postage – printed letters were
pricked on a prearranged plan so as to send messages in code; old
newspapers were used as a preconcerted signal of the occurrence
of some event, or small changes in the addressee's name or title
would be used to convey trade information. Finally, since payment

was made by the recipient of correspondence and not the sender, the recipient could decline payment and refuse to accept the letter, because by virtue of the letter having been sent the recipient would know that the sender was still in the land of the living. The select committee's report helped introduce the Penny Post, which eliminated evasion and turned the Post Office into a very large cash generator for successive governments until very recent years.

A contemporary and equally perverse folly is the practice of tackling drug culture by putting drug users in prisons where they can easily obtain supplies and where they are likely to meet dealers and forge connections, so that upon release they may get into the supply side as well. A splendid example of governments' addiction to un-joined-up government was evidenced when the then Conservative Prisons spokeswoman gave a rousing speech against drugs at the Tory Party conference before joining her colleagues on the platform to celebrate her birthday with champagne. She was happy to flaunt her own use of a recreational drug in public while condemning the users of other recreational drugs. Drugs are now big business, and as sensible and sober commentators such as *The Economist* have pointed out, until there is no money to be made, business will continue to be booming. More alcohol was consumed in America during prohibition than before.

The failure of dumb Chancellors of the Exchequer down the ages to recognise the futility of policies that encourage smuggling is only matched by their obstinacy in believing, against all the evidence, that they alone can impose an enforcement regime of sufficient ferocity to end smuggling. Each new haul of drugs or alcohol is heralded as the sign of the triumph of the policy, instead of being admitted as all too convincing evidence of its failure. Gilbert and Sullivan, in their operetta, *Iolanthe*, suggested that MPs had to leave their brains outside the House of Commons: one can't help wondering if something similar occurs in the foyer of the Treasury each morning.

By comparison, the policy of levying penal rates of tax on

motorists while grossly underfunding the transport infrastructure seems a minor folly. It has been estimated that the government takes some £42 billion a year in taxes on motorists, yet the central government road budget is not quite £7 billion. As the National Audit Office has pointed out, the Highways Agency spends less than 12 per cent of its budget on making better use of the existing infrastructure, while the economic cost of road congestion has reached some £3 billion a year. Most of the time the UK's road network is adequate enough to meet demand, but quite often it is not; yet with a minimal amount of effort (others have shown the way) and for little cost, significant improvements could be made. The penal imposts on motorists might be acceptable if the government used the money to fund improvements to public transport, but although the UK has the fastest rate of growth in train passengers in Europe, the government has refused to spend the large sums needed to offset the years of previous underfunding of the rail network since nationalisation in 1948.

Such stresses are by no means unique to the public sector; they can also be seen in industry in the endless battles between purchasing, manufacturing and sales departments. But in the commercial world the stresses are subject to the discipline of profit – and ultimately of bankruptcy; in government, the contradictions can co-exist for years funded by the luckless taxpayer. During the 1950s and 1960s, for example, the UK economy was held back by a preoccupation with the balance of payments (a result of maintaining a fixed parity for the pound) masterminded, according to the economist Andrew Shonfield, by 'government officials who make it a point of professional pride to keep their eyes blinkered against all considerations other than the balance of payments'. The private sector was berated for failing to invest adequately while, to finance the balance of payments, successive governments directed tax policy so as to penalise investment and research and development. It is doubtful that a company which pursued unsuccessful strategies with such consistency would last for twenty years.

One feature of the propensity to work in watertight compartments is particularly annoying to the public. It consists of not providing relevant information unless asked for it specifically and correctly. It is rather like the children's party game of pinning the tail on the donkey, except that the public often are not told of the existence of the donkey, let alone the tail. It is something that drives businessmen to distraction and many of the least advantaged to the courts, and often into jail.

A significant number of those accused of benefits fraud, for example, would have been better off claiming the correct benefit than they were in fraudulently claiming the wrong one, but too often they do not receive adequate, understandable or appropriate advice to enable them to make a correct claim. Sometimes this is because staff administering the benefit lack an adequate understanding of the system themselves because of its complexity (a problem Lord Rayner noted in the 1980s when he was appointed to run the Efficiency Unit), but sometimes it is because staff are unhelpful.

The public may feel that they are uniquely disadvantaged in this way, but in fact some bureaucrats delight in playing the same game with their fellow workers. The failure of individuals in different authorities to cooperate in preventing tragedies to children in care is a different, and awful, example of this sort of attitude. Often enough such tragedies are blamed on a failure of the authorities to cooperate, but of course this means that individuals failed to cooperate. It is depressing that this particularly pernicious failure of government has been openly supported by two heads of the Home Civil Service – Sir Robert Armstrong during his evidence in the prosecution of the author of *Spycatcher*, when he seemed quite pleased to have been 'economical with the truth', and Sir Robin Butler in his evidence to the Scott Inquiry on Arms Exports to Iraq, where he thought it appropriate to disclose only 10 per cent of the picture so long as the 10 per cent was accurate. If top public servants think it appropriate not to disclose the full picture, why should some harassed clerk take a more lofty view?

In the United Kingdom, the reports of the House of Commons Public Accounts Committee provide a regular catalogue of administrative catastrophes, and for those with an interest in blood sports the transcripts of the committee proceedings are well worth reading. The committee's forte is to subject Permanent Secretaries to a public grilling, often for the sins of their predecessors. The committee's position was put forcefully by Alan Williams MP, when a new accounting officer was incautious enough to say he could not answer for questions which predated his arrival.

> Yes, you do. Excuse me, that is what you are here to do; that is the accounting officer's role. It is why we do not haul all your predecessors out of retirement, and when we try, to get screams from the Cabinet Office at our attempts to do so. Your job is to answer for your predecessors as well as yourself.

By this time the accounting officer had got the message, and explained that what he had intended to say was that he didn't know why a certain decision had been taken. An extreme example of this process was provided by the newly appointed Permanent Secretary of the Department for the Environment, Food and Rural Affairs, Brian Bender, trying to explain in 2003 why nothing had been done about a recommendation on foot-and-mouth disease that had been made in 1967! His answer was that no one in the department now understood the point at issue.

One thing that particularly aggravates the committee is that the same issues crop up time and time again. Their very special bête noire is the practice of extending contracts without going to tender. This is widely done to save time and effort, but it does tend to keep costs up. The problem is not a new one; in 1835, the commissioners appointed by Parliament to examine the Post Office found the cost of buying mail coaches was too high because the purchase contract was not open to competitive bidding. They recommended that the contractor, who had held the contract for some forty years, be given an extension of his current contract for six months only, and that models and drawings for improved mail coaches be invited. When the contractor declined to accept such an extension of his contract, the third report of the commissioners recommended that the Post Office ask for bids and that he be banned from the process. This change was effected by Parliament in the same year.

Normally the Treasury takes a fairly tough line on such matters, but in 1873 the Chancellor of the Exchequer, Robert Lowe again, managed to get personally involved in awarding the Post Office contract for the Zanzibar mail service, without any proper tendering process and for a vastly inflated sum. This time the driver was Lowe's dislike of his Financial Secretary, and of the red tape which the latter clearly enjoyed. Lowe was also impatient with the Postmaster General, who objected to the whole scheme, which had been dreamed up as a cut-price way of bribing the Sultan of Zanzibar into stopping slavery.

The ensuing parliamentary rumpus (coinciding with financial irregularities at the Post Office) led Lowe to resign as Chancellor. He did himself no favours with a truly lamentable performance at the dispatch box when the matter was first raised in the House. One MP commented that 'a speech less calculated to conciliate the judgement of the House, or to persuade it that this arrangement was for the public advantage, he had never heard'.

A hundred years later, in 1967, the Public Accounts Committee complained that the Post Office was obtaining only 25 per cent of its telephone equipment and 10 per cent of its exchange equipment by competitive tendering. The rest of the equipment was obtained under 'bulk supply agreements' with groups of manufacturers who negotiated common prices with the Post Office and allocated production among themselves. The committee welcomed the news that the Post Office did not intend to renew the agreement for telephone apparatus when it expired in 1968.

Between July 1992 and February 1993, the Departments of Health and Social Security relocated a substantial amount of their head-quarters' work to new, purpose-built offices in Leeds – Quarry House. The Department of Social Security led the management of the construction project. Quarry House was constructed within the budget of £85.2 million and occupied by the planned date of February 1993. However, the building was designed in such a way as to have 1,850 square metres less space than the department had specified; even after the contractor had fitted out the roof space free of charge there still remained a shortfall of 460 square metres. When members of the Public Accounts Committee looked into the matter, they concerned themselves mainly with this shortfall and other design deficiencies. But they also noted and criticised the fact that, during the project, consultants' contracts were re-newed without retendering.

As well as addressing specific cases, the Public Accounts Com-mittee looks at the lessons to be learned from them in general. Unsurprisingly, committee members have concluded that de-partments should base policy-making on sufficient and reliable information considered by staff with appropriate research and analytical skills; that departments should test how the policies are likely to work in practice; that they should consider the impli-cation of proposed policies on existing policies of their own and other departments; and that those involved in delivering policies should be consulted at an early stage of policy development. As a set of precepts for good policy-making they are sound; the evi-dence suggests they are not widely observed in Whitehall.

The repetitive nature of the issues that come before the Public Accounts Committee reinforces the point that there is little inter-est among civil servants in learning from the mistakes of others. Although more senior civil servants are aware of the committee, its reports are not widely read and so it is not too surprising that the lessons are not absorbed. Detailed knowledge of the activities of the Public Accounts Committee is far more limited than its members might care to believe, and in particular a vast army of middle-ranking staff and outsourced service providers, who between them place a large volume of contracts, are almost totally oblivious of the committee's concerns about their everyday actions.

It is a bit odd that in a knowledge-based economy the Public Accounts Committee does not take steps to ensure its views are more widely known; the existing feedback system that was adequate for a civil service of the size Gladstone knew is no longer adequate for one which now numbers some 450,000. The formal position is that the Treasury respond to each report advising the committee of their response to recommendations. The appropriate changes are then made to the formidable tome known as government accounting, which sets out the rules for all financial matters relating to central government and is never referred to by most civil servants at any point in their careers, and whose existence is probably only known by a select few in central finance departments.

The disinclination to learn lessons from the past not only means that mistakes are repeated, but that good examples of effective administration are not copied. Lord Rayner, while in charge of the Efficiency Unit, understood that many civil servants did have a great deal of useful knowledge and regretted that it was not tapped more widely by ministers; all too often it is not tapped by their colleagues either. Lord Rayner probably also realised that while knowledgeable civil servants can be of assistance to governments when devising new policies, they can be of even greater value when the government is in a hole.

Given the penchant for everyday detail shown in his diaries, it is not surprising that Samuel Pepys provides a good example of a bureaucrat doing a stalwart job in just such circumstances. In 1667, following a disastrous war with the Dutch during which British naval vessels were burnt by the Dutch in the Medway, Pepys, as Secretary of the Navy Board and Surveyor-General of Victualling, had repeatedly advised King Charles II about the woeful state of the navy; he was totally ignored. Following the debacle in the

Medway, a humiliating peace treaty was signed. Parliament established a committee to investigate what had gone wrong. Pepys was hauled before the committee for what was expected to be a pretty brutal mauling, but delivered a three-hour tour de force and won universal plaudits. He was able to do this because of the huge effort he put into understanding his work: visiting the dockyards for which he was responsible, getting to know the people who ran them, and having all the facts and figures at his fingertips.

At that time, such detailed understanding of government business was pretty rare. Fortunately, it is less rare now, but it is not common. A good contemporary example of how powerful such command of the facts can be is provided by the epidemic of foot-and-mouth disease in the spring of 2001. By the end of March that year, the government's recently appointed chief scientific advisor, Professor David King, knew from computer modelling which he had commissioned at three universities that the disease was out of control, and that a cull of animals was the only thing that would bring it to heel. The policy was hugely contentious, but it was adopted and proved to be successful. It was adopted because the facts were established in a way which gave them immense credibility, and they were then presented persuasively.

Not all problems are caused by poor advice; they may arise if the advice offered and the facts upon which the advice is based do not fit the required political solution, or the current perceived wisdom as to the nature of the problem itself. This is not a new phenomenon either. In 1833, the government of Earl Grey appointed a royal commission under the chairmanship of the Protestant Archbishop of Dublin, Dr Whately (a political economist), which sat from 1833 to 1836 and made a close examination of social conditions and attitudes through the land. The commission produced a wide-ranging paper on the Irish economy and made a number of sensible proposals. The commission had examined carefully the issue of workhouses and concluded that as the problem in Ireland was one of too little available work, they could not recommend the system 'as at all suited to Ireland'. The conditions in Ireland were vastly different from those in England and Wales, where plenty of work was available for those who wished to do it, and it was therefore wrong to adopt the same plan for relieving poverty.

By the time the commission presented its report, the government had changed and the Home Secretary, Lord (John) Russell, did not like the commission's findings. 'They have bestowed too great a degree of consideration to the question by what means, and by what State resources, you can improve the general welfare of the country, and have not confined themselves entirely to the destitute classes, which was more particularly put into their hands.' The commission's report was shelved, and the government decided that relief of the destitute in Ireland should be investigated by someone with knowledge of the English Poor Laws; it was not thought necessary that the person should also know something of Ireland. George Nicholls, one of the English Poor Law commissioners, was appointed to carry out the investigation. He ignored the conclusions of the report of the royal commission, and on the basis of a six-week stay (having never been in Ireland before), he produced a report recommending that the well-thought-out reasoning in the commission's report be set aside in favour of the introduction of workhouses.

The report was in the early stages of implementation when Ireland was hit by famine. By this time the government had changed yet again, and Peel was Prime Minister; he had some knowledge of Ireland and took reasonably speedy steps to address the problems the Great Famine caused. Loans were advanced to give the destitute employment, and cargoes of maize brought from America and sold at cost price. Work funded by the Treasury was created to provide employment. It was not vastly different from what Dr Whately's commission had recommended. But Peel had committed political suicide by repealing the Corn Laws; his government fell and Lord John Russell became Prime Minister. The starving poor of Ireland now fell into the charge of Charles

Trevelyan at the Treasury, who believed the Irish were getting their comeuppance from God for being lazy. He recommended to the Cabinet that the distribution of subsidised food should be drastically reduced, that the programme of works be increased but locally financed, and that the supply of corn should be left to the free market.

Given Lord John Russell's earlier views, it is not surprising that Trevelyan was given pretty much a free hand on the matter. In November 1847, the Commissary-General, who was on the scene and could see what was happening, proposed that the export of corn from Ireland to Britain should be stopped. But Trevelyan, operating from his comfortable office in the Treasury, firmly rejected the suggestion. It is estimated that at least a million people died from starvation and other diseases during the Great Famine of 1845–52, while a further million emigrated. The workhouse system in Ireland almost collapsed under the strain and a number of workhouses closed, leaving their occupants without any means of support. George Nicholls could not be blamed for the famine, but if he had not dismissed the proposals of the Irish Commission of Poor Inquiry, the country might have been better able to cope.

Some seventy years later, at the Versailles peace conference in 1918, the British Prime Minister Lloyd George, the French President Clemenceau and President Woodrow Wilson of the United States ignored the advice of an impressive array of special advisors (including John Maynard Keynes, Henry Cabot Lodge, John Foster Dulles, Jan Smuts and Herbert Hoover) with consequences that are still proving fatal in the Balkans and the Middle East.

Many experts visited the relevant areas and brought back valuable local knowledge, but the three leaders in their Parisian hotels set this knowledge aside and stitched up deals on the basis of prejudice and ignorance – even ignoring their own foreign ministers in the process. For six months, three people who imagined themselves to be the most powerful in the world, and who perhaps were the most powerful, gave the most awful demonstration of the evils of giving power to those who do not understand how to seek and take advice.

More recently, in the period since the Second World War, there have been two spectacular instances of Prime Ministers hurling themselves to a premature political death in the teeth of well-informed advice. Officials were pretty well united in opposing Anthony Eden's decision to attack Egypt in 1956 after President Nasser nationalised the Suez Canal, and were particularly outraged by the despicable way in which the secret deal with Israel and France was cooked up. Eden drove his law officers to the brink of resignation by not seeking their advice as to the legal basis for his action (and at a meeting with them failed to persuade them he was acting legally), but his obsession with Nasser drove him to ignore advice he did not want to hear. Less damaging to the country in international terms, but nearly as divisive internally, was Mrs Thatcher's attempt to resurrect the poll tax. She was persuaded to launch this kamikaze policy initiative by academics with little experience of government, against the advice of many of her colleagues and her civil servants – particularly those in the Treasury.

The results were predictable. When a previous poll tax had been introduced way back in 1381, two of King Richard II's councillors, Archbishop Sudbury and Treasurer Hales, were killed in the ensuing revolt. The 1990 version of the poll tax also gave rise to riots, and while no politicians were killed this time around, it was as a direct consequence of the tax fiasco that Mrs Thatcher met her political death.

# CHAPTER 15

# WHERE WILL IT ALL END?

That the civil service has a widespread problem with leadership and management is beyond dispute. The apparent inability of either ministers or top civil servants to introduce the necessary cultural change to alter this state of affairs is, in no small measure, a result of their failure to understand the nature of the Victorian reforms of the civil service, and of the implications of those reforms for the direction that the civil service subsequently took. The generally held view of those reforms would probably run along the lines of an editorial in *The Times* of 27 October 1933:

> The time came when amateurs could no longer cope with the work ... The Civil Service, as we know it, dates only from 1855. At that date the British people – with the gravest misgivings, which their Queen shared – made up its mind to have its laws administered by professionals. And, since it had to submit to that necessary evil, it decided to have the best professionals in the world.

But this view is quite wrong. The reforms of 1855 made little or no difference to the sort of people who ran Britain. The creation of the Civil Service Commission was a helpful step in starting to eliminate entry into the civil service of the totally unfitted, but patronage continued with only the most modest element of competition, and civil servants still came from the same back-grounds and with the same range of abilities.

The date when something really significant did happen was November 1854, when Sir Charles Wood fell for the chicanery of the Rev. Dr Benjamin Jowett and destroyed Haileybury, the establishment that had been producing professional civil servants for nearly fifty years. Without any consideration of the implications of the decision for the government of India, the government resolutely turned its back on the idea of a professional civil service and decided instead to put the day-to-day running of India into the hands of classical scholars who had spent three years rubbing shoulders with similar men, and whose only claim to administrative competence was an ability to construe Latin and Greek rather better than their peers; as Macaulay himself put it so well, they were the men 'who understood the Cherokee best, who made the most correct and melodious Cherokee verses – who comprehended most accurately the effect of the Cherokee particles'.

Benjamin Jowett's successful attack on professionalism was given a new lease of life with Robert Lowe's reforms of 1870, which applied to this country the same prescription that had been applied to India. The possibility of establishing a professional civil service here had never been contemplated by Queen Victoria or anyone else. The question was simply whether the top administrative jobs were filled by patronage or by competition. The Queen did have doubts about that, but Gladstone's crusade against patronage carried the day. Robert Lowe was less concerned with the battle against patronage; his aim was to use competition as a means of ensuring that the lower orders were firmly barred from the top jobs.

The reforms instituted by Lowe, and more particularly his protégé Lingen, failed to achieve Lowe's aim, since this was based upon a quite false premise that poor people could not be clever. But the reforms did eventually restrict recruitment into the civil service to those with a particular set of qualifications, even though these qualifications were not unique to civil servants, and had little or no relevance to the work that was increasingly being carried out by them. By the end of the nineteenth century, virtually all top posts were filled by promoting sharp young classicists from Oxbridge who had entered the service straight from university, had no experience of work elsewhere and, as Deputy Prime Minister Clement Attlee put it in 1944, had 'little opportunity of taking a critical and informed view of the methods of doing business'. This situation had been foreseen by one of Trevelyan's critics back in 1854. In commenting upon the Northcote–Trevelyan Report, Captain O'Brien (the Private Secretary of the First Lord of the Admiralty) had written, 'Who so narrow-minded as mere college men? Who so unfit to manage human affairs generally as the mere learned and scientific!' O'Brien was perhaps overreacting to Trevelyan's plan, but Attlee's more measured comment was right on target.

The impact of Lowe's handiwork took some time to affect all parts of the civil service, as there were many young people in posts in 1870 who did not have an Oxbridge classics background, and it took time for Lingen and his successors in the Treasury to reduce the number of posts which might be recruited by selection as opposed to competition. By the 1930s, however, the process was fairly well complete. The apprehensions of those like Rowland Hill, who had opposed Trevelyan's original proposals to select administrators solely on the basis of a 'literary' exam, had been thoroughly substantiated. As the century progressed, detailed knowledge of the Victorian reforms was lost and the nature (and shortcomings) of the civil service were increasingly attributed not to the practice of selecting recruits from such a narrow range of people, but to a non-existent grand design of the Victorians. An editorial in *The Observer* on 7 October 1945, for example, noted that 'the civil service was built up as a defensive body, safeguarding the old way of life, not as a creative body laying down the pattern of a new way … The Victorian state … asked of its officials care, deliberation and thrift, and the whole civil service technique was fashioned to provide these.'

But that assertion is not borne out by the facts; the civil service became defensive and inward-looking because its intake came from such a narrow base. The civil service of the nineteenth century had been particularly proactive in a number of fields, notably in employment legislation, safety at work and public health, and in developing the postal services. It was perhaps no coincidence that it was in those departments – the Board of Trade, the Factory Inspectorate and the Post Office – where women made progress in gaining more senior jobs.

The ability of Frank Scudamore to realise the potential of the women recruited to the Post Office was not that of a man 'safeguarding the old way of life'. He was not alone. Hubert Llewellyn Smith came second in the open competition of 1886 and was offered a post in the War Office, but his Quaker connections caused him to turn it down. He then turned his energy to social affairs in the East End of London, and to involvement with various organisations concerned with social, political and economic questions. He established a significant reputation and when Anthony Mundella, the president of the Board of Trade, came to establish a new labour department, he secured the services of Llewellyn Smith as the first labour commissioner. Llewellyn Smith attacked the work with energy and with the benefit of seven years' experience of working in the East End. His department analysed the reasons for unemployment as well as recording the jobless statistics; strikes and lock-outs were also recorded and within a year the first annual abstract of labour statistics was published. Even before that, the department had commenced production of the *Labour Gazette*, with the novel aim of providing workers with a means of obtaining prompt and accurate information on labour issues. This was not by any stretch of imagination the work of a 'defensive body safeguarding the old way of life'; it was a bold and highly effective administrative development which was to lead directly to the establishment of labour exchanges, to the beginnings of employment protection legislation and, some seventy years later, to the establishment of Acas (the Advisory, Conciliation and Arbitration Service).

While particular individuals and departments continued to make a positive impact on administration, the constricting effects of confining recruitment to one special group of people created a general trend towards conservatism that accounted for the long-term discrimination against women, and opposition to the very thought of establishing a civil service staff college. It produced the complacent remoteness over the victims of the Blitz that so riled *The Observer* in 1946.

Complacent remoteness was not a criticism that could have been levelled at Anthony Trollope as he roamed the countryside, determining postmen's rounds and checking up on local postmasters. Nor was it one that could have been levelled against early women factory inspectors like Hilda Martindale, as they took on the sweatshops and the employers of child labour. But it was a criticism that could certainly have been levelled against Balliol men such as Francis Palgrave and Matthew Arnold, who used the Education department as a means of financing their literary ambitions, and whose interest in the education of the children of the labouring classes was limited or non-existent. Such men set an unfortunate precedent, and while their successors were not as universally useless as Jowett's early protégés, there was certainly a tendency to value being clever over being effective.

Criticism of the civil service became more widespread during the 1950s, particularly by those on the political left, and gave rise to the jibe that Britain was being administered by gifted amateurs. One of the most notable blasts came from economist Thomas Balogh in his essay 'The Apotheosis of the Dilettante: the Establishment of Mandarins'. Ironically, Balogh was a senior tutor and fellow of Balliol; he seemed unaware that the 'dilettantes' who had provoked his ire were the creation of Jowett, his predecessor at Balliol, not as part of any grand design for the governance of the country, but simply as a career path for graduates who did not want to join the Church or become lawyers.

Balogh regarded the civil service as the creation of the Victorians and as part of an overall scheme of negativity; an attempt to suppress initiative and create what he termed a 'night watchman state'. As already noted, the facts simply do not support this analysis; Frank Scudamore, for example, showed such initiative that it cost the Chancellor of the Exchequer his job! But by the 1950s the narrow range of recruitment, combined with a failure to employ specialists such as economists and statisticians in significant numbers, and a reluctance to let such specialists as there were get their hands on policy-making, was becoming a serious problem. This was particularly so in the context of governments which sought to extend the boundaries of the state and to manage the economy. Balogh's criticisms, though they rested on a faulty understanding of the history of the Victorian reforms, were not misplaced. The Balliol juggernaut was running out of steam.

Not only were the mandarins recruited from a narrow base, but the split between them and the rest of the civil servants remained as firm as ever; there was little if any promotion from the other ranks, despite the presence in these ranks of many people who could have taken over from the mandarins with ease. This was the point Thomas Farrer had made in his response to Robert Lowe's proposals in 1870, when he noted the need to ensure that good staff in the junior grades would be able to progress to the first division. There were those within the civil service who understood the problem. In 1941, a senior civil servant in the Ministry of Pensions wrote to the secretary of the Civil Service Commission in the context of the committee looking at the postwar civil service. He pointed out that 99 per cent of assistant principals were promoted to principal by the age of thirty 'even if they are not really fit for advancement'. He then outlined two major problems:

Some of the young men and women who come into the service are extremely superior – in fact they regard themselves as Brahmins. In some departments nothing is done to knock this idea out of their heads, with the result that they become more and more superior and more and more contemptuous of the world at large which they regard as their intellectual inferiors. They may well be right, but it does not make them good administrators … the young administrator should have more practical education in his early years. In other words, he starts right in on paper and never stops: he is never called upon to do a practical job of work.

It was a lucid description of the legacy of the Victorian reforms. It was a problem that could have been reduced by promoting executive class officers to the administrative grade. In the 1950s and 1960s, junior staff often had extensive management experience. Even more importantly, they often had extensive experience of dealing with the public, including sections of it which would have been totally unfamiliar to many of the mandarins. They could have brought wider perspectives to the top posts. But such a move was anathema to the mandarins; the brahmins had to maintain the caste system. The position was worsened by the impact of the reduction in the numbers of civil servants under the Conservative governments of the 1950s and '60s; with recruitment and promotions scarce or non-existent, the civil service was ageing. When I joined the Ministry of Power in the last months of Harold Macmillan's stint as Prime Minister, the department had just had its first promotions for fifteen years. It all reinforced the general level of stultification.

My purpose is not sociological; I am concerned with the way the civil service is organised and how this affects its ability to carry out the activities required of it. While it is true that the scope of the work of the civil service had, by the 1960s, changed out of all recognition since the 1860s, the work of the 'intellectuals' had not changed in terms of process, only in terms of the subject matter; this still holds true forty years later. Bismarck is supposed to have said that only two people understood the Schleswig-Holstein question, of whom one was mad and the other dead; Victorian civil servants who had to brief on the issue might be thought to have been every bit as taxed as a modern counterpart briefing a minister on an EU directive specifying the right radius for a banana.

The work of a senior civil servant today would have been readily understood by members of the Playfair Commission of 1870, who saw that 'those higher posts involved responsibility, discretion and power to direct work and deal with the outside public in such a manner as to uphold the credit and efficiency of their departments'. It is mianly senior civil servants who deal with the vast army of government relations experts employed by private sector companies, trade associations and special interest organisations. It is senior civil servants who decide how replies to ministerial correspondence and parliamentary questions are to be drafted. It is they who take responsibility for briefing ministers and attending key policy meetings. They must be adept at précis and drafting, and quick-witted enough to deal with sudden shifts of policy – often in response to events outside their control. They spend a high proportion of their time at meetings of one sort or another, so they need to be smooth operators in that environment. Above all, they need to understand the mindset of their ministers. These are the unchanging requirements of those who work closely with ministers; such requirements would not only have been recognised by the Victorians but by those in similar positions as far back as the Tudor era. While the context and the subject matter may have changed out of all recognition, the requirements of the work have not.

The same is not true of work at the lower levels. In 1870, the 'mechanical' work, as noted above, was basically that of the 'accountants and copy-boys' who allegedly caused such annoyance to the Duke of Wellington, and while such work is still to be found, most of it is carried out by computers and photocopying machines; the great majority of those employed below the level of the senior civil service are nowadays engaged in far more demanding work, which has a great impact on what the Playfair Commission called 'the outside public'. It is these civil servants who take the decisions as to how working tax credits and a whole raft of other benefits apply in particular cases; who decide whether specific highly complex equipment needs an export licence; who investigate breaches of company law; who assess the capabilities of weapons systems; who manage major works projects; and organise the distribution of overseas aid. These are not mechanical and monotonous tasks of the sort envisaged by the Playfair Commission, which they thought would be 'rarely calculated to develop superior capabilities'. The work is precisely the sort that involves 'responsibility, discretion and the power to direct work and deal with the outside public in such a manner as to uphold the credit and efficiency of their departments.' In short, when performed well, it is the type of work the Playfair Commission envisaged being done by the more senior staff, and certainly those who do perform it well make excellent candidates for the senior civil service.

The premise that policy work is more difficult than any other type of work is false, but because so few civil servants have experience of both, the myth persists. One reason for this is that the intellectuals tend to see only the work of their immediate support staff, who do indeed tend to do the sort of work denominated by Trevelyan as mechanical. But outside the immediate vicinity of the intellectuals' offices, a whole range of work is carried out that is highly complex, intellectually demanding and usually fairly invisible to the top management. A bright, fast-stream civil servant who was put in charge of a major project to move some 400 staff into new accommodation was invited to report on progress to her department's top management; she told them in forceful terms that the task was by far the most difficult she had faced in her career. Within the civil service it would be difficult to think of a task further removed from the normal range of fast-stream experience than accommodation, and yet, if the top brass only knew it, such work can pose the most demanding problems, and provide first-class opportunities for learning how to cope with complex and fast-moving situations.

The same levels of complexity would be posed by any number of Trevelyan's 'routine' operations, as the staff of many executive agencies and non-departmental public bodies (quangos) could testify. Yet most senior civil servants have been nowhere near this sort of work during their formative years, and thus they arrive in the senior civil service with little experience of management or of how routine work is done at all, let alone how it is done well. My own experience can stand as a good example. For some twenty years I worked in small units, never managing more than eight staff. When I reached what is now the senior civil service, I was put in charge of some 240 people, including 180 technical staff dispersed round the country. It was expected that I would be able to manage them, although it was not anticipated that this would take up much of my time, which was to be mainly devoted to relevant policy issues – which were the only reason for having a senior civil servant there in the first place. One of my colleagues had a similar experience. When he was appointed to a new post, he was told that managing the work of a large group of staff en-gaged in licensing would only occupy about 10 per cent of his time, whereas the small group of staff engaged on trade policy work would require virtually all his attention. Licensing was an area of work that was clearly seen as of little importance and less glamour; the magic word 'policy' indicated important work and lots of opportunities for ministerial contact (and overseas travel).

As it happened, the licensing work in question involved ex-ports of arms, and within a few weeks my colleague was up to his neck in Matrix Churchill, the supergun saga, and, just for good measure, the row over the export of Antonio Canova's statue, 'The Three Graces'– and by that time so was I. Mechanical work turned out to be every bit as challenging as policy-making! Civil service fast-streamers are generally not given practical experience of mechanical work, and they are not provided with practical training in management. As one put it to me, 'We are being trained for the civil service of twenty-five years ago.' But it could be argued that this person is wrong, and that it is actually the civil service of 1870 for which the training is really provided.

The training provision for fast-streamers is heavily skewed towards the traditional top civil service skills of being good on paper. As Trollope put it in his novel *The Three Clerks*:

> Mr Précis' peculiar forte was a singular happiness in official phraseology ... He knew well, none perhaps so well, when to beg leave to lay before the Board – and when simply to submit to the Commissioners. He understood exactly to whom it behove the secretary 'to have the honour of being a very humble servant,' and to whom the more simple 'I am, sir,' was a sufficiently civil declaration. These are qualifications great in official life.

They are indeed, but they do little to address the pronounced weakness in management skills brought about by the recruitment process. It is a weakness that has been noted in departments' investors-in-people assessments and has recently been vividly illustrated in the evidence to the Hutton Inquiry, and in the bizarre occurrences at the Department of Transport in the wake of special advisor Jo Moore's gaffe about it being a good day to bury news.

The civil service has no monopoly on bad management, as the evidence of employment tribunal cases up and down the country regularly demonstrates, but because of the nature of its work, any weakness can be more damaging in its consequences. The civil service is a very large service organisation, and in service organisations staff attitudes have an enormous impact, and poor management produces poor staff attitudes. As a former director-general of the Institute of Directors noted, 'There is almost no extreme of poor performance which cannot be reached by a person or group of people given sufficient lack of encouragement.' If top civil servants don't look after their own staff, what hope can their customers have of a fair deal? A junior civil servant who publicly humiliated a benefit-seeker responded to a remonstration by a third party with the words, 'You can't complain; we treat everybody this way!' It is perhaps no wonder that in a recent survey of those asked which profession provided particularly good examples of leadership, only 3 per cent mentioned the civil service.

I once asked the head of human resources at a well-known car hire company how they managed to maintain high standards of customer care. Her answer was that they had created a climate in which those people who did not care about customers didn't feel comfortable working for the company. I was struck by the contrast with my experience of the civil service, where, despite the presence of a good number of really helpful staff, the time-wasters and time-servers did not feel uncomfortable. Despite all the rhetoric, the civil service still does not have enough people who understand how to manage, and certainly not enough who want to manage. I once heard an under-secretary complaining to his minister, 'Why don't you let me stop mucking about with all this management nonsense and get on with my real job?' That lack of understanding and interest feeds all the way down to the most junior levels. Within such a large organisation there will always be beacons of excellence, but poor management is often a major cause of delivery failures. And when poor management is coupled with silly political deadlines (or just silly politicians), or inadequate or inappropriate resources, the scene is set for a first-class cock-up.

The failure to create a culture of management excellence is not the exclusive preserve of the civil service; other parts of the public sector are equally affected. There are, as I have pointed out, many hard-working and conscientious people in central government, and there are very many also in other parts of the public sector.

They, too, are often let down by colleagues who simply do not care and by management that fails to weed out the unsuitable or challenge inappropriate behaviour.

The 2003 report of the inquiry into the death of Victoria Climbié, while she was under the supposed protection of Haringey Social Services, revealed an awful but instantly recognisable picture of work that had fallen completely into the hands of those without any real aptitude or ability to even begin to address the difficult tasks they faced. A major problem was that the top managers were out of touch with their staff and therefore did not understand the extent to which they, as senior managers, were risking the lives of those who were in their charge. The terrible consequence of this particular failure rams home the point that the impact of bad management is not something which is contained within an organisation, but has direct and significant impact on the outside world. Since so much of government (prisons, courts, the health service, childcare, benefit systems, supervision of the public utilities) impacts directly on peoples' lives, it is simply not acceptable to allow poor management to continue to be a feature of the public sector. But if the top management possess poor management skills themselves, and their political masters none at all, then it is difficult for them to know how to effect change for the better.

That there have been changes is true, and many of these have been changes for the better. People with practical and successful experience outside Whitehall are now being recruited, and many are having a beneficial impact. But Gladstone and Trevelyan's concerns about costs have been realised. In one of his last appearances as Cabinet Secretary, Sir Andrew Turnbull drew attention to the dangers of the two-tier pay system developing in Whitehall, which he suggested might well become indefensible. Other changes have turned the clock back to the mid-Victorian period, most notably the reversion to paying staff in different departments different rates of pay for the same work.

The bureaucracy in this country can trace its origins to Norman

England. In all that time there has only been one detailed, systematic and effective attempt to assess the task of administration and to tailor the recruitment, training and promotion of administrators to meet that task. The Fulton Committee did a reasonable job, but its aim of creating an open system under which staff needed only to demonstrate competence to get to the top has been extensively subverted by the creation of the senior civil service. While the top posts are no longer the preserve of white males with Oxbridge degrees, the Civil Service College has not survived. Training is available to all grades, and the need for policy-makers to have a better grasp of statistical analysis is recognised a little more widely. It has to be admitted, however, that recognising the need for better analysis is not the same as getting better analysis bedded into the culture. It would be interesting to know how many civil servants have even heard of the 'Adding It Up' report, or how many have read it and sought to apply its principles.

It is probably true that the civil service is now more effective than the service that Jowett and Trevelyan undermined, and it is certainly a great deal more effective than the civil service examined by the Fulton Committee. But there is still a long way to go for it to become truly fit for purpose.

Many of the remaining problems facing the civil service stem from the continuing elitist split between the intellectuals and the mechanicals. This split was based on a totally outdated perception of the nature of the work, and upon an irrational fear of democracy which has no place in an open and quite reasonably democratic society. The flawed thinking which has kept it in place has been increasingly undermined by the move towards open recruitment for the top jobs. This development has demonstrated that there is no requirement to have a double-first from Oxbridge to be able to hold down a top job, and that what counts is the ability to deliver the goods. There is no reason why a graduate-entry fast stream should not continue, so long as ways can be found of preventing the selection process remaining discriminatory. Women and members of ethnic minorities are just as likely to make good administrators as white Oxbridge males.

But the continuance of the fast stream should be balanced by giving mainstream civil servants the opportunity to develop their full potential and to rise as high as their abilities allow, without creating elitist obstacles to progress. Equally, fast-streamers need to be given a much wider range of relevant experience – in management and policy delivery in particular – so that they can compete against mainstream civil servants and outside recruits on the basis of achievement, rather than by academic excellence and attendance at the right university.

The British civil service, for all its faults, contains many really able people. But for the greater part of the past 130 years, it has been organised to get the least out of most of them. Perhaps the time has come to think about making the most of the available talent; it is not always present in the obvious places. Some thirty years ago, a young scaffolder got married. His wife grew concerned at the risks he ran each day and so, with scarcely an O level to his name, he became a clerk in the civil service. By chance, he landed in a section which vetted his department's forms for clarity and ease of use; he took to the work like a duck to water and became adept in turning the ambiguous and confusing drafts submitted to him into models of clarity. The drafts came from people with all levels of educational achievement, but he could wipe the floor with the lot of them when it came to presentation.

If we are to continue to have government run by amateurs, we should at least ensure that the most effective amateurs get to the top. As Trevelyan wrote to Northcote in March 1854, 'As regards promotion there will not, except in rare cases, be any examination after admission, and what is wanted to entitle to promotion is not literature ... but sustained application to business and its fruits, experience, skill and mature judgement.'

# BIBLIOGRAPHY

Ackroyd, Peter, *Chaucer*, Vintage, 2005

Abbott, Evelyn & Campbell, Lewis, *The Life and Letters of Benjamin Jowett*, John Murray, 1897

Air Ministry, Costal Command, *The Air Ministry Account of the Part Played by Costal Command in the Battle of the Seas*, HMSO, 1942

Asquith, Margot, *The Autobiography of Margot Asquith*, Penguin, 1937

Aye, John, *Humour in the Civil Service*, Cecil Palmer, 1928

Barrington, Emilie Isabel, *The Servant of All*, Longmans & Co., 1927

Balogh, Thomas, 'The Apotheosis of the Dilettante' in Thomas, Hugh (ed.), *The Establishment*, Anthony Blond, 1959

Bindoff, S. T., *Tudor England*, Penguin, 1961

Briggs, Asa, *Victorian People*, Penguin, 1982

Brooke, Christopher, *The Saxon and Norman Kings*, Batsford, 1963

Campbell, James, *The Anglo-Saxon State*, Hambledon & London, 2000

Chapman, R. A. & Greenaway, J. R., *The Dynamics of Administrative Reform*, Croom Helm, 1980

Cheeseman, E. C., *Brief Glory*, Harborough Publishing Co., 1946

Chester, Sir Norman, *The English Administrative System 1780–1870*, Clarendon Press, 1981

Christopherson, Derman & Baughan, E. C., 'Reminiscences of Operational Research in World War II by Some of Its Practitioners', *Journal of the Operational Research Society*, Vol. 43, No. 6, pp. 569–77

Clarke, Peter, *The Cripps Version: The Life of Sir Stafford Cripps*, Allen Lane, 2002

Clifford, Colin, *The Asquiths*, John Murray, 2003

Cobbett, William, *Cottage Economy*, C. Clement, 1822

Cohen, Emmeline W., *The Growth of the British Civil Service 1780–1939*, Allen & Unwin, 1941

Compton, John M., 'Open Competition and the ICS 1854–1876', *English Historical Review*, Vol. 83, No. 327, 1968, pp. 256–84

Cornish, W. R. & Clerk, G. de N., *Law and Society in England 1750–1950*, Sweet & Maxwell, 1989

Coward, Barry, *The Stuart Age: England 1603–1714*, Longman, 1994

Crick, Michael, *Michael Heseltine*, Hamish Hamilton, 1997

Cross, Claire, Loades, David & Scarisbrick, J. J. (eds), *Law and Government under the Tudors*, Cambridge University Press, 1988

Crossman, Richard, *Diaries of a Cabinet Minister*, Jonathan Cape, 1976

Crystal, David, *How Language Works*, Penguin, 2005

Dodwell, H. H. (ed.), *Cambridge History of India*, Vol. 6, Cambridge University Press, 1932

Edwards, Michael, *The Battle of Plassey*, Batsford, 1963

Elton, G. R., *The Tudor Revolution in Government*, Cambridge University Press, 1953

Farrington, Anthony, *The Records of the EIC Haileybury and Other Institutions*, HMSO, 1976

Ferguson, Niall, *The Cash Nexus*, Penguin, 2001

Foreman, Susan, *Shoes and Ships and Sealing-Wax*, HMSO, 1986

Grieve, M., *A Modern Herbal*, Jonathan Cape, 1931

Hart, Jennifer, 'Sir Charles Trevelyan at the Treasury', *English Historical Review*, Vol. 75, 1960

Hennessy, Peter (ed.), *Ready Steady Go! Labour and Whitehall*, Fabian Society, 1997

Hennessy, Peter, *The Prime Minister*, Allen Lane, 2000

Hennessy, Peter, *Whitehall*, Fontana, 1990

HMSO, *Staffs Employed in Government Departments*, 1921–60

HM Treasury, *Digests of Civil Service Staff Statistics*, 1947–56

Hoskins, W. G., *Local History in England*, Longmans, 1984

Hobsbawm, Eric, *Age of Extremes*, Abacus, 1995

Hurd, Douglas, *Memoirs*, Abacus, 2004

Ingham, Bernard, *Kill the Messenger*, Fontana, 1991

Ireland, Bernard & Grove, Eric, *War at Sea 1897–1997*, HarperCollins, 1997

Jobson, Adrian (ed.), *English Government in the Thirteenth Century*, The Boydell Press/National Archives, 2004

Johnson, Paul (ed.), *The Oxford Book of Political Anecdotes*, Oxford University Press, 1986

Kearney, H. F. (ed.), *Origins of the Scientific Revolution*, Longmans, 1966

Kirby, M. & Capey, R., 'Air Defence of Great Britain, 1920–1940', *Journal of the Operational Research Society*, Vol. 48

Lawson, P., *The East India Company: A History*, Longman, 1993

Le Fleming, H. M., *Warships of World War I*, Ian Allan, 1959

Lewis, Michael, *The History of the British Navy*, Penguin, 1957

Linklater, Magnus & Leigh, David, *Not With Honour*, Sphere, 1986

MacArthur, Brian (ed.), *The Penguin Book of Historic Speeches*, Penguin, 1996

Macaulay, Thomas Babbington, *Warren Hastings*, Cassells, 1885

MacCulloch, Diarmaid, *Reformation*, Penguin, 2004

MacDougall, Donald, *Don and Mandarin*, John Murray, 1987

Marmot, M. G. et al., 'Health inequalities among British civil servants: the Whitehall II study', *The Lancet*, Vol. 337, 1991

Martindale, Hilda, *Women Servants of the State 1870–1938*, Allen & Unwin, 1938

Moore, R. J., 'The Abolition of Patronage in the Indian Civil Service and Closure of Haileybury College', *Historical Journal*, Vol. 7, 1964

Monier-Williams, M. (ed.), *Memorials of Old Haileybury College*, Constable, 1894

Morley, John, *The Life of Cobden*, T. Fisher Unwin, 1910

Mullen, Richard, *Anthony Trollope: A Victorian in His World*, Duckworth, 1990

Myres, J. N. L., *The English Settlements*, Oxford University Press, 1995

Neale, J. E., *Queen Elizabeth I*, Penguin, 1952

O'Connor, John, *The Workhouses of Ireland*, Anvil, 1995

Ollard, Richard, *Pepys*, Sinclair-Stevenson, 1991

O'Malley, L. S. S., *The Indian Civil Service 1601–1930*, John Murray, 1931

Parkinson, C. Northcote, *Parkinson's Law*, Penguin, 1986

Paxman, Jeremy, *The Political Animal*, Penguin, 2003

Perkin, H., *The Rise of Professional Society in England Since 1880*, Routledge, 2002

Regan, Geoffrey, *Historical Blunders*, Andre Deutsch, 2002

Regan, Geoffrey, *The Guinness Book of Military Blunders*, Guinness, 1993

Robinson, Howard, *The British Post Office: A History*, Princeton University Press, 1948

Rolt, L. T. C., *Red for Danger*, Pan Books, 1986

Sampson, Anthony, *The Arms Bazaar*, Coronet, 1991

Schonfield, Andrew, *British Economic Policy Since the War*, Penguin, 1958

Stanley, Martin, *How to Be a Civil Servant*, Biteback Publishing, 2016

Strutt, Sir Austin, *The Home Office 1870–1896*, Home Office, 1960

Sutherland, Gillian (ed.), *Studies in the Growth of Nineteenth-Century Government*, Routledge & Kegan Paul, 1972

Sutherland, Lucy, *The East India Company in Eighteenth-Century Politics*, Oxford University Press, 1952

Tanenhaus, Sam, *Whittaker Chambers: A Biography*, Random House, 1997

Tomalin, Claire, *Samuel Pepys*, Viking, 2002

Tuchman, Barbara, *The March of Folly*, Knopf, 1984

Tuck, P. (ed.), *The East India Company 1600–1858*, Routledge, 1961

Tupp, Alfred C., *The Indian Civil Service and the Competitive System*, R. W. Brydges, 1876

Uglow, Jenny, *The Lunar Men*, Faber & Faber, 2003

Vincent, Benjamin, *Hayden's Dictionary of Dates*, Edward Moxton & Co., 1866

Walsham, Alexandra, *Providence in Early Modern England*, Oxford University Press, 1999

Winter, James, *Robert Lowe*, University of Toronto Press, 1976

Woodham-Smith, Cecil, *The Great Hunger*, NEL, 1977

Woodham-Smith, Cecil, *Florence Nightingale*, The Reprint Society, 1952

Wright, Maurice, *Treasury Control of the Civil Service*, Clarendon Press, 1969

## HANSARD

HoL, 1813, XXV, 710, Grenville on Reform of Indian Civil Service

HoL, 10 July 1833, cols 524–6, Macaulay on the Need for Competition

25 June 1853, CXXVIII, cols 746–58

22 July 1853, col. 685, Wood on Haileybury College

8 August 1853, CXXIX, col. 1448, Granville on Haileybury

8 August 1853, CXXXV, cols 1456–7, Wood on Haileybury

15 July 1855, col. 2090, Northcote on patronage after CSC set-up

HoL, 13 March 1854, CXXXI, cols 640–655, Debate on N/T report

9 April 1869, Vol. 195, col. 488, Civil Service Lower Class

19 July 1859, Vol. 155, col. 14, Compulsory Vaccination

10 July 1861, Vol. 164, cols 674–7, Compulsory Vaccination

9 June 1873, Vol. 216, cols 686–711, The Zanzibar Mail Contract

19 June 1873, cols 1198–1206, The Zanzibar Mail Contract

24 June 1947, Attlee on the Civil Service

16 May 1952, Debate on Equal Pay for Women Civil Servants
25 January 1955, R. A. Butler on Equal Pay for Women Civil Servants

## PARLIAMENTARY PAPERS

The fifteen reports of the Commissioners for Examining the Public Accounts published in the Journals of the House of Commons between November 1780 and December 1786

The ten reports of the Commissioners for Enquiring into Fees, Perquisites, and Emoluments in the Public Offices (England)

PP 1809 II, Select Committee on EIC and Patronage

PP 1828 XVI, Return of the Number of Persons Employed and of the Pay or Salaries granted to such Persons in all the Public Offices or Departments in the years 1797, 1805, 1825 etc.

PP 1833 XXII, Return of the Establishments of the Public Departments and Offices, 1821–32, respectively, showing reductions which have been carried into effect since 1821 etc.

PP 1847–48 XVIII, Commons Select Committee on Miscellaneous Expenditure

PP 1852–53 XXXII, India Bill

PP 1852–53 XXVII, India Bill

PP 1854–55 XX, Northcote–Trevelyan Report and Papers

PP 1854–55 XXVII, Reports of the Committees of Inquiry into Public Offices and Papers Connected Therewith

PP 1854–55 XL, Macaulay's Report on Examinations

PP 1857–58 XIV, Railway Safety

PP 1867 XXXIX, Correspondence between the Treasury and the Board of Trade

PP 1873 VIII, Post Office Purchase of the Telegraphs

PP 1873 VII, Civil Service Reform

PP 1873 VII, Select Committee on Civil Service Expenditure, Appendix 9

PP 1875 XXIII, Playfair Committee

PP 1902 LXXXIII, Return Showing the Total Number of Persons in the Established Civil Service, 31 March 1902

PP 1911 I, Return Showing the Total Number of Persons in the Established Civil Service, 31 March 1911

PP 1912–13 XV, Cd 6210, Cd 6535, MacDonnell Commission

PP 1917–18 VIII, Cd 8657, Leathes Committee

PP 1920 XXVII, Memorandum on Present and Pre-War Expenditure with Particulars of Government Staffs at Certain Dates

PP 1929–30 XXII, Staffs Employed in Government Departments

PP 1937–38 XX, Staffs Employed in Government Departments on 1 April 1938

PP 1954–55 XII, Cd 9380, Equal Pay for Women

PP 1967–68 XVIII, Cd 3638, Fulton Report

PP 1981–82, Cd 8620, Control of Manpower


***Committee of Public Accounts***

Fifth Report Session 1966–67, 647

Fourth Report Session 1996–97, HC, 69

Fifty-First Report Session 2001–02, HC, 684


**INDIA OFFICE LIBRARY**

Wood Papers 3, Jowett to Wood, 2 February 1854

Wood Papers 5, note of 27 November 1853 re Exams

Wood Papers 51, Jowett's letters of 23 & 26 July to Gladstone


**PRO PAPERS**

30/29/21, Granville PPS

30/29/66, 1870 Order in Council; Railway Safety

T 1/6971A, Replies to Treasury letter on 1870 Order in Council

T 1/7258B/19279, Lowe and Lingen on implementing the Order in Council of 1870

T 162/475, Miss Tostevin and the Marriage Bar

T 162/602, Post-war Civil Service

T 215/306, Treasury Brief for Priestley Commission

T 273/9, Permanent Secretaries' Meeting

T 222/21, Civil Service Numbers

T 222/500, Staff Inspection
PREM 8/17, Proposals for Civil Service Staff College
PREM 11/4520, Macmillan Cabinet Meeting
PREM 13/ 3241, Wilson/Balogh
PREM 13/2126, Department of Economic Affairs
PREM 13/14, Wilson tribute to Civil Service
PREM 13/764, Fulton Committee
PREM 13/1357, Training in the Civil Service
PREM 13/1973, Prime Minister's Correspondence
PRO Board of Trade E3492, Subpoena Clerks
CAB 184/121, Ministerial Fatigue
T 216/944, Fulton Committee
T 330/147, Fulton Committee

## NEWSPAPERS
*The Times*, 15 April 1793
*The Times*, May & June 1793
*Civil Service Gazette*, 13 May 1854
*Civil Service Gazette*, 6 January 1855
*The Economist*, 12 May 1860
*Saturday Review*, 16 April 1864
*The Times*, 7 February 1868
*Civil Service Gazette*, 11 June 1870
*Civil Service Gazette*, 3 August 1872
*The Observer*, 7 October 1945
*The Listener*, 22 November 1984
*Sunday Telegraph*, 14 September 1986
*The Times*, 13 October 2005
*The Times*, 29 November 2006

## GLADSTONE MSS
Add MS 44216, fo. 192, Northcote applies for vacancy in BoT inquiry
Add MS 44333, fo. 123, from Trevelyan 31 January 1854
Add MS 44333, fos 91–4, Thoughts on Patronage 17 January 1854

Add MS 44376, fos 210–15, Jowett 14 December 1853
Add MS 44301, fos 70–71, Lowe to Glad re. Trevelyan
Add MS 44301, fo. 104, Lowe to Gladstone, 10 November 1869
Add MSS 44301, fo. 106, Lowe to Gladstone, 22 November 1869
Add MSS 44637, fo. 113, Cabinet Minute, 10 November 1869

## BODLEIAN LIBRARY
### *Trevelyan Letters*
**1853**
20 May to Col. Courtblat
19 July to Dr Vaughn
9 September to J. Parker
9 September to Mr Dinwiddie
13 September to Gladstone
3 October to B. Jowett
11 November to C. Wood
25 November to C. Wood

**1854**
28 January to S. Northcote
28 January to B. Jowett
2 February to C. Wood
4 February to Delane
27 February to B. Jowett
14 March to A. N. Bather
14 March to Rt Hon. J. Parker
15 March to Bishop of Manchester
17 March to Prof. Thompson
18 March to S. Northcote
3 May to Vaughn
9 May to F. Parratt
12 June to B. Jowett
13 June to B. Jowett
13 June to C. Wood

20 November to Head Coastguard

**1855**
12 January to A. Y. Spearman
26 January to H. Roberts
14 February to B. Hawes
24 February to Delane
27 February to T. Walrond

**1858**
23 February to Lord Shaftsbury
15 April to Gladstone
13 October to Lord Chancellor of Ireland

# NOTE ON THE SOURCES

I should like to record my gratitude to the staff of the Bodleian Library, the British Library, the National Archives and the Newspaper Library. Thanks are also due to Min Tong at the Institute of Directors, Richard Wood at the Parliamentary Archives, John Woolf of Redbridge Library Services and the late Andrew Hambling, archivist of Haileybury School.

The attribution of most of the quotations in this book is clear from the text. Instances where the sources are not clear are mainly private information, often from comments made to me by colleagues over the years. I cannot therefore guarantee them, but I have no reason to doubt what I was told. Most of my sources would not want to be identified; I have thought it proper not to name any.

# INDEX